BEING BERLUSCONI

BEING BERLUSCONI

THE RISE AND FALL FROM COSA NOSTRA TO BUNGA BUNGA

MICHAEL DAY

palgrave macmillan

BEING BERLUSCONI

First published in 2015 by PALGRAVE MACMILLAN® TRADE in the United States—a division of St. Martin's Press LLC, 175 Fifth Avenue, New York, NY 10010.

ISBN: 978-1-137-28004-6

Library of Congress Cataloging-in-Publication Data

Day, Michael, 1966–
Being Berlusconi : the rise and fall from cosa nostra to bunga bunga / Michael Day.
pages cm
ISBN 978-1-137-28004-6 (hardback)
1. Berlusconi, Silvio, 1936– 2. Prime ministers—Italy—Biography. 3. Businesspeople—Italy—Biography. 4. Italy—Politics and government—1994– I. Title.
DG583.B47D38 2015
945.093'11092—dc23
[B]
2014044328

Design by Westchester Book Composition

First edition: July 2015

10 9 8 7 6 5 4 3 2 1

Printed in the United States of America.

CONTENTS

ACKNOWLEDGMENTS

Heartfelt thanks to my brilliant friend, journalist and editor Jonathan Dyson, for his patient and thoughtful appraisal while I was writing the book. Special thanks as well to colleagues in Italy, including Jennifer Clark, Michele Novaga and many others at the Foreign Press Association offices in Rome and Milan. The help and advice of Italian journalists including Piero Colaprico of *La Repubblica,* Marco Travaglio and Marco Politi both of *Il Fatto Quotidiano,* have also been invaluable. I should also thank the misanthropic wit of Fabio Vassallo, who encouraged my own irreverence—*al punto giusto,* I hope.

Several members of the magistrature have been extremely helpful, as have many parliamentarians, past and present, including Giuliano Urbani and Laura Garavini on the Anti-mafia commission. A number of Italian academics have also been very generous with their time and advice including Giorgio Sacerdoti and Emanuele Lucchini Guastalla of Bocconi University, Justin Frosini of the joint Johns Hopkins–Bologna University law department and Renzo Orlandi, also at Bologna University. Thanks, too, to the late James Walston of the American University of Rome, whose insights illuminated the murk of Italian politics for me and dozens of other journalists, and who is sorely missed by all of us. A shout-out, as well, to my agents, Jane and Miriam at Dystel & Goderich, and my editor, Karen Wolny at Palgrave Macmillan, for her patience and support, and also *The Independent,* which has let me wander around Italy for the past six years, witnessing so many interesting things. And finally, a huge thank-you to Annalisa and Giovanni and Enrico and Vincenzo and Elis and the hundreds of other Italians, who, through their kindness and cheerfulness, have made my time here so much easier and more enjoyable.

PROLOGUE

For someone with such a dubious, albeit global, reputation, three-time Italian prime minister Silvio Berlusconi has collected a surprising number of awards during his controversial career—although we're not talking Nobel Prizes. In 1977 he was made a Knight of the Order of Merit for Labor, in recognition of his entrepreneurial skills, hence his nickname "Il Cavaliere" (The Knight). Others followed: little-known knighthoods and gongs from Romania, Latvia and Poland, plus medals that you'd be even less likely to shout about, from the likes of Saudi Arabia and Libya.

But Il Cavaliere's last prize came on the evening of July 19, 2010, high up on the unlikely roof terrace above the main aisle of the city's cathedral, Il Duomo, when he received the "Grande Milano" award, a prize that marked him as the city's outstanding citizen of the year. The cathedral, a monumental tribute in marble to Northern Italian gothic, glowed pink in the setting sun as Milan's great and good were hauled unceremoniously up the southern flank of the vast structure, 20 at a time, in a makeshift elevator, to see the prizegiving.

Pretty young stewards armed with clipboards and insect repellent welcomed politicians, journalists and hoary TV celebrities, some accompanied by young female companions tottering in six-inch heels, as they stepped onto the roof of the cathedral.

The sun sank and the eastern sky turned mauve, but the mercury didn't budge from the 86-degree mark. Swarms of mosquitoes danced around sweating guests, whose eyes darted around anxiously—and in vain—for evidence of a bar.

If ever there was an awards ceremony in which the speeches needed to be brief, this was it. The provincial president, Guido Podestà, seemed to think so: in his introduction of Berlusconi he gushed only briefly about the lascivious wheeler-dealer's "extraordinary charisma, exceptional human qualities and entrepreneurial skills," before welcoming the mogul onstage at the far end of the roof terrace, under the gaze of saints and gargoyles.

As with many of the good things to come Berlusconi's way over the years, a payment figured in the proceedings; Podestà had suggested as much when he praised the winner's "entrepreneurial skills." Shortly into his bloated acceptance speech, Berlusconi announced another €5 million ($6.5 million) a year from state coffers to maintain the vast cathedral, which, like the Golden Gate Bridge, is in a perpetual state of restoration.

Sitting at the far end of the ceremony with the other journalists, I felt my shirt stick to my back in a big wet patch as I turned to a reporter from *La Repubblica* and asked how long she thought the speech would last. "Forever," she scowled.

Berlusconi has always loved the sound of his own voice: only a month earlier, noting his tonsils' "sensual" quality, he employed them to launch the tourism ministry's latest promotional campaign for Italy. Now, in the suffocating heat, accompanied by a hundred inward groans among fidgeting guests, Milan's man of the year, billionaire, criminal suspect and prime minister, had plenty to say.

He attacked the judges who were trying to make him accountable to the law, or what little there was left after he'd manipulated it to his own ends for the best part of two decades; he talked up his largely inconsequential and frequently embarrassing performance on the world stage—"maybe it's because I'm the oldest that I'm the wisest and most knowledgeable," he said; he vowed to press on with plans to limit law enforcement's use of wiretaps—proposals that threatened investigations into organized crime; and he promised to rewrite the constitution.

Since that night in 2010 his plans to change the constitution have come to nothing; he's been kicked out of office for good and the judges have had the last laugh. In retrospect, the occasion and the speech have acquired a valedictory air, a final public gathering of the cronies and political allies who hitched a ride with the Silvio Berlusconi show. All of Milan's conservative political establishment was present that evening, accompanied by a cast of characters ranging from the controversial to the ridiculous: "post-fascist" ministers, the city's high-society mayor, a seedy impresario, a pimping TV news anchorman, a Rottweiler newspaper editor. The unholy assembly had one thing in common: unquestioned loyalty to the media mogul—all of them, in various ways and to different degrees, owed him something.

The mogul's highly paid TV mouthpiece, Emilio Fede, was in the audience, as was Fedele Confalonieri, his college friend and faithful TV executive, who had been with him his entire, spectacular, scandal-struck career, since playing in a band with Berlusconi in their college years.

Berlusconi's vaudeville side was on show too. When the evening's special guest, veteran French crooner Charles Aznavour, failed to show up on time, the prime minister assumed the role of host. "I seem to find myself presenting the show," he told the audience, before half joking that he'd decided not to sing with Aznavour "because I don't want to show him up." No one doubted that he'd have crooned happily for half an hour.

Berlusconi actually shared the Grande Milano prize that year. The joint winner that evening at Il Duomo was another shady character in Milan high society, the 90-year-old priest, tycoon, philanthropist, crook and hospital director Don Luigi Verzè, who met Berlusconi when the pair worked on controversial real-estate projects in the 1970s. Don Verzè had tended to Berlusconi's spiritual needs when the tycoon was hospitalized at the priest's hi-tech San Raffaele hospital seven months earlier after being hit over the head with a miniature copy of Il Duomo by a demented protestor.

"A man hit you over the head with the Duomo. Now you're standing on top of the Duomo. It's a sign from God," the priest told Berlusconi and the audience. Berlusconi said of his old friend, "He gives me absolution without even hearing my sins, because he already knows them. I hope Don Luigi rests in eternity because if there is a person that deserves it, he does."

Don Verzè, who built up overseas slush funds and sent his hospital and research center €1.5 billion ($1.8 billion) into the red, had been rumored to be trying to buy his second private jet (with money that probably wasn't his) when he died on New Year's Eve in 2011, taking many of his secrets and those of Berlusconi with him to the grave. The papers said it was unclear whether the would-be philanthropist/priest was a "Saint or Devil."

But with Berlusconi the picture is clearer. The mountain of evidence we already have on the billionaire TV mogul suggests there is nothing remotely saintly behind his winning smile, not even by the standards of morally malleable Italy. The real questions are: What on earth has happened in the last 20 years? How did he get away with it for so long? And how did they finally nail him?

PART I

THE RISE

CHAPTER 1

STARTING AS HE MEANT TO CONTINUE

Milan, Italy's gritty design and finance hub, is the City where people get things done: they graft, they sell, they make and design, they earn. It's not like Rome, the beautiful capital, in which locals sit around waiting for the tourists to come and drop money in their laps, and where Italy's gilded and venal political class line their pockets and enjoy long lunches. Milan-born Silvio Berlusconi understood the potential of both his hometown and the Eternal City—that is, money and power, respectively. And he cashed in spectacularly.

If becoming a hedonistic multimillionaire politician were easy, then we'd all be at it. It's a testament to Berlusconi's genius as a businessman and politician—and key to his popular and vicarious appeal—that he started with very little and rose to become Italy's richest man and dominate its politics for two decades.

Like many exceptional individuals, his background was anything but. Berlusconi's father, Luigi, worked as a clerk in the one-branch Rasini bank in Milan. His mother, Rosella, was a housewife, although, by most accounts, she ruled the roost. According to friends of the family, it is from his mother that Silvio Berlusconi got his get-up-and-go. His affectionate nature was probably due in large part to a loving bond with his father, Luigi.

Berlusconi recalled the day his father finally returned home after a long absence during the Second World War. Young Silvio waited anxiously at Como railway station, north of Milan, before finally seeing his father get off the train. He remembered racing along the platform to embrace his dad. "That moment has remained in my memory as the most agonizing and the happiest of my life," he once said.[1] Some reports suggest Berlusconi's high opinion of himself was probably thanks to both parents, who eschewed any criticism for constant praise and adoration. "Our Silvio is better than all of them" was the message drummed into him in his impressionable early years.[2]

He was born in 1936 in what was then the city's northern edge. Today the area, Isola, is Milan's most up-and-coming neighborhood. Trendy bars and shops buzz in the shadow of skyscrapers that are continually sprouting up in the giant construction site around the nearby Garibaldi railway station. These days when he's in Milan, Berlusconi, the former real-estate magnate, no doubt casts a wistful glance at the gleaming edifices. "If I were just starting up now," he might tell himself, "I'd make a killing." Who would doubt it?

Young Silvio's parents packed him off to a strict Catholic boarding school in the city at the age of 11. Berlusconi rose at 7 every morning to study mathematics, history, philosophy, languages and religion, with the rosary after lunch. He always obtained good grades. It didn't go unnoticed, however, by the Salesian priests who ran the establishment, that his religious conviction was somewhat lacking. A school friend recalled how Berlusconi would drift away during prayers; his lips "moved mechanically; his thoughts were clearly elsewhere."[3]

This was probably the earliest recorded evidence of the vexed relationship with religion that has marked his career. Berlusconi's political instincts have told him that in Vatican-influenced Italy, he needs to keep the Church on board. But playing at being a good Catholic has always been at odds with his libertine personal philosophy. The result has been numerous shows of fake piety—until finally, toward the end of his career, the documented tide of sleaze that engulfed Berlusconi was such that any religious posturing became pointless.

Back at the prayer sessions in the Sant'Ambrogio Salesian Institute, the young Berlusconi probably had business in mind. In his early teens he was already doing the homework of slower or lazier classmates in return for their pocket money. This conservative educational institute probably drummed into him the anticommunist rhetoric that he would continue to spout for the rest of his life. And it was at this boarding school that the future tycoon met lifelong friend Fedele Confalonieri. More than sixty years on, Berlusconi and Confalonieri—who now runs the mogul's TV empire—remain as thick as thieves. Berlusconi's second wife would compare their relationship to that of two brothers. The friendship also set a pattern that has seen Berlusconi stick by key associates with unswerving loyalty—loyalty that is mutual and underpinned, no doubt, by a shared knowledge of where all the skeletons are hidden.

Confalonieri, the dour straight man to Berlusconi's vaudeville act, shared with his school friend a passion for music. By the age of 16 the pair were putting on improvised shows, with Confalonieri on piano and Berlusconi twanging the double bass and crooning standards made popular by Frank Sinatra, Nat King Cole and Yves Montand.

By the late 1950s, when Berlusconi had to pay his way through Milan's Statale University, he was earning extra money as a singer and host on Mediterranean cruise ships, putting his natural charm to good use, effortlessly entertaining large groups for hours at a time with songs, jokes and patter. With his hair slicked back and his winning smile never more than a couple of seconds away, the young entertainer made up for his short stature (he's just five feet five inches) with his boy-next-door good looks and easy charm. Confalonieri has attested that Berlusconi never had any difficulty wooing the ladies.

Berlusconi graduated in law in 1961, with top honors. His thesis on the contractual aspects of advertising even won an award from a local advertising agency.

And so, in the early 1960s, Berlusconi, the ambitious young graduate, found himself in the right place at the right time. The postwar expansion of the Italian economy was in full flow. And Milan, the country's business capital, was the hottest spot of all. Thanks to the city's entrepreneurial spirit, good links with the rest of Europe and an abundance of cheap labor arriving from the poorer south of the country, there was money to be made—and Berlusconi knew it.

After graduating, Berlusconi sold vacuum cleaners for a while. But it occurred to him that selling property would be easier—and a lot more profitable. He just needed enough cash to get things going. He managed to convince the head of his father's bank, the tiny Banca Rasini, to guarantee the loan needed to build his first apartments in Via Alciati in Milan. His famous powers of persuasion were next in evidence when he sold the first Via Alciati property to Confalonieri's grandmother.

His next project was a step up in size and ambition. A planned complex in Brugherio outside Milan would provide homes for several thousand people. The investment needed for this project was an order of magnitude greater than he'd needed for the Via Alciati apartments. Berlusconi again managed to get his hands on the cash, but this time it was less clear from where—or from whom—the money came, thus setting a pattern for the next ten years.

The would-be real-estate mogul founded a company, Edilnord, from which to base the venture. Once again, the little Rasini bank helped out, but its assistance wasn't enough for a property development of this size: additional funds flowed in from a Swiss company, FRA of Lugano. This firm's real proprietors have never really been identified.[4] And it was at this point that the whispers began: rumors concerning the origins of Berlusconi's investments. When large, opaque cash flows are involved in Italy, the word "mafia" inevitably surfaces.

But Berlusconi just got on with selling the properties, and the tycoon's sales patter was more than up to the task. The Brugherio apartments were not in a very attractive spot. It was a swamp. There were few amenities in the vicinity, but plenty of factories and industrial plants. Plus, the economy was cooling a little by 1964, when the properties went on the market. Still the mogul made a success of it—his key break came when he sold a block of the apartments to a pension fund investor before they were finished. Within five years, Berlusconi had found owners for 1,000 new homes.

The property development that really made Berlusconi's name, however, was Milano 2. Even its name indicates the confidence—some would say presumptuousness—of its creator. It wasn't, in fact, another version of Italy's neoclassical finance capital. Nonetheless, its selling point was its nominal status as a self-contained satellite "town," with its own security and homes for 10,000 people. It had its own shops, schools, a church, a cinema, a central piazza and its own artificial lake. Milano 2 apartments, on the eastern outskirts of the city and not far from the small Linate airport, were marketed as homes "in Milan without the smog and the traffic." They were also well away from the student protests and riots, and the sense of dread that occupied Italy's big cities during the 1970s—Gli Anni di

Piombo (the years of lead), a time marked by violence and deadly terrorist attacks as far-left and far-right activists fought viciously over their bankrupt ideas. Milan's burgeoning but anxious middle class, their numbers swelled by a boom in design, advertising and telecommunications, liked the sound of Italy's first gated community and snapped up the properties as the complex grew over the 1970s.

But where did the money come from for this vast real-estate venture? Bank of Italy inspectors, intrigued by the tsunami of cash flowing into Berlusconi's project, discovered labyrinthine account arrangements and various companies within companies that resembled a series of Russian nesting dolls. *The Economist* had a go at unraveling the nature—and provenance—of the investments.[5] At one point the august finance journal warned its high-powered readership to concentrate ("what happened next is complicated . . .") as it sought to explain the fiendishly clever and complex financial web that Berlusconi and associates had woven in order to conceal the identities of those funding Milano 2 and those profiting from it.

In one part of its special report, *The Economist* noted that Berlusconi's name was "nowhere to be seen" in the company filings of the main developer, Edilnord, or in the filings of Sogeat, the group overseeing the commercial part of Milano 2. At that time, strict currency exchange laws meant that profits made in Italy on behalf of Swiss investors had to return to their country of origin. The report noted, however, that Silvio Berlusconi, his brother, Paolo, and the mysterious Swiss company behind Edilnord all had bank accounts at Banca Rasini, the single-branch institution in Milan where Berlusconi's father had worked for most of his life. It would later emerge that some senior figures in Cosa Nostra, the Sicilian mafia, also held accounts there.[6]

To cut to the chase, the Bank of Italy officials' probe suggested that both Edilnord and Sogeat belonged to Berlusconi. Suspicious of what was happening, they sent in the finance police, the Guardia di Finanza, whose officers found that between 1974 and 1978 the two companies made profits of 5.74 billion lire ($3.8 million), which had not been returned to Switzerland as the law demanded.

It fell to Massimo Maria Berruti, a young captain in the finance police, to interview Berlusconi on October 24, 1979. The property magnate explained that he was simply an external consultant to the two companies, although it was increasingly obvious to anyone who'd studied the evidence that the two companies and the mysterious "Swiss investor" were, as *The Economist* described them, "Berlusconi's alter-egos."

Despite strong evidence that Berlusconi had violated exchange-control regulations on a huge scale—a crime that could invite a long jail sentence—no legal action was taken against him. Berruti made his report, which was signed off by a finance police general, who soon after became a member of the secret P2 masonic lodge—a subversive society to which, as we'll see, Berlusconi himself had links. Not long after, Berruti himself quit the Guardia di Finanza. Deciding it was time for a raise, he went to work for Berlusconi—the first of many to choose the tycoon over the state. Berruti would be sentenced to eight months in jail in 2001 for aiding and abetting Fininvest, Berlusconi's holding company, in the corruption of public officials.[7]

Although substantial evidence emerged that Berlusconi was the immediate source of the Milano 2 investment, as well as its beneficiary, the probe didn't explain the provenance of the original funding. But already, a great many people had their suspicions. Opaque investments and unexplained circular flows of money through shell companies at home and abroad suggested that Berlusconi was using highly disreputable sources—namely, the Mafia—to kick-start his burgeoning real-estate empire. It was a suspicion that was to grow ever stronger over the coming years.

How Berlusconi paid for his Milano 2 and Brugherio apartments wasn't the only cause for concern. The Brugherio development wasn't supposed to exceed five stories, but upon completion it was eight floors high. The Brugherio official who had been in charge of town planning, Edoardo Teruzzi, was, strangely enough, brought onto Berlusconi's payroll as project manager. He later dismissed the illegal height of the development, which boosted Berlusconi's profits considerably, as a "misunderstanding" that was easily resolved by Berlusconi's company "paying 200 million lire and offering to build a nursery school for free."[8]

Milano 2 didn't have Brugherio's downside of being situated in a grim industrial zone, with few or no facilities. Its well-heeled inhabitants would be able to jog by its lake and use the new town's swimming pools and shops, while private security kept out the riffraff. The thunderous din emitted by aircraft landing and taking off from nearby Linate airport was another matter, though. Berlusconi even managed to sort that out, however, when it became apparent that the noise was repelling potential buyers. He persuaded parliamentarians in the notoriously corrupt Christian Democrat Party—the centrist Catholic political movement that would implode 15 years later in the massive "Tangentopoli" bribes scandal—to propose new flight paths that spared Milano 2 residents the worst of the noise, while making life suddenly very unpleasant for thousands of people in other towns and villages in the region.

Berlusconi combined this re-routing coup with a second masterstroke, establishing a hospital, the San Raffaele, right by Milano 2. Thus, when his emissaries went to Rome to cajole slippery *deputati* and senators into altering the flight paths, they were able to do so ostensibly for the sake of the sick. In reality, the San Raffaele would be a private, profit-making clinic; not a single brick had been laid when Berlusconi's minions were making their cynical diplomatic sorties to the Italian parliament. The San Raffaele would be developed by another shady character in Milan society, Don Luigi Verzè. The larger-than-life priest was also a real-estate magnate, a friend of Berlusconi, a self-proclaimed philanthropist and a crook. Much of the medical research in the hospital he helped establish would be highly respected. But Don Verzè's hubris and greed would also see the hospital enveloped in a scandal involving slush funds and the suicide of a senior official that even tainted the Vatican.[9]

Back at Milano 2 the first 200 residents could sleep tight. The flight routes were changed for their benefit—and that of thousands of potential Milano 2 homeowners. The petition signed by 3,000 outraged residents in the nearby town of Segrate was ignored, as were concerns by Alitalia pilots that the new routes would make takeoff and landing more dangerous.[10] Ironically, another community to complain of being "bombarded by noise" as a result of the altered flight paths was Brugherio, the location of Berlusconi's first big property development.

Berlusconi didn't lose much sleep over this, however. Research published by the Polytechnic University of Milan declared that the final flight paths represented the best compromise in terms of minimizing environmental disturbance; it subsequently emerged that Berlusconi himself paid the engineers who'd written the report. But the future prime minister was sitting pretty, with two huge property developments to his name, and basking in his new nickname, the "King of Bricks."

The decade from the mid-1960s to the mid-1970s had seen key developments in Berlusconi's personal life, too. He'd married Carla Dall'Oglio in 1965. The couple had met the year before, when Dall'Oglio, then a

24-year-old shop assistant, caught Berlusconi's eye in a street near Milan's Central Station. The mogul has never shied from pursuing what he wants, and he immediately turned on the charm. It might not have worked the first time, but soon after, when he spotted her getting on a bus, he jumped in his car and sped after it, determined to get her attention.[11] His persistence paid off.

The couple had their first child, Marina, in 1966. Their second child, Pier Silvio, was born three years later, in 1969. Both would enter the family business. Marina, in particular, soon showed evidence of her father's business acumen, if not his charm.

The Berlusconi family lived in a comfortable apartment on the western edge of the city, close by the original Via Alciati development. Other relatives moved into the same block with them. By the mid-1970s, however, with the Brugherio development completed and the mighty Milano 2 project in the offing, Italy's fastest-rising entrepreneur needed a home rather more in keeping with his perceived status and ambitions. If such a place were available at a bargain price, even better. Berlusconi had just the right man to help him—someone who would enable him to cut a deal so squalid that even now it beggars belief.

The story begins in August 1970, with a grisly multiple murder among Italy's aristocracy. The Marchese Camillo Casati Stampa di Soncino, 43, shot and killed his second wife, Anna Fallarino, 41, and Fallarino's 25-year-old student lover, Massimo Minorenti, before turning the gun on himself, in a tragedy that transfixed Italy for months.

The magnificent Casati Stampa estate, including the 145-room Villa San Martino, in Arcore, near Milan, with its art collection featuring works by Tintoretto and Tiepolo, was due to pass to the Marchese's traumatized daughter, Annamaria, then just 19 years old. But to everyone's surprise the sister of her murdered stepmother turned up with other ideas. She declared that if Anna Fallarino had outlived her killer/husband by even a few minutes, then the estate would have passed from husband to wife—and thus as the sister, she, rather than Annamaria, would be in prime position for the inheritance. Forensic tests showed that the father had, as everyone expected, been the last to die. And these put paid to the fanciful plan. But Cesare Previti, the lawyer and brains behind this cynical money grab, wasn't finished. He simply switched sides, somehow persuading the young Marchesa Annamaria to hire him.

Annamaria, now 23, had moved to Brazil in an attempt to start a new life. In order to pay the inheritance taxes on the family estate, she had to put Villa San Martino on the market, but stipulated that the library, the art collection and the grounds were not to be sold. Previti, her lawyer and the co-executor of her estate, had his own plans, however. He eventually called his client in Brazil to inform her that a potential buyer had come forward in the form of Silvio Berlusconi. The price offered by the up-and-coming tycoon was an absurdly low 500 million lire, at that time the equivalent of $850,000, an offer that included the library, the land and the art collection—the latter was thought to contain several paintings worth more than $1 million each. The naïve young woman agreed.

Berlusconi even managed to defer payment to the Marchesa for six years after taking possession. This meant the Marchesa continued paying taxes on the property long after the mogul had moved in. Previti neglected to tell the Marchesa that by 1977 he was on the board of Hydra Real Estate, the Berlusconi company buying Villa San Martino from her. Previti had, in fact, also been on the statutory board of auditors for Berlusconi's Fininvest holding company since 1975.[12]

Previti and Berlusconi weren't finished with the Marchesa yet, however. In 1979 the mogul bought another chunk of the Casati Stampa estate, 800 acres of land, including a castle near the town of Cusago. This time the naïve young aristocrat wasn't even paid in cash. Instead she was offered shares in one of the mogul's numerous shell companies, represented as being worth $2 million. But since the firm was not traded on the stock market, the shares' real value was hard to estimate. Smelling a rat, she ordered the shares to be sold. But they were simply bought back by another Berlusconi financial entity for less than their original estimated value.[13]

At this point, upon learning about the completion of the Villa San Martino sale and how it had been carried out, a family member, the Marchesa's sister-in-law, the Countess Beatrice Rangoni Machiavelli, flew to Brazil with evidence that Annamaria had been swindled by her lawyer. The Marchesa finally dumped Previti, cancelling his power of attorney, and handed control over to her sister-in-law, the Countess.

The Marchesa has never commented on the controversy, preferring to concentrate on her new life on the ranch in Brazil, where she is married with a family. But in 2010, Countess Beatrice, a former member of the European Parliament, gave her damning verdict in an Italian press interview. Berlusconi and Previti, the Marchesa's own lawyer, had "swindled" the young woman and "robbed her twice"—of her home and then her land, she said.[14]

And thus Cesare Previti joined the top table of Silvio Berlusconi's cronies. Here was a character so squalid that if a politician in any other major Western country spent more than three minutes alone in a room with him, his or her political career would go down the toilet. Berlusconi did more than spend three minutes with this unscrupulous lawyer; he employed him to perform various forms of dirty work over decades, and even made him a minister in his first government in 1994. Finally, in 2007, more than 30 years after Berlusconi and the lawyer became acquainted, Previti was jailed, convicted of bribing a judge in Rome in order to help Berlusconi win a takeover battle.[15] Berlusconi rewarded Previti for his services by changing the law to ensure he spent less than a week behind bars.

Thanks to the attorney's double-dealing, Berlusconi now had a home fit for a king—at a ridiculously low price; an acquisition whose sleaziness would set the tone for events there over the next four decades. As we'll see, the vicissitudes of Silvio Berlusconi are indelibly tied to the comings and goings in his Arcore mansion: from the earliest intrigues concerning his association with mobsters, right up until the Rubygate sex scandal that would make him an international laughingstock. This is the story of a shady but brilliant businessman dubbed the King of Bricks who became the decadent proprietor of a country, only to be laid low by his own obsessions and hubris.

CHAPTER 2

DIRTY CASH

Several years before the truth emerged about Berlusconi's purchase of Villa San Martino, the husband of the young, bereaved Marchesa, Pierdonato Donà dalle Rose, called around at Arcore to inquire after the fate of the Marchesa's artwork and of one work in particular, the celebrated Fourteen Stations of the Cross by Bernardino Luini. He was met at the gates by a tall, unsmiling man with a rifle and a heavy Sicilian accent, before eventually being given the brush-off by the villa's smarmy new owner.[1]

More than anything, it was the presence of this gun-toting employee at Arcore that would set tongues wagging and have prosecutors setting up wiretaps as fast as they could get their hands on the equipment and, of course, the permission of a judge. The tall man, Vittorio Mangano, was a mobster from the powerful Porta Nuova clan of Cosa Nostra, the Sicilian Mafia. The fact that Berlusconi employed such a character—officially as the villa's stable master—would have been enough to fatally blight the career of an aspiring politician in any other Western country, yet Berlusconi survived. In Berlusconi's case, however, hiring a mafioso was indicative of both the tycoon's hubris and his willingness to adapt to the prevailing conditions in a country in which organized crime holds sway in a manner that most non-Italians fail to comprehend. Still, it appeared to offer the first concrete evidence of Berlusconi's links to the mob.

The mogul's Sicilian connections stemmed from his university friendship with Palermo-born Marcello Dell'Utri, the man who would go on to head Berlusconi's money-spinning TV advertising division, Publitalia, and who would help mastermind the tycoon's entry into politics, before becoming a senator himself. By the mid-1970s, Dell'Utri was already a member of Berlusconi's innermost circle, along with Fedele Confalonieri and Cesare Previti. Given the job of overseeing Villa San Martino's upgrade from exquisite seventeenth-century villa with art by old Venetian masters to arriviste dream with an indoor pool subtly enhanced by a bank of TV screens at one end, Dell'Utri set to work. He was also charged with management of the villa's day-to-day affairs.

And in one of his first moves as general manager of Villa San Martino, Dell'Utri hired Mangano, the "stable master." True, there was a stable—with one horse—at the mansion. But no one believed that was the real reason for the mafioso's menacing presence at the estate of the newest member of Italy's financial aristocracy. It was speculated then, and generally accepted now, that the lugubrious Cosa Nostra figure was there to warn off other criminals—and other mafia clans—seeking to tap into Berlusconi's rapidly multiplying millions.

Kidnappings involving the children of rich businessmen were rife in Italy in the 1970s. Berlusconi said in an Italian newspaper interview that kidnappers tried to take his young son Pier Silvio in 1974. It didn't escape people's notice that one of Mangano's duties was to drive his boss's children to and from school. Berlusconi would later admit Mangano's real role to Indro Montanelli, the editor of his own newspaper *Il Giornale*. "I was afraid of kidnapping then. Who would be better able to protect me than a Mafioso? He was in the business."[2] And yet, Mangano's presence hinted at a darker and more complex association between the tycoon and the mob.

In the 1970s, the Mafia's gaze was focused ever more intently on the wealthy north of the country, and not just for the potential rich pickings from kidnappings—of which there were 72 high-profile cases in Milan alone between 1973 and 1979. Mob bosses needed to infiltrate legitimate businesses in order to launder earnings that were spiraling, thanks to the drug trade.[3] In addition, many senior mafiosi were exiled to the north of Italy while awaiting trial in their native Sicily. Thus, the state inadvertently gave the Mafia the manpower it needed in the north to build ties with "respectable" financial organizations.

When the news broke that there was a gangster at Arcore, Berlusconi and Dell'Utri claimed they had had no idea who Mangano was, they insisted he was given the boot as soon as his background became apparent. Neither claim bears much scrutiny. It is true, however, that the chaotic manner in which news of Mangano's presence at Arcore emerged is at odds with the view that his employment was planned to the last detail. Mangano's hiring came to the authorities' notice some months after the Marchesa's brother paid a visit. The pivotal event was the attempted kidnapping of one of Berlusconi's dinner guests in the early hours of December 7, 1974. The victim, a fake aristocrat from Naples named Luigi D'Angerio, managed to flee after his captors crashed their car. The kidnappers, it turned out, were mafioso pals of Mangano. But if you employ a scary mobster with a charge sheet as long as your arm, you can probably expect a few personnel problems.

When the police arrived and demanded to know who had been to dinner that night, Berlusconi neglected to mention the presence of Mangano. But the police found out anyway and returned to arrest Mangano three weeks later; there was already a warrant out for him in relation to crimes committed in Palermo. Berlusconi claimed during his 1994 election campaign that he fired Mangano immediately after the attempted kidnapping. But when police turned up several weeks after the kidnapping attempt, Mangano was still at Arcore. The mobster also returned to Berlusconi's mansion after a month in prison; police even found him living there several months later.[4]

If that wasn't bad enough, it seems that Dell'Utri, one of Berlusconi's most senior lieutenants, liked the gangster Mangano so much he decided to stay in touch. Five years after the bungled Arcore kidnap attempt, police tapped into Mangano's phone calls during his stay in a Milan hotel and were surprised to hear not one, but several, chats with Dell'Utri. Mangano was suspected of organizing large-scale heroin shipments and laundering the dirty cash through Milan's financial community. The telephone surveillance was designed to keep track of Mangano's activity as Cosa Nostra's "bridgehead in the north of Italy," according to Palermo prosecutor Paolo Borsellino in an interview with French journalists on May 21, 1992. The prosecutor was killed by a Mafia bomb two months later.[5]

In one of the calls recorded by police, Mangano tells Dell'Utri: "I have a deal to propose to you and I have a horse that is right for you."

"Dear Vittorio," Dell'Utri replies, "for a horse I need cash and I don't have any."[6]

Suspicions about the real nature of Mangano's "horses"—"horse" being slang for heroin—increased after another call from the same hotel room, during which Mangano attempted to sell fellow mafioso Rosario Inzerillo "Arabian horses." Mangano assured the other mafioso it was a good deal: "Pure blood, they cost 170 million—you know what I'm saying."

Prosecutors probing Dell'Utri's connections with Cosa Nostra later found a note in Dell'Utri's diary recording that the mobster paid him a visit in Milan in 1993—this despite it being public knowledge that Mangano had been sent to prison by magistrate Borsellino for much of the 1980s and despite the fact that at the time of the 1993 visit Dell'Utri was busy organizing Berlusconi's first general election campaign. Dell'Utri subsequently told prosecutors that he had merely "socialized" with the senior mobster and drug runner, and would do so again.

Mangano eventually returned to Palermo to become head of the Porta Nuova clan of Cosa Nostra. He died in a jail in 2000 while serving a life sentence for murder, drug offenses and Mafia association. At least *he* didn't get a job in politics or Berlusconi's TV empire. Dell'Utri's rise continued, however (although his eventual fate wouldn't be so different). Despite "mistakenly" bringing a dangerous gangster into the household, and continuing to associate with him for another two decades, Dell'Utri was rewarded with top jobs in the Berlusconi business empire, helped the mogul launch his political career and entered parliament himself.

Berlusconi might have needed to employ Mangano to protect his family from kidnappers, as he claimed. But there's a price for everything, particularly where the Mafia is concerned. The evidence accumulated over decades is damning. Almost 40 Cosa Nostra informants have now told investigators that the Mafia used Berlusconi's burgeoning empire to launder its money, and that there had been a "charge for assistance" for nurturing his businesses. But where assistance stopped and extortion began, we'll probably never know.

In May 2014, after a 20-year legal battle, Italy's highest court, the Supreme Court of Cassation in Rome, sentenced Dell'Utri to seven years in prison for Mafia association, upholding the Palermo appeals court verdict from the year before. The Palermo judges, Dino Lo Forti, Daniela Troja and Mario Conte, said in their 476-page opinion that the former senator's pivotal role as Berlusconi's envoy to Cosa Nostra, in which he helped "pour millions of euros of Berlusconi's money into the Mafia's coffers," was "beyond reasonable doubt."

The pivotal episode in the shady association, they said, was the meeting in Milan in 1974 between up-and-coming businessman Berlusconi, Cosa Nostra associate Gaetano Cinà and high-ranking boss Stefano Bontate, an encounter that Dell'Utri organized and attended. It was at this meeting that a deal was struck, Berlusconi received protection from other mafia clans plus backing for his construction business and protection of broadcasting plans in Sicily in return for large amounts of cash.[7] But in addition, it seems likely that Cosa Nostra benefitted by having somewhere to launder its dirty money while reaping the returns as a secret shareholder in one of Italy's fastest-growing financial empires.

Finally facing prison, Dell'Utri wasn't taking any chances. Just before the Supreme Court was to rule definitively on his conviction—and with the distinct possibility it would confirm the lower court's sentence—he packed his bags and fled. Interpol agents found Dell'Utri on April 12, 2014, in a five-star hotel in Beirut, Lebanon, with €30,000 ($40,000) in cash and 110 pounds of luggage, five days after Italian authorities sounded the alarm. Several weeks later he was hauled back to Italy to begin his jail sentence in Palermo.[8]

Despite the raft of evidence against him, including his close ties to Dell'Utri, whom judges said had "a natural predisposition to actively enter into contact with Mafiosi," Berlusconi himself was not tried for mafia association: the statute of limitations does not allow prosecution of alleged crimes that occurred more than 20 years earlier (unless they carry a life sentence). Magistrates just beat the clock when they nailed Dell'Utri, who was shown to have been in contact with Mangano until 1994. But for Berlusconi, it was too late to press charges for mafia links said to have occurred in the 1970s and 1980s.

As the Palermo judges noted, the shady dealings were not restricted to Berlusconi's construction business. TV was the sector that truly propelled him to national and international fame—and notoriety—and it appears even this activity may have been tainted from the start. One Mafia informer said that from 1978 onward Berlusconi's Fininvest holding group paid some $130,000 a year in protection money to keep its TV transmitters in Sicily operational. Another high-profile informant, Giovanni "The Pig" Brusca, claimed that Berlusconi poured as much as 600 million lire ($400,000) a year into Cosa Nostra's coffers, which was "tied to his business activities in Sicily."[9]

The mogul's broadcast career started at Milano 2. One of the new town's novelties was its own cable TV station. In 1974, the year that Berlusconi sat down for a chat with Sicilian underworld figures Gaetano Cinà and Stefano Bontate, Telemilano was beamed into the shiny new homes at Milano 2. Pompous broadcast plutocrats at Rai, Italy's stuffy state broadcaster, probably scoffed. Although the unlikely maiden broadcast—an interview with the head of the Kurdish resistance in Iraq, conducted in French—was a long way from the ratings-grabbing lowbrow fare that would launch his TV channels into the big time, Berlusconi would soon be laughing at Rai's expense.

It seems likely that, at first, Berlusconi wasn't thinking much further than employing new cable TV technology to add another luxury amenity to his Milano 2 development. At that time, laws enshrined a strict monopoly for Rai, the state-owned broadcaster, and private operations had to be very small to remain under the radar. This all changed in 1976, when Italy's Constitutional Court paved the way for local commercial broadcasting, although Rai would retain its monopoly on national TV and radio. Berlusconi, never one to miss a good business opportunity, responded to the court's ruling by purchasing another local station, TVI Television International of Milan, and merging it with Telemilano to create Telemilano 58, which began broadcasting over the local airwaves. He wasn't the only one to enter the new market; over 400 small private TV outfits sprouted up. The vast majority were no-hopers, without the resources or the know-how to make a decent go of it.

Three networks, launched by the big publishing houses, Mondadori, Rizzoli and Rusconi, seemed to have the most going for them. They may well have sneered at Berlusconi, the arriviste real-estate mogul, as he attempted to conquer the airwaves without their literary and intellectual credentials. In reality, it was the publishing houses that never stood a chance. Part of Berlusconi's genius was that he understood, from a business perspective, that it was essential to give viewers what they wanted, not what paternalistic journalists thought they needed.

The mogul's TV insight was all the more impressive given that most Italians didn't yet *know* what they wanted. But when Berlusconi introduced his trashy but addictive diet of *Dallas*, *Baywatch* and topless quiz shows, viewers soon realized what they'd been missing. Berlusconi, the entertainer, had notched up another victory. He started as he meant to go on, stealing one of Rai's best-known entertainers, Mike Bongiorno, its

American-Italian middlebrow "Chat Show King," and making him "artistic director." Italy's cultural elite sniggered. But Berlusconi knew exactly what he was doing. "Remember that the audience or our listeners, as they say in America, have about an eighth-grade education and were not top of the class," he told his sales team in a 1980 pep talk.[10]

With viewers switching in droves to his stream of trash and cheap US imports, Berlusconi was able to turn his nascent broadcast business into a fabulous cash cow. Crusty old Rai looked down on advertising as a vulgar necessity in its attempt to educate the nation with documentaries and programs on the arts and history. Would-be advertisers had to ingratiate themselves with the mostly leftist or pious Christian Democrat figures in charge of the various Rai channels for the privilege of paying to promote their goods or services. Even then, advertisers had to ensure their commercial spots didn't offend the Christian Democrats' Victorian sanctimony or the leftists' rigid worldview. Any suggestion of hedonism or even consumerism—the whole point of advertising, after all—was frowned upon. Hence firms seeking the power of TV to advertise underarm deodorant (intimate and embarrassing), dog food (extravagant when Third World children were starving) and cars (Italy's Fiat should be protected from competition) were not allowed.[11] It's little wonder that Berlusconi's less hidebound advertising arm, Publitalia, was able to clean up. Publitalia was founded in 1979; at the end of 1980 it posted revenues of 12 billion lire ($10 million). By the end of the 1980s income had soared to 2,167 billion lire ($1.8 billion).

From the beginning, Berlusconi pushed his luck with the law. In order to deliver these extraordinary revenues, he had to expand his TV station from a local outfit to a national operation. Unfortunately, the 1976 ruling by the Constitutional Court stated that private broadcasters could operate only locally.

Renato Brunetta, one of Berlusconi's key political advisers, noted that "what Berlusconi did was what he always does. He cut to the core—and the core was that the purpose of television was to sell advertising nationally."[12]

Berlusconi came up with a crafty way around the ban on national programming by private corporations. He retained what was nominally a group of local TV stations but had them broadcast the same programs a few seconds apart. "The idea was pure genius," said Brunetta, who has remained loyal to Berlusconi through innumerable scandals to this very day. Through parallel scheduling—from Canale 5 in the north and Canale 10 in the south—Berlusconi achieved a national TV station in all but name, and one that stood to clean up in the hugely under-exploited advertising market. His chief rivals, Mondadori's Rete 4 and Rusconi's Italia 1, responded in kind. But neither could regain the lost ground in the advertising war—and neither could compete with Berlusconi's seemingly bottomless pockets. By 1984, they had both sold out to him. In the span of six years, the real-estate mogul had built up three "national" TV channels, giving him a virtual monopoly in private TV, which would power his business and political success over the next three decades.

A major hiccup occurred in October 1984 when magistrates in three regional capitals—Rome, Turin and Pescara—declared that Berlusconi's TV channels were for all intents and purposes national networks, and therefore in breach of the 1976 ban and had to be shut down. Berlusconi critics may have wondered why it had taken the law so long to work this out. Nonetheless, on October 16, 1984, distraught viewers in three entire regions found themselves without *The Smurfs*, *Dynasty* and Pamela Anderson in a red swimsuit.

Berlusconi was quick to underline the gravity of what had happened: "The television, apart from being a great communal activity for the family, is the instrument thanks to which the quality of life is improving."[13] His Fininvest TV shows, which continued to broadcast to the rest of Italy, fanned the flames of outrage. They demanded that citizens be free to choose with their TV remote controls. Not for the first time in the scheming mogul's still-young career, at the sign of real trouble he was able to call on the right person to help him. Berlusconi's crony this time was none other than Italy's prime minister, Bettino Craxi.

As the historian Paul Ginsborg noted, Craxi "reacted with a speed and determination that could only have been called exemplary had they been employed for another and worthier cause."[14]

The prime minister, who was probably in Berlusconi's pocket by this point, told journalists: "As a TV viewer, it annoyed me to see blank screens." He didn't address the question of illegality. Instead he called an emergency cabinet meeting for Saturday, October 20. This meeting produced one of Italy's all-too-common emergency decrees—laws that neatly skirt the need for parliamentary scrutiny and thus avoid the obvious inconveniences associated with the democratic process. The Craxi decree allowed national commercial television broadcasts to resume, and

Berlusconi's millions to continue pouring in. Berlusconi thanked the prime minister with a business *billet-doux:* "Dear Bettino, thank you from my heart for what you've done. I know it wasn't easy and that you had to put your credibility and authority on the line. I hope to have the opportunity to make it up to you." Berlusconi needn't have worried.[15]

Craxi, who in 1983 had become Italy's first socialist prime minister, was not an old-school left-winger of the type that a *laissez-faire* businessman like Silvio Berlusconi might be expected to frown upon. This politician, who pulled his party away from the grip of the communists and toward the center, was a power-hungry pragmatist and a bully, who believed the means justified the ends. Unlike his political opposition on the left, he had no compunction about making money and made little effort to disguise this.

Craxi had been named leader of the Socialist Party just as Berlusconi launched his TV business. By the late 1970s, with Berlusconi's star as a property magnate rising, Craxi was a regular dinner guest at the tycoon's opulent San Martino mansion in Arcore. Both of them ambitious and feisty, they became close friends—Craxi would be Berlusconi's best man at his second wedding. More than any other, it was perhaps this unholy alliance, between an unscrupulous businessman and a corrupt politician, that would lift Berlusconi's career into the stratosphere and taint three decades of Italian history.

CHAPTER 3

REALPOLITIK

Critics of Berlusconi remember the 1980s as the decade in which he stitched up Italy and cemented his status as a billionaire media magnate. From the tycoon's point of view, however, it was a time of constant anxiety as he fretted over the fate of his fledgling broadcast empire. The emergency decree issued by his pal Craxi in 1984 gave his national TV operation legal cover for only six months. For the rest of the decade the tycoon hoped and prayed that when it eventually arrived (and it was late—even by Italian standards), legislation to deregulate Italy's private broadcast free-for-all wouldn't emasculate his TV business.

To improve his chances, Berlusconi made sure he kept some of Italy's most powerful people close—in his pocket, in fact. And of course Craxi, Italy's prime minister from 1983 to 1987, was one of them. For the leader of a nominally left-wing party, Craxi enjoyed an unashamedly luxurious lifestyle. When he wasn't dining with Berlusconi at Arcore, he might be found at his swanky homes in New York or Barcelona. If the humdrum business of running the country called for him to be in Rome, he would slum it in the city's five-star Hotel Raphael. In fact, Craxi and his Socialist Party cronies commandeered an entire floor in this opulent Rome institution for ten years. Who paid the bill—and how—was anyone's guess, although honest graft rarely figured in the speculation. It was from the Hotel Raphael that Craxi fled, on April 30, 1993, showered with coins (an insult reserved for thieves) by outraged citizens, to head abroad.[1] Given that Berlusconi's Fininvest had poured nearly 23 billion lire (around $16 million) into the corrupt politician's offshore slush funds, at least he didn't have any financial concerns.

During his heyday, Craxi the champagne socialist demanded numerous favors from Berlusconi. Craxi received lots of friendly coverage on Berlusconi's Canale 5 channel. After the tycoon purchased Rete 4 and Italia 1, these, too, were accommodating to Craxi, which couldn't have hurt his successful election campaign in 1983. Craxi also relied on Berlusconi's financial muscle to settle industrial scores.

When the state-owned food company SME was to be privatized in 1985, the communist-baiting Craxi learned to his dismay that the left-leaning industrialist Carlo De Benedetti, with whom Berlusconi would go on to spar for years, was poised to buy it. Out of the blue, Berlusconi, who'd never shown any interest in the food industry, stepped in to bid 600 billion lire ($300 million back then) for the state-owned firm—100 billion lire more than Benedetti had promised. Berlusconi admitted afterward that Craxi had "begged" him to intervene.[2] When De Benedetti later withdrew his legal challenge, Berlusconi simply walked away from the sale. The SME affair turned what was a growing competition between Berlusconi and fellow media baron De Benedetti into a toxic rivalry. Their backgrounds gave them even more reason to hate each other. De Benedetti, a traditional member of northern Italy's left-leaning bourgeoisie, regarded Berlusconi as a vulgar and unscrupulous arriviste, which was true. But De Benedetti wasn't Snow White in the business scruples stakes—as his subsequent admission of paying big bribes would indicate.[3] For his part, Berlusconi saw his rival as part of the snobbish, sanctimonious left-wing elite he despised, and hoped to give him a bloody nose at every opportunity.

The SME mugging set the scene nicely for the takeover battle of the decade, as the moguls locked horns again over the possession of Italy's biggest publishing house, Mondadori.

In 1986, De Benedetti grabbed a 16 percent stake in the publisher, which also printed the country's biggest-selling news magazine, *Panorama*. Berlusconi already owned 7 percent and began schmoozing Leonardo Mondadori, who controlled an additional 25 percent of the publisher, which he soon sold to the media mogul. The sudden death of the company's CEO, Mario Formenton, a year later, however, provoked the takeover war between the two tycoons. The outcome of this struggle would leave Berlusconi in an even more powerful position and underline the sleazy methods on which his burgeoning business empire was based.

At first, De Benedetti appeared to have the upper hand. In April 1988 the left-wing magnate acquired a majority stake in Mondadori. With this, De Benedetti was able to add *Panorama* to his media empire, which already included the big-circulation center-left publications *La Repubblica* and *L'Espresso*, making him the most powerful media magnate in Italy. The thought of having a natural enemy with so much media clout appalled Craxi. Berlusconi also felt threatened. The furious mogul suggested to Fininvest lawyer Vittorio Dotti that they cover the publishing house in shit. "Metaphorically speaking," said Dotti. "No, really," Berlusconi replied. "We could organize a lorry full of manure to spray over the building."[4]

With just weeks to go before the completion of De Benedetti's purchase of Mondadori, the Mondadori-Formenton family announced it had changed its mind and would now sell its shares to Berlusconi. This volte-face may have been due to the intervention of Formenton's lawyer, who felt that his client had been unhappy about the plans De Benedetti had for Mondadori.[5]

But a furious De Benedetti claimed the way in which his deal had been cast aside was illegal. At the third and final court case in the protracted legal battle, Berlusconi won control of the giant publisher, thanks largely to the efforts of his crooked lawyer, Cesare Previti. Several years later it emerged that Previti had bribed some of the Roman judges hearing the case. So effective were Previti's methods that, incredibly, the final ruling in 1992 favored Berlusconi more than he could have dreamed when he began the legal tussle: the corrupted panel of judges even ruled that *La Repubblica* and *L'Espresso* should be handed over to the mogul.

Subsequent investigations found what appeared to be early versions of the crooked judges' ruling in the offices of Berlusconi's legal team.[6] It seemed that even the judiciary was prepared to sell itself for Berlusconi's millions.

Faced with the prospect of Berlusconi having this much control over the Italian media—including virtually half of its television programming, two major daily papers and the two biggest weekly news magazines—even his political fixers balked. Seven-time (and then incumbent) Christian Democrat prime minister Giulio Andreotti sent emissaries around to Arcore and persuaded Berlusconi it might be a good idea to hand *La Repubblica* and *L'Espresso* back to De Benedetti. At that point in Italy's history, the Machiavellian Christian Democrat bigwigs were still the real powers behind the scenes. Berlusconi agreed. He was already incredibly successful. Why be greedy—or in any case, too greedy? By adding the number one publishing house and the biggest-selling news weekly to his portfolio of three TV stations, he was now Italy's biggest media baron.

Previti's subsequent trial for bribery suggested that a range of underhanded methods were in play to ensure Berlusconi's preeminence in the Italian media. One of the witnesses called for the trial was Enrico Manca, the president of Rai. The state-controlled broadcasting company was in theory Berlusconi's bitterest rival; after all, it was on Rai's lawn that Berlusconi had parked his tanks, stealing millions of viewers and taking full advantage of the paternalistic network's inability or refusal to exploit the Italian advertising market.

Strange, then, that Manca should have a Swiss bank account, managed by Previti, containing the equivalent of over $500,000. Manca said the account existed "only" to avoid tax payments. Berlusconi's critics noted, however, that the account was opened in 1986—the year Manca assumed the powerful position at Rai.[7]

Manca was appointed president of the state broadcast network by Berlusconi's political fixer, Craxi. Previti was reported to have hosted the meeting between the mogul and the newly appointed Rai president that produced a sort of pact, or truce, between the two networks. This became known as the Pax Televisiva. And, looking back, there's not much doubt it worked rather more in Berlusconi's favor than in Rai's. Fininvest audience share grew from a third to nearly a half during this period.

But elected politicians and judges were not the only powerful and influential people to help Berlusconi's business interests. He may also have received support from a secret society known as P2 (Propaganda 2). His involvement in this masonic organization would later lead to one of his first serious brushes with the law.

In October 1990 the appeals court in Venice found Berlusconi guilty of perjury, his first and—until August 2013—only unchallenged conviction, albeit one not confirmed at the Supreme Court level. Berlusconi hadn't helped himself by ignoring the judge's call for him to "be brief" when he made a spontaneous declaration to the court. The mogul loved the sound of his own voice so much he spoke for half an hour.[8]

The mogul had lied in court while trying to sue two Italian journalists, Giovanni Ruggeri and Mario Guarino, over their claims concerning his activities as a freemason. He had been a member of the shadowy P2 masonic lodge—a secret society of politicians, judges, policemen, journalists, dodgy businessmen and various right-wing crackpots. P2's stated aim was to save the country from the Italian Communist Party, by infiltrating trade unions, political parties and the media.

Berlusconi insisted he had joined the P2 lodge only shortly before it was discovered in 1981 and that he hadn't even paid his subscription—thus intimating he hadn't been a serious participant. The documented evidence convinced the court in Venice, however, that the mogul was initiated into the P2 lodge in early 1978 and had paid the 100,000 lire membership fee. Not for the first time in recent Italian history, luck favored the brazen, and Berlusconi's conviction was quashed under a handy amnesty, designed to relieve pressure on the country's overstretched criminal justice system.

But what was Berlusconi doing mixed up with this subversive and unsavory organization? According to the historian Paul Ginsborg: "probably nothing much." The academic suggests that rather than play any sort of strategic role, or take part in its subversive activities, the mogul merely hoped the group might offer the chance to extend his contacts and win personal favors for his business empire.[9] But once again, Berlusconi's dishonesty, and his willingness to keep such grubby company, must call into question his fitness for high office.

His involvement in P2 came to light when two magistrates in Milan, Gherardo Colombo and Giuliano Turone, discovered a partial membership list in 1981—with Berlusconi's name on it—in the process of another investigation. Predictably the P2 list contained a big slice of Italy's power elite—the heads of the secret services, 34 generals, eight admirals, plus police, bankers, magistrates and civil servants and 44 parliamentarians. Victor Emmanuel, the son of Italy's last king, was also on the list. But nobody had heard of Licio Gelli, who headed the organization.

The group has been ridiculed in some quarters. But Gelli and another P2 member, Pietro Musumeci, were found guilty of attempting to impede police investigations into the August 1980 bomb attack that killed 85 people at the Bologna railway station. Right-wing terrorists were convicted for the atrocity.

So, was P2 just a motley assortment of reactionary individuals who dreamed of bashing the left while making some deals for themselves on the side or, as some insist, something far more alarming and more powerful—"a shadow government"? Philip Willan, an author of two books about the role of the lodge in Cold War Italy, told me: "The P2 was both a mutual assistance society for its professionally ambitious members and an important secret instrument for the global battle against communism, both in Italy and Latin America." He added that when the lodge's power was at its height, "no major business operation could go ahead in Italy without a green light from Licio Gelli."

P2 certainly had a predilection for money: of the 1,000 or so names on the incomplete membership list found in Gelli's office in 1981, 119 were drawn from the treasury and finance ministries and from the banks. The heads of the armed forces and the main intelligence agencies were also represented in the lodge. Gelli told Willan that as head of P2 he had been in personal contact with the heads of the CIA in Italy.[10]

By 1977, P2 even had its tendrils well and truly wrapped around *Corriere della Sera*, the country's stately newspaper of record. In the late 1970s, *Corriere* had run into financial difficulty. In desperation, the newspaper's publisher, Rizzoli, accepted Gelli's offer of money and in return pledged to fire the editor and ensure the paper's editorial line shifted radically to the right.[11]

Soon inexplicable stories, which are now thought to have been coded messages to and from various intelligence organizations, began appearing on the paper's usually sober news pages. During the 55-day period between March and May of 1978, in which Christian Democrat ex-premier Aldo Moro was held hostage by the Red Brigade terrorists, one editorial in this traditionally moderate newspaper called for democratic rights to be suspended and suspected leftist sympathizers to be rounded up.[12] Thus, for a bizarre but mercifully brief period *Corriere della Sera* resembled the in-house journal of Augusto Pinochet. A subsequent cross-party parliamentary report declared P2 had dedicated itself "to the pollution of the public life of a nation."[13] And around this time—in 1978—Berlusconi became an unlikely financial commentator in this highbrow daily.

Even if Berlusconi didn't share the P2's subversive ideals, there is evidence that he may have enjoyed significant benefits from membership. In 1979, when the finance police officer Massimo Maria Berruti questioned Berlusconi over the nature of his real-estate finances, he turned to his superior officer Salvatore Gallo before deciding to shelve evidence that Berlusconi had dodged currency control laws. Gallo was initiated into the P2 lodge in July 1980.

In the 1970s, Berlusconi's business empire appeared to have remarkably good access to capital in Italian finance houses. One such house was the Monte dei Paschi di Siena bank. Its general manager, Giovanni Cresti, was a member of P2. Later Monte dei Paschi di Siena's statutory board of auditors concluded that "inspectors who have looked at the loan book have made an accurate analysis of it that allows the conclusion that there was significant favoritism toward [Berlusconi's group]."[14]

Geoffrey Robinson, a Touche-Ross accountant who worked on the liquidation of a Luxembourg subsidiary of the P2-controlled Banco Ambrosiano, told Roman magistrates in 2004 that some of the bank's investments that helped Berlusconi were evidently made for political rather than business reasons. "The reasons for this share purchase can only be understood in the light of the Italian political situation at the time, since the operation made no sense in itself; it was a bit like throwing money out of the window," Robinson said of one transaction.[15]

In addition to sharing his opinions on economic matters with readers of *Corriere della Sera*, which was and remains the country's biggest-selling newspaper, Berlusconi was also buying up a daily paper for himself. In 1977 he purchased a 12.5 percent stake in *Il Giornale;* within ten years, he'd increased this to a majority holding. Its editor, Indro Montanelli, one of Italy's most distinguished journalists, shared with Berlusconi an aversion to communism. He left *Corriere della Sera* in the 1970s—before its brief infiltration by P2—because he thought the paper was becoming too tolerant of the far left. Convinced that the country needed a strong conservative daily, he founded *Il Giornale*.

Unlike his new boss, however, Montanelli had respect for democracy and due process. His journalistic integrity ensured he attacked those on either side of the political spectrum when he spotted cant or hypocrisy. This proved a constant source of bafflement and irritation for the tycoon-publisher. But Berlusconi's relationship with Montanelli was unlike any he had with other employees. The tycoon, despite being immeasurably richer than his editor, held his contrarian editor in a degree of veneration—without ever appreciating his need for journalist independence. Once, when he called around to admonish his editor over yet another off-message article, he found that the elderly journalist was unwell. He washed his employee's feet in a basin, repeating over and over: "This is something I wouldn't even do for my father."[16]

In many ways the complete antithesis of Berlusconi, the tall, skeletal and intellectual Montanelli was famous for his sardonic wit—from which even his employer was not spared. "He lies as he breathes," the journalist famously declared of Berlusconi at a later date. Berlusconi wasn't the only person riled by Montanelli's irreverence. By 1983, Craxi was raging about Montanelli's attacks against his person and his party.

After becoming prime minister, Craxi rang Berlusconi (in a conversation wiretapped by magistrates fishing for evidence of the mogul's links with the mob) to warn his mogul-friend that he considered *Il Giornale* to be "hostile," and he said that there would be "consequences." Coming from his political fixer-in-chief, "consequences" sounded a lot like no more protection from hostile antitrust media legislation. Berlusconi replied in the same conversation that he would "show his claws" and "we'll tell him [Montanelli] to fuck off."[17]

But Berlusconi, fearing a direct confrontation with such a distinguished and formidable employee as Montanelli, preferred instead to go behind his back. He set about encouraging more malleable senior staff members of the newspaper to toe the line, well aware that even an editor as experienced as Montanelli couldn't exercise complete control over all the pages of a major daily newspaper.

But in the following decade as Berlusconi was preparing for his own entry into the political arena, Montanelli's criticism was deemed no longer simply irritating, but unacceptable.

Berlusconi continued to talk up his own hands-off approach as a press baron. "My TV networks and my newspapers are free spaces in society where everyone—I repeat—everyone, even those who think differently to how I do, has and will continue to have, the right to speak . . . impartiality is my rule."[18] But for the leading journal of the right, anything other than *Il Giornale*'s fulsome support for Berlusconi's political aspirations would be very damaging. Berlusconi has always courted popularity, however. And sacking a national journalistic treasure such as Montanelli presented a problem. As ever, and as the next chapter shows, the smiling media mogul with the bottomless pockets had the right cronies to do his dirty work—and forced the redoubtable Montanelli to fall on his sword.

Ironically, in the late 1980s, while Berlusconi was fretting over his editor's failure to concentrate his fire on the political left, the mogul was entering into a lucrative and—even today—little-known business venture with his supposed *bête noire*, the Soviet Union. Montanelli, the arch-anticommunist, wouldn't have approved. Not surprisingly, though,

Berlusconi didn't draw attention to the fact that he had sent his senior lawyer Vittorio Dotti and two high-ranking Publitalia executives, Dario Rivolta and Giorgio Maino, over to Moscow in the spring of 1998 to firm up a deal to produce TV advertising for the monolithic Soviet state network Gosterlaradio.

The Soviet TV apparatchiks accepted the Berlusconi executives' proposals to produce spots for Western firms as part of a joint Italian-Soviet venture, although the commercials had to be at least six minutes long and contain the right information/propaganda. Dotti explained that an advertisement for Fiat cars, for example, "had to begin by showing the plant where the cars were built. You had to show the workmen and engineers in action and it was necessary to talk about the materials and the production processes. In other words, you had to produce a little film."[19]

But the mogul was fine with that, according to Dotti: "For Berlusconi, ideology wasn't a problem." Crucially, the new advertising spots raked in an "impressive" 100 million lire ($68,000) a pop. The oddball Soviet-Italian operation even produced its own little manifesto, with a TV screen next to the Soviet flag complete with hammer and sickle. So, even as his future friend Vladimir Putin was busy doing the KGB's dirty work in East Germany, the *laissez-faire* mogul was making hay in Mother Russia.

In the early days at least, Berlusconi was smart at managing his public image as well as dealing with his political opponents. He knew that a large part of his appeal lay in his image as a man of the people, albeit one who flew by helicopter from one luxury pleasure palace to another. In 1986, even as he was scheming and fretting over the fate of his media empire, the millions pouring in from TV advertising meant he was able to buy a football (soccer) club. And not just any football club. Berlusconi became the owner of mighty AC Milan, one of the aristocrats of the sport.

In the mid-1980s the team was going through a lean period. But national interest in football was greater than ever thanks to Italy's triumph in the 1982 World Cup. The purchase, which was to prove one of the tycoon's most inspired, was probably a mixture of heart and head. Berlusconi, a life-long supporter of Milan, imagined a rejuvenated team, flush with his cash, and he saw how the team's success might rub off on him. Berlusconi the businessman was also quick to see how much he stood to make from advertising in football-mad Italy.

But the decision to take the leap was a torturous one. He'd actually been considering buying the football club for several years. Back in 1982 a clairvoyant he consulted, known as Moro, had warned that the portents were against the purchase of AC Milan.[20] "My mystic told me that it would bring me bad luck," he told associates.

But unable to shake the obsession with owning the prestigious club, he convened another meeting in January 1986 with his most trusted associates to discuss buying it. Not one to do things in half measures, the mogul rented a huge villa in the top ski resort St. Moritz, in the Swiss Alps, which had belonged to the former shah of Iran. After a weekend of examining and reexamining the pros, and many potential cons, of purchasing AC Milan, Berlusconi and his aides agreed the move was too risky. The morning after, however, when the group had just taken their business-class seats for the flight back to Milan, Berlusconi suddenly declared: "Oh to hell with it. I'm going to buy it."[21]

Thus in July 1986, to the accompaniment of Wagner's "Ride of the Valkyries," the new Berlusconi AC Milan squad flew into the stadium by helicopter to meet the fans. In the following 1986–87 season, the club sold a record number of season tickets.

Berlusconi's AC Milan made shrewd purchases from overseas, including the Dutch stars Ruud Gullit and Marco Van Basten. The purchase of Gullit was particularly interesting. This flamboyant black player, famous for his flowing dreadlocks, was confronted by Italian football crowds—which are often racist and violent. However, Milan fans were soon dazzled by Gullit's skills and charm and in their own, politically incorrect, way showed their appreciation by blacking their faces and wearing dreadlock wigs during the matches. Of course Berlusconi was quick to claim the credit for this transformation.

"I explained to them it was possible to support a club without being violent or racist. That mentality had to go." Unfortunately, you don't have to go very far to see such attitudes elsewhere in Italian football. But to its credit, Berlusconi's AC Milan, in purchasing Gullit and, more recently, black players like Mario Balotelli, has been more active than most clubs in fighting racism on the terraces. It was noted, however, that Berlusconi's unlikeable and mentally unspectacular brother, Paolo Berlusconi, undid some of the good work in February 2013 when he referred to Balotelli, Milan's new $28 million striker, as "the little negro of the family."[22]

Berlusconi basked in the glow of the revitalized club—and notable triumphs, including the Italian championship in 1988 and the European Champion's Cup the following year, for which the club provided a ship, an airplane and 450 buses to ensure 26,000 Milan fans were in Barcelona to see the victory.[23]

As he had hoped, Berlusconi profited mightily from the symbiotic relationship that TV enjoys with the sport. The more that football was broadcast and discussed—with endless hours devoted to match highlights and analysis—the greater the interest created. This meant bigger AC Milan ticket sales as well as more viewers and greater TV advertising revenue for the mogul's TV channels.

In addition to making huge quantities of cash, AC Milan would also prove a vital source of inspiration and popular appeal in the 1990s, when Berlusconi made his move into politics. With the trophies piling up, Berlusconi's fame soared; he was surprised—but utterly delighted—to receive praise bordering on adulation from Milan fans. He liked to recall how one supporter had told him: "Silvio, you're God; you're the Messiah." The suggestion of divinity obviously struck a chord with the vain and egotistical tycoon, who'd be further buoyed by polls suggesting he was better known among Italian children than the Son of God. In 2006, explaining why Italians ought to reelect him after five years of crass and inept leadership, Prime Minister Berlusconi said: "I am the Jesus Christ of politics . . . I sacrifice myself for everyone."[24]

Football wasn't the mogul's only major move in the 1980s in which his emotions played a major part. For family man Berlusconi it was love—or probably lust—at first sight at the start of the decade. In March 1980 he saw a voluptuous young actress named Veronica Lario, née Miriam Raffaella Bartolini, give a topless turn in Fernand Crommelynk's stage comedy, called (rather appropriately as things would turn out) *Il Magnifico Cornuto* (the magnificent cuckold). The smitten tycoon dashed backstage after the show (he owned Milan's Teatro Manzoni, after all) to tell the 24-year-old from Bologna how much he'd appreciated her performance.

The pair became lovers. Lario moved in, together with her mother, to the residential part of Berlusconi's Milan business headquarters. He kept the relationship secret from his wife, Carla Dall'Oglio, until 1984, when Lario gave birth to Berlusconi's third child, Barbara. With the affair out in the open, Berlusconi and Dall'Oglio separated within a year. Relations between Dall'Oglio and the tycoon appear to have remained amicable over the years, and Berlusconi has continued to show her the generosity and concern that he typically displays to those close to him. This undoubtedly is one of his more attractive character traits.

Lario gave up acting after her appearance in the 1982 slasher film *Tenebre,* by cult horror director Dario Argento. Rather than making a home at Arcore, however, Lario chose, from 1992 onward, to bring up her three children in the opulent Villa Belvedere, north of Milan. Lario bore two other children to Berlusconi after Barbara: Eleonora and Luigi were born in 1986 and 1988, respectively. Lario, an interesting and feisty personality, never assumed the dowdy role of politician's wife. She rarely accompanied Berlusconi on state visits and had no compunction about criticizing his conservative politics, including Italy's role in supporting the invasion of Iraq. For most of the 1990s their marriage was seen as successful, if unconventional. But by the early 2000s they had entered into a cordial separation. This became a spectacularly messy and bitter divorce in May 2009, when the extent of Berlusconi's libido hit the front pages.

But back in the mid-1980s, with billions of dollars of advertising flowing in, a beautiful new partner and AC Milan football club to his name, everything was going right for Berlusconi. He just needed his political allies to sort out the business about the media antitrust law.

After eight years of sweating and scheming and greasing the palms of every venal official or parliamentarian who intimated that he stood to make life easier or harder for the TV baron, things suddenly threatened to turn sour for Berlusconi in 1988, after the fall of Craxi's government.

The bolt from the blue was the election to the prime minister's office of the left-wing Christian Democrat Ciriaco De Mita, who made little effort to hide the fact that he considered Berlusconi a vulgar opportunist. He swiftly appointed a new head of Rai, Biagio Agnes, who tore up the Pax Televisiva. But De Mita's premiership lasted only a year, and he was replaced by Giulio Andreotti, a more malleable politician, who, along with another Christian Democrat figure, Arnaldo Forlani, and Craxi, formed the unofficial CAF (so named after the trio's initials) pact, which would keep the leftists at bay—and help Berlusconi shore up his TV empire.

Finally, in 1989, after a decade of virtually uncontrolled private broadcasting, clear new regulations on the limits of media ownership and activity were imminent. Berlusconi had three of the six major national TV channels, a newspaper, and important news magazines. He'd also sewn up 60 percent of Italy's burgeoning TV advertising market. It fell to Republican Party member Oscar Mammì, a small but respected member of the coalition government, to draw up the legislation. Rumors swirled around the Italian parliament and in the columns of the newspapers that Berlusconi would be forced to give up one, or even two, of his TV channels in order to undo his domination of the Italian media.

Jaws dropped when the proposals finally emerged. The limit on the number of TV channels that could be controlled by an individual was three—the number Berlusconi already had. The mogul, who was no doubt grinning from ear to ear, would, however, have to relinquish his national newspaper, *Il Giornale*, which he did by handing it over to his brother, thus keeping it in the family and maintaining his influence.

Even better for the tycoon, by banning the simultaneous ownership of a TV channel and national newspaper (but not, note, news magazines, which Berlusconi owned), the antitrust proposals would prevent his main media rivals and critics—principally the owners of the daily newspapers *Corriere della Sera*, *La Repubblica* and *La Stampa*—from joining Berlusconi in the lucrative TV market.

Prosecutors later discovered that the man who drafted the legislation for Oscar Mammì, Davide Giacalone, received a payment of 600 million lire (then worth $500,000) from Berlusconi's Fininvest holding company. He maintained that it was a consulting fee. Prosecutors also investigated the claim that another much bigger payment of 10 billion lire ($8.3 million) originating from Fininvest was given to Giacalone and his political party. But Rome had jurisdiction over the probe, and in the capital city, it would later be revealed, Berlusconi's lawyer Previti had at least one very influential person in the important preliminary investigations court in his pocket. No indictments against Giacalone for accepting bribes were ever made.[25]

These bribes were, in fact, small beer compared with the quantities of cash that may have been splashed out to ensure the "Save Berlusconi" legislation passed through parliament unscathed. In 1991, Fininvest channeled the equivalent of $70 million of Italian treasury notes through different banks in the tax haven of San Marino, before converting them to cash and ferrying the money back to Milan in a series of armored trucks, and then using the money to buy new treasury bonds.[26] The tortuous path of this huge amount of money no doubt would have resulted in payments that were very difficult to trace.

Asked about the reasons for this Fort Knox–style operation involving such enormous amounts of money, one senior Berlusconi employee, Mario Moranzoni, the treasurer of Fininvest, was said to have replied: "Politicians cost a lot. The Mammì law is up for discussion."[27] Up for discussion, yes, but with that much cash thrown at its potential critics, it certainly wasn't really under threat.

Prosecutors later discovered another big single payment—of around $18 million—to an offshore account belonging to the former prime minister, Bettino Craxi. Thus, seven years after the crooked Socialist leader threw Berlusconi's nascent TV empire a lifeline with his emergency decree, he was there again, cap in hand, to ensure its future. Craxi didn't know it then, but his days were already numbered.

Thanks to Craxi's venality, however, Il Cavaliere was now in the position to fleece a nation.

CHAPTER 4

ESCAPE ROUTE

With his money-spinning TV empire shored up by the 1990 Telecommunications Law, Berlusconi looked set for life. Although his shady business methods had left a trail of incriminating evidence as long as the Milan-Rome autostrada, it was clear that Italy's politicians were unable or unwilling to challenge the mogul and his virtual monopoly on commercial television.

One group, however, not only smelled a rat, but set out to do something about it. Italy's magistrates made their first real moves against Berlusconi in the early 1990s, launching a legal war that continues to this day. Concerns about the opaque nature of the investments that launched him into the big time had ensured the tycoon was never really off the prosecutors' radar. Before battle was truly joined, however, Italy's powerful judiciary took on and defeated an even bigger foe. And in doing so, they unwittingly provided Silvio Berlusconi with an escape path—in practice a political vacuum into which the mogul would slip with astonishing ease.

People with only a passing interest in world affairs at the time were probably aware of the Tangentopoli (bribe city) mega-scandal that engulfed Italy in 1992–1994. Cynical Europeans looked on and shook their heads at news reports that appeared to confirm their impression of Italy as a country mired in graft. But even long-suffering (and in many cases, participating) Italians were shocked at what prosecutors found. Following the trail from a single incident of bribery, magistrates uncovered a vast web of corruption that enmeshed Italy's ruling political class. So clamorous was the outcry that within 18 months the centrist Socialist and

Christian Democrat parties, which between them had ruled Italy for half a century, imploded completely. This political cataclysm would signal the end of Italy's First Republic—only to see it replaced with something startlingly different but depressingly similar.

The Mani Pulite (Clean Hands) investigation that uncovered Tangentopoli began on February 17, 1992, when magistrates in Milan arrested Mario Chiesa, a Socialist Party official, as he tried to flush a $6,000 bribe from a cleaning firm down the toilet. The payment didn't seem that big in the grand scheme of things, but prosecutors were intrigued to discover that this party apparatchik, who had designs on the mayorship of Milan, had also managed to squirrel away $10 million in Swiss bank accounts.

After the news of Chiesa's arrest broke, Socialist Party chief Bettino Craxi publicly disowned him; he was a bad apple in an otherwise whiter-than-white political organization. This was the worst thing Berlusconi's political fixer could have done. Galled by his superior's chutzpah, and resigned to an inevitable conviction when magistrates found his Swiss slush funds, Chiesa began spilling the beans on political corruption so endemic it is thought to have been worth $4 billion a year.[1] Chiesa told investigators that all the major political parties regarded bribes as an extra "tax"—for their benefit.

Some economists calculated that this sleaze factor added about 5 percent to the cost of every business transaction carried out in 1992.[2] Magistrates in Milan, where the giant corruption scandal first centered, had the bit between their teeth and went all out to catch the crooks in the ruling Socialist and Christian Democrat parties. Rapidly moving up the food chain, they discovered that politicians expected—and got—big kickbacks on everything imaginable, from cleaning contracts to the construction of new roads.

It's worth noting, without in any way excusing the rampant corruption of Tangentopoli, that bribes had figured in Italian politics for as long as anyone could remember. The use of kickbacks was ramped up during the Cold War period as a means to fund the political parties; the Christian Democrats and the Socialists in particular skimmed off millions to fight the growing strength of the Italian Communist Party—the largest in Europe. But, even as the fall of the Berlin Wall signaled the threat had passed, establishment politicians became greedier. Craxi and his colleagues wanted more and more—and much of the cash went into their own pockets or overseas slush funds.

The Clean Hands magistrates were helped in their quest by the national mood at the time. Following a series of lesser scandals, the public's disgust at their crooked politicians was already at the boiling point. Hence the emergence of protest parties. Most prominent of these was the populist Northern League, rising from nowhere to demand secession from what it saw (with some justification) as the corrupt, lawless south of Italy and Rome, "La Ladrona" (the big thief), where—it said—diligent northern workers' taxes disappeared into a bottomless pit.

In Milan alone, the Clean Hands investigations resulted in 1,408 definitive convictions for white-collar crimes including bribery, abuse of office, illegal funding of political parties and false accounting.[3] But the investigations soon fanned out: at one point more than a third of Italy's parliamentarians were under investigation, and judges dissolved 400 town councils. When then justice minister Giovanni Conso sought to downgrade the seriousness of bribery-related offenses in order to take the heat off scores of endangered lawmakers—the so called *colpo di spugna* (wipe the slate clean) proposals—baying crowds surrounded the Ministry of Justice and the parliament building.[4] The government soon ditched the proposals. Parliamentarians also voted to impede the arrest of their colleagues by Mani Pulite magistrates, but soon thought better of it. Many businessmen who'd had to pay the bribes were lining up to give evidence, but some of those complicit in the web of corruption took their own lives, as did at least one parliamentarian.

In the December 1992 local elections, support for the two main political parties collapsed. The day after the elections, magistrates officially placed the biggest fish of all, Socialist Party leader Bettino Craxi, under investigation. The former prime minister was charged with corruption and involvement in illegal funding of political parties. The evidence of his criminal greed mounted; he was soon facing 11 indictments. His infamous excuse, "*Così fan tutte*" (everyone does it), didn't go down well. In May 1994, he fled Italy for his villa in Hammamet, Tunisia. The Italian courts convicted him in his absence on two counts of corruption (with over 40 charges still pending) and sentenced him to 27 years in jail, reduced to nine years on appeal.[5] Craxi died in exile in 2000 from diabetes-related complications.

Berlusconi's recalcitrant newspaper editor, Indro Montanelli, meanwhile, hailed the Mani Pulite investigations as "a peaceful revolution by civil society" and printed daily developments with gusto—to the chagrin of Berlusconi's political chums. Berlusconi may have allowed himself a wry smile as he saw politicians who had been pestering him for money for a decade being taken away in handcuffs.

The mogul was also aware of the huge popular support enjoyed by the magistrates leading the purge. One prosecutor, Antonio Di Pietro, who produced the pivotal confession from Chiesa, became a star overnight and enjoyed the sort of hero status that had been thrust upon Berlusconi when he stepped in to revitalize AC Milan.

Di Pietro certainly stood out from the series of gray-haired men who slipped in and out of Milan's forbidding Palace of Justice every day. Solidly built with a not unhandsome but lived-in face of a boxer, Di Pietro was immediately recognized by the way he spoke, with his strange accent and odd inflexions he'd carried from the little—and little-known—region of Molise in the southeast of the country. His background also helped set him apart from other prosecutors. Unlike his boss, the chief prosecutor, Francesco Saverio Borrelli, Di Pietro wasn't from Milan's *borghesia*, but from a poor rural family. He studied law at night school and served as a policeman before joining the judiciary.

The Italian public loved him. "Go on Di Pietro" slogans appeared everywhere. Traders saw Di Pietro T-shirts fly off the shelves. But unlike the mogul selling AC Milan kit, Di Pietro was working for the good of society—and, as he was to find out, at no small cost to his own career. He also moved into politics, but, unlike his media mogul nemesis, he would never be slippery enough to succeed in the Machiavellian world of Italian politics.

For Berlusconi, though, the immediate downside of Di Pietro's diligence was a rapid depletion in the ranks of his political fixers. Without their support, his media empire wouldn't have existed. And with their demise, how long would his empire last?

The fall of Craxi was bad enough for Berlusconi, but he had even more to worry about in June 1993, when magistrates arrested Davide Giacalone, the ministerial aide who had drafted the Berlusconi-friendly media legislation and received a $500,000 "consulting fee." Soon after Giacalone's arrest, a Fininvest executive, Aldo Brancher, was held for offering bribes to the health ministry in order to win a larger share of lucrative public health advertising on the Berlusconi networks. Investigators were not stopping at politicians: policemen and even a judge were arrested as part of the monumental anti-corruption purge. Berlusconi knew that his nemeses, the magistrates, were getting closer and that, without his crooked friends in positions of power, the left would make a bid to destroy his TV business.

By the end of 1993 the financial health of his Fininvest empire was adding to Berlusconi's woes. The TV advertising revenues were still pouring in, but the tycoon had overstretched himself by purchasing the Standa supermarket chain, an over-staffed and old-fashioned outfit that never took off, even under the dynamic tycoon's ownership. And there were the ill-fated ventures into French TV: Berlusconi bought pay channel Telepiù and the lowbrow Tele Cinq—dismissed by the snooty French as "Coca-Cola TV." These failures cost him hundreds of millions of dollars.

Between 1987 and 1993, Berlusconi's Fininvest empire saw its audience share rise and its turnover rocket fivefold. In the same period, though, its debts shot up by 1,200 percent and its profitability collapsed.[6] Berlusconi didn't have a cash-flow problem. Rather, he'd demonstrated a monumental ability for overdoing it—a tendency that, along with his uneasy relationship with the law, would come to define him.

A general election was not far off, and with the anticommunist Christian Democrats and Craxi's centrist Socialist Party swallowed up by the Tangentopoli black hole, Berlusconi dreaded a left-wing surge in the national polls. In the December 1993 local elections, the left even won the traditional center-right strongholds of Palermo and Naples. What a government made up of not-very-ex-communists might do to his private TV monopoly put the fear of God into Berlusconi. Given the huge debts that Fininvest had already racked up, he knew it wouldn't take very much to sink the business.

The left was already making noise about dismantling two of the mogul's networks. In addition, the center-left coalition government wanted to follow the rest of Europe and ban the tacky advertising spots in the middle of quiz and light-entertainment shows, which saw presenters segue effortlessly from interviewing guests to promoting prosciutto. This advertising deviance had, of course, been pioneered in Italy by Berlusconi—and it earned his Fininvest empire a whopping $350 million a year.[7]

Fininvest hit back using the very same TV programs that were threatened by the ban. Stars and presenters attacked the government and talked up the on-air promotional spots as if they were public information films. This succeeded in killing the proposed law change; and in retrospect it might be seen as an out-of-town tryout for the Fininvest boss's own general election campaign the following year.

The national political situation remained precarious, though, for Berlusconi. The center-right was in free fall and the left in the ascendant. Things were further complicated by proposals, widely backed by the public and parliament, to replace Italy's rickety form of proportional representation with a type of first-past-the-post system of the kind used in Britain and the US, albeit one that recognized solid coalitions as single groups. Berlusconi commissioned Giuliano Urbani, an expert at Milan's Bocconi University, to predict what the outcome would be in a general election. To the mogul's horror, the political scientist predicted a landslide for the opposition.

Il Giornale editor Montanelli later revealed that, in a moment of candor during the 1994 election campaign, Berlusconi had told him why he had decided to make a bid for power. "If I don't enter politics I'll end up in jail and fall into debt."[8] Sixteen years later Fedele Confalonieri, Berlusconi's faithful pal, and Mediaset president, was equally frank: "If Berlusconi hadn't entered politics, if he hadn't created Forza Italia, today we'd be sitting under a bridge or in prison accused of mafia offences."[9]

Demonstrating his Olympic-level chutzpah, the mogul declared in November 1993 that the inevitable conflict of interests that would arise from his participation in politics, as a media magnate, meant he would not be standing in the general election. "It would be in complete contradiction with my principles and unfair to the other candidates."[10] In fact, by refusing to name himself a prime ministerial candidate, Berlusconi was under less pressure to answer tricky questions on what he would do to turn around Italy's moribund economy or cut debt levels sufficiently to ensure the nation qualified for entry into the single European currency, the euro.

Only on January 26, 1994—just two months ahead of the general election—did the mogul officially enter the playing field (*scendere in campo*), after months of increasingly unconvincing denials. But it's almost certain he'd made the decision several months earlier. A key stage was a secret meeting at Arcore in July 1993, with close friends and advisers. Two of them, Fedele Confalonieri and another high-ranking Fininvest executive, Gianni Letta, counseled against Berlusconi's political involvement. But the hawks, led by Dell'Utri and Previti, appeared to have won out.[11]

Berlusconi may have realized a year earlier, however, that his fate—and his salvation—lay in politics. In 1992 his wife, Veronica Lario, certainly appeared aware of his political ambitions, telling *Corriere della Sera* that she had no intention of becoming "a Hillary Clinton," a statement that would prove prophetic when the worst of the scandals struck 18 years later.[12]

Berlusconi employed the full force of his marketing and business machine to create a new political party, one that he would lead to a general election victory. In November 1993, Team Berlusconi began setting up the National Association of Forza Italia! (Go Italy!) clubs. The name Forza Italia! was inspired by the chants of supporters of the national football team. A catchy title—even a little vulgar. Crucially, though, it was entirely different from the language of the political establishment that had just imploded.

By December 1993, the mogul's Forza Italia clubs were present in virtually every major town, and the movement had 200,000 members. For a political movement that was light on policies and heavy on imagery—principally Berlusconi's status as an energetic self-made man—there was something disturbing about the military precision, reminiscent of the days of Mussolini, with which Forza Italia clubs sprung up around Italy. The official plan, however, was not to mimic fascist recruitment strategies, but to ape the Catholic Church by establishing 8,000 outposts to match Italy's 8,000 parishes.[13]

Berlusconi's mafioso advertising chief, Dell'Utri, was charged with employing his formidable marketing and organizational skills as campaign chief. Dell'Utri had first touted the idea of involving Fininvest more closely in politics as early as 1992, shortly after the Tangentopoli scandal broke, when the group's political contacts appeared to be in trouble. The campaign chief had already dispatched his top Publitalia men to scour the country for 600 or so parliamentary candidates to represent Forza Italia. Nearly all were from business and many had direct or indirect links with Fininvest.

The political debutants were all expected to make a contribution to the new party and also had to pay for their "candidate's kit"—rather steep at $700, for little more than a case, a videocassette of Forza Italia's program and some campaign and promotional material. But also included were the Forza Italia theme song in both regular and karaoke versions. All the candidates were drilled on the importance of tidy appearance, fresh breath and the need to avoid sweaty palms at all costs—tips right out of Berlusconi's salesman's handbook. The Forza Italia sales team was preparing for battle.

That a corrupt, self-serving tycoon, with little or no record of interest in politics or public service, could buy his way to the prime ministership of one of the world's biggest democracies, was—and is—shocking. But this phenomenon—without equal in modern history—bears testament not only to the mogul's wealth and TV power, but also to the brilliance of his campaign, his mendacity and the peculiar social circumstances in which Italy found itself in the early 1990s. The Socialist and Christian Democrat elite thought they had the right to power. But the new boy on the block, Berlusconi, was as energetic and thorough as the ex–political establishment had been complacent.

The politicos still standing after the Mani Pulite tsunami were for the most part more honest than their former colleagues. But they were minor-league players, without the political skills of the characters they'd replaced. Berlusconi watched the political talk shows on his bank of TV screens at Arcore and saw a bunch of boring, gray-haired men who couldn't sell hamburgers at McDonald's. He, on the other hand, could sell just about anything. And selling himself to the masses ought to be child's play. Right-hand man Confalonieri, who later noted that Berlusconi had "achieved Napoleonic things," thought at the time that "Berlusconi's superiority complex got the better of him."[14] But Silvio Berlusconi, who gave "Coca-Cola TV" to the masses, was about to sell them his brand of anti-politics.

The legwork, then, was well under way when on January 26 Berlusconi sent a nine-and-half-minute videotape announcing his candidacy to all the TV networks and Reuters.[15] Berlusconi, now 57, with his hair receding, but still looking fit and in form in his trademark navy suit, was the model of quiet purpose and sobriety as he began with the words: "Italy is the country that I love. Here I have my roots, my hopes, my horizons . . . never as in this moment does Italy need people of a certain experience, with their heads on their shoulders, able to give the country a helping hand and make the state function . . ." In those days, before political and judicial pressures had taken their toll, and with the surgeon's knife yet to restrict his facial expressions, Berlusconi had the unusual—almost unsettling—tendency to smile broadly after almost every phrase. But for his candidacy, perhaps helped by nerves, he reined in the grins.

The speech, which was full of marketing-approved words such as "freedom" and "hope," avoided any policy specifics. The general thrust was that Berlusconi was stepping into the breach to save Italy from the communists. The speech also went on too long, another Berlusconi trademark; to the egotistical mogul more is always more where he's concerned. His own channels gave the performance extravagant coverage—just a few months after the mogul had denounced suggestions he might seek political advantage from his media ownership. Even his opponents on Rai, aware of the hullabaloo, felt obliged to show highlights.

Berlusconi had at last thrown his hat in the ring and there was no going back. He knew he couldn't get a majority in parliament by himself, so instead he planned to form a solid alliance with two other parties. This in itself was logistically difficult and fraught with danger. For a start, the two groups with which he hoped to form a coalition, the Northern League and the Alleanza Nazionale, hated each other. And both—particularly the "post-fascist" Alleanza, in large part, an unsavory Mussolini fan club—were far from the respectable mainstream that Berlusconi ostensibly sought to attract. But not for the first time the mogul showed that political ideology wasn't really important to him. He probably would have been willing to get into bed with anyone or anything if it meant he could keep control of his business empire and stay out of jail. The Alleanza Nazionale leader Gianfranco Fini insisted—even in 1994—that fascist dictator and mass murderer Benito Mussolini was "the greatest statesman of the century," thereby undermining his attempts to present his party as a modern center-right force. The Northern League and its rabble-rousing leader Umberto Bossi weren't fascists but did have strong xenophobic tendencies. Twenty years later the League's deputy, Senate Speaker Roberto Calderoli, would compare Italy's first black minister to an orangutan and attempt to laugh off the resulting condemnation.[16]

Unlike Fini's strongly nationalist party, however, the League wanted greater autonomy for the North of Italy. The unholy alliance of the League, the Alleanza and Forza Italia decided on the pompous name of The Pole of Freedoms. Anyone could see the partners would make a coalition government from hell.

Berlusconi's primary concern, though, was winning power, not worrying about what would happen afterward. His left-wing opponent Achille Occhetto led a steady but unremarkable campaign. He pointed to Berlusconi's conflict of interest and past links with disgraced ex–prime minister Craxi; even some Northern League supporters liked to refer to Berlusconi as "Craxi with a toupee."

Berlusconi hit back with impossible but headline-catching promises of one million new jobs and lower taxes—without cuts to public services. His TV audience, fans of *High Noon*, *Dynasty* and *The Smurfs*, had no reason to doubt him. And more importantly, he had three national TV channels at his disposal to promote himself as the man who got things done: the man who built a real-estate empire from nothing, sparked a TV revolution and revitalized the AC Milan football club—and provided more TV coverage of the sport than ever before, even for supporters of Juventus or Roma. The campaign's quintessential exchange occurred when Berlusconi faced Luigi Spaventa, his center-left opponent for a parliamentary seat in Rome. Spaventa, an economist, challenged the mogul over the financial illiteracy of his election promises. Berlusconi retorted: "How many Intercontinental [football] cups have you won?"[17] After this exchange, surely Italy knew what it was letting itself in for?

Berlusconi was the first Italian politician to speak the language of ordinary people; he wasn't elitist; he didn't come from the old self-serving political establishment. And the significance of this perceived break with the past, although hard to quantify, was surely a huge plus factor in a country that had lived through two inexplicably grim decades.

The great paradox of Italy in the 1970s and 1980s was that one of the world's most beautiful, prosperous and socially stable countries, which had been riding high, thanks to the economic miracle of the preceding decades, should find itself gripped not just by endemic corruption but also by a strange paranoia and under siege from political violence, as shadowy right-wing forces blew up banks and railways stations in Milan and Bologna, and the far-left Red Brigades tried to kneecap or shoot dead anyone who didn't agree with them. The Brigades' abduction and murder of former prime minister Aldo Moro in 1978—a leader who, ironically, had been making overtures to the far left—came to define the era: one of fear, amoral violence and relentless conspiracy theories, involving everyone from the CIA to the Vatican.

In the 1970s, Rome's criminal Magliana gang became a byword for viciousness; in the early 1980s "the Second Mafia War" saw hundreds die as the Corleonese boss Salvatore Riina stamped his authority on Cosa Nostra. Riina's eventual capture in 1993, following his murder of police and magistrates, sparked retaliatory bomb attacks in mainland cities.

By 1994, Italians had had enough of politicians on the make and of strikes and protests and bloodshed. Berlusconi appeared to be a leader from another world—one who was aspirational but reassuring. Many pundits noted that with television and business triumphs going back 20 years, the mogul had had two decades to create an impression on the public—to condition it, even. Berlusconi, the smiling family man and dashing entrepreneur who had brought light entertainment and glossy American soaps into their living rooms after decades of dreary, didactic state TV, probably seemed like a messiah. He was certainly the first transatlantic Italian prime ministerial candidate.

An easier factor to quantify was the colossal media firepower Berlusconi had at his disposal. In Italy, political advertisements are not allowed in the final month of an electoral campaign. But that left the mogul with four weeks to blitz Italian television, practically half of which he owned.

His other crucial advantage was the ban on political spots maintained by Rai state TV that limited the options of his opponents. Berlusconi's center-left political opponents didn't know how to react to the promotional onslaught of Forza Italia ads and the blatant pro-Berlusconi bias of the Berlusconi-owned networks. Research by Pavia University showed that Rete 4, generally seen as the least partial of the Berlusconi networks, devoted 68.3 percent of its election coverage to Forza Italia, to the disadvantage of opposing parties.[18] In the end Berlusconi's opponents decided against paying for spots on the enemy's TV channels. Not only would it have been galling for them to swell the mogul's coffers, but it occurred to them—probably with reason—that their earnest ads probably wouldn't have much impact on a Berlusconi audience that was addicted to *Dallas* and admired Italy's own J. R. Ewing. Subsequent research showed that the number of hours a person spent viewing Berlusconi's TV channels correlated with the likelihood they would vote for him. The trend was particularly pronounced among women: 75 percent of female ex–Christian Democrat voters who watched more than four hours a day of Mediaset television put their "X" next to Berlusconi. Only 40 percent of those who watched less than four hours a day voted for him, however.[19]

He consulted, used and abused opinion polls to great effect. Indeed, persuasion was probably a principal aim of the barrage of opinion polls produced by the research company Diakron, which was owned by the mogul himself. Berlusconi insisted the pollster was independent. But the pollsters kept producing remarkably positive results for the tycoon, and Berlusconi was also quick to exaggerate, or even lie, about the findings.

As the mogul prepared for the brief two-month election campaign, there were still thorns in his side. Indro Montanelli, the editor of the Berlusconi newspaper *Il Giornale*, was as uncontrollable as ever. As demanded by the 1990 law limiting media ownership, Berlusconi had handed the publication over to his younger brother, Paolo, a sort of Mini-Me to the mogul, who lacked his big brother's business brain but shared his uneasy relationship with the law. But there was never any doubt whose paper it really was. With an election two months off, there was now too much at stake, and Berlusconi decided his recalcitrant editor had to go.

His use of TV attack dogs to dispose of Montanelli underlines how Il Cavaliere's permanent smile and nice-guy act was simply that—an act; the front of a hard-nosed businessman whose loyalty to his nearest and dearest was matched by his disregard for everyone and everything else.

The most unpleasant of these TV cronies, and the one who underlined Berlusconi's ruthlessness, was Vittorio Sgarbi. Even today the ubiquitous Sgarbi is the guest of choice for TV talk shows seeking some ratings-boosting fights. Like a pseudo-intellectual with Tourette's syndrome, this vaguely unhinged individual parades his credentials as an art critic, name-drops cultural figures and then screams obscenities at anyone with whom he disagrees. In recent years his favorite rejoinder to dissenting debaters, "*pezzo di merda*" (piece of shit), has gradually been replaced by "*capra*" (goat), which apparently he considers less likely to result in further defamation payouts. Unlike well-known art historians like Robert Hughes or David Sylvester, who were happy to let their writing and cultural insights do the talking, Sgarbi wanted notoriety. He was more than willing to join Berlusconi's payroll as a political attack dog, specializing in unfair and spiteful abuse, delivered at high volume—and having had the misfortune to be on a live TV show in which Sgarbi was yelling abuse at the guest sitting next to me, I can testify to the volume.

From December 4 to 6, 1994, Sgarbi stepped up attacks on Montanelli in his daily 20-minute slot on Canale 5, dismissing the editor as a fascist (due to his youthful dalliances with the far right) in three vituperative episodes.[20] The fact that Sgarbi's paymaster, Berlusconi, was currently cozying up to Italy's far-right "post-fascist" Alleanza Nazionale was something he chose to overlook. In one of his regular TV rants, he called Montanelli's refusal to quit "pure cowardice."

Another crony to weigh in was Emilio Fede. Short, seedy and implausibly tanned—like Berlusconi—but with none of his tycoon friend's charm and business acumen, Fede read the news on Berlusconi's awful Rete 4 channel, a TV graveyard of the worst US repeats, on which Chuck Norris's *Walker, Texas Ranger* would remain a daily highlight thirty years later.

Still, Rete 4 had—and still has—millions of older viewers, a key Berlusconi constituency. And as Il Cavaliere rode into political battle, his lapdog Fede (which means "faith" in Italian) began taking potshots at the boss's "ungrateful" newspaper editor. Fede, whose ineptitude at reading the news was matched only by his sycophancy, declared that Montanelli was disloyal to his owner Berlusconi and that he deserved the boot. "If I were his publisher I would relieve him of his post," he said. Montanelli demolished his attacker with a single swipe. "In Berlusconi's place, I wouldn't be able to fire Fede," he said, "because I would never have hired him."[21]

Although Berlusconi did not join in the attacks on Montanelli as they reached full flow, he made little or no effort to dissociate himself from them. Distancing himself from aggressive attacks on perceived enemies by employing the worst elements of his media outfits to do the dirty work is a technique Berlusconi continued to use over the decades.

As the 1994 election campaign began, with Berlusconi allowing one of his own TV news programs to publicly attack Montanelli, the writing was on the wall for the veteran journalist. Berlusconi appeared in person at the offices of *Il Giornale* two days later and promised better funding and wages for the paper if it toed his line. Montanelli quit.[22] As mendacious as ever, Berlusconi denied that he had forced Montanelli out or that Fede had acted with his approval. He said that he'd been hoping Montanelli would stay, writing his front-page editorials for *Il Giornale* for eternity. Instead it would be Montanelli's withering put-downs of Berlusconi that would stand the test of time.

Other tricky moments in the run-up to polling day concerned the legal predicaments of Marcello Dell'Utri. Magistrates said they had evidence the Publitalia chief had falsified accounts in order to divert company money into slush funds. Berlusconi dismissed the probe as an "ignoble political attack"—a riposte that he'd repeat like a broken record over the decades. More dangerously, rumors grew that magistrates in Palermo might make a move against Dell'Utri because of his mafia ties.

Bizarrely, however, Berlusconi was even able to turn this embarrassment to his advantage. When *La Stampa* printed comments from the left-wing head of the parliamentary Anti-mafia commission, Luciano Violante, confirming that Dell'Utri was indeed officially under investigation for mafia-related offenses, the Berlusconi TV stations howled in outrage that this confidential information had been improperly leaked to hurt the tycoon's election chances.[23] Violante threatened to sue the journalist Augusto Minzolini (who would later figure as a key Berlusconi media crony), claiming he'd been set up. Soon, however, Violante quit his commission post. Incredibly, the furor over the news leak came to overshadow accusations that a would-be prime minister had a mafioso campaign organizer.

Certainly, plenty of Italians who went to the polls on March 27, 1994, weren't that bothered. Berlusconi's Forza Italia took 21 percent of the vote. This was a bit less than some pundits had predicted, but it still made Forza Italia the biggest single party—an incredible achievement for a group of political ingénues whose party hadn't existed six months earlier. Together with the 13.5 percent received by the Alleanza Nazionale and the 8.4 percent of the Northern League, the center-right coalition had a majority of seats in the lower house of parliament, the Chamber of Deputies, and was just a whisker short of a majority in the upper chamber, the Senate. And Berlusconi felt sure he could persuade some malleable senators to swap sides. Incredibly, 50 of Berlusconi's parliamentarians were ex-Publitalia staff. The rest of the democratic world looked on agog as Berlusconi and his TV advertising team prepared to run the country. When Emilio Fede announced the news of his boss's election victory, on his Rete 4 TV news show, his eyes welled up with tears.

There had been another announcement, made with much less fanfare, four months before the election. In November 1993, Milan's chief prosecutor, Francesco Saverio Borrelli, the driving force behind the Mani Pulite investigations, made a less-than-oblique declaration in *Corriere della Sera* to people considering entering politics. "Those who want to run for office should look inside themselves. If they are clean they can proceed without fear. But those who know they have skeletons in their closet, secrets from the past . . . then open the closet and then step aside . . . Step aside I say, before we arrive."[24]

Berlusconi never had any intention of stepping aside. Despite some temporary decisions by *deputati* to waive immunity at the height of the Mani Pulite investigations, magistrates still needed permission from parliament in order to arrest its members. The tycoon knew he would be safer in Montecitorio, the seat of parliament.

What, then, had the Mani Pulite investigations achieved? Not so much, according to Italian political scientist Alberto Vannucci: "The Mani Pulite inquiries courageously exposed, but could not solve the issue of widespread corruption in Italy. An enduring improvement in the quality of public ethics would have required the specific interest and consequent action of leading political actors, or strong and enduring social support for an anti-corruption agenda. Neither condition, however, has ever been realized."[25]

Strong, enduring support for an anti-corruption agenda? Berlusconi was now in power. Things could and would get a whole lot worse. And a twenty-year legal war was shaping up.

CHAPTER 5

GETTING HIS HANDS DIRTY

For someone whose prowess in running a football club played a big part in his election campaign, Berlusconi could claim to have got off to a good start as prime minister. Just ten days after being sworn in, on May 18, 1994, AC Milan won the hallowed European Cup. In June, the post-election honeymoon saw Berlusconi's Forza Italia increase its poll ratings from the 21 percent at the time of the vote to nearly 31 percent. It wouldn't be long, however, before Berlusconi discovered that actually running the country wasn't nearly as easy as he made it sound on the pre-election TV campaign spots. In a nutshell, Berlusconi's first attempt at governing would prove inept, sordid and short: his administration collapsed by the end of the year.

In July 1994, Berlusconi decided it was time to wind up the Clean Hands investigations before he got dragged in. His stooges in government prepared a decree to be forced through parliament that would end the arrests of Tangentopoli suspects. Unusually, magistrates took to the television to protest, with greater coverage afforded them on Rai, naturally. The public, still furious over the Tangentopoli scandal, reacted furiously and the government backed down, rescinding the law.

Milan's prosecutors made their first big move against the prime minister in November 1994. Their timing was exquisite—so exquisite, in fact, that Berlusconi's friends and foes alike asked whether the moment was chosen for maximum embarrassment. The crooked tycoon was basking in the spotlight as host of a United Nations conference on organized crime, with international leaders including Bill Clinton and François Mitterrand in attendance, when it emerged that chief prosecutor Borrelli's team wanted him in for interrogation on suspected bribery. Whatever Berlusconi thought of their timing, the magistrates could justly claim to be performing their jobs. But the Forza Italia politicos and Berlusconi's media outlets were apoplectic. Some accused the judiciary of a coup d'état. Battle with the mogul had truly been joined. Berlusconi had already been preparing for the inevitable confrontation, however.

As soon as he had his feet under the desk at Palazzo Chigi, the imposing official Rome residence of the Italian prime minister, the mogul began to draw up a list of powerful positions to be filled by his key cronies. Berlusconi's personal tax lawyer, Giulio Tremonti, suddenly found himself finance minister of a G7 economy. Before long, he was thanking his boss by writing legislation that resulted in Fininvest enjoying a 250 billion lire ($130 million) tax break.[1] Berlusconi's chief corporate lawyer, Vittorio Dotti, became Forza Italia's leader in the Camera dei Deputati, the lower chamber of parliament.

Best—or perhaps worst—of all, Berlusconi had big plans for his personal legal adviser, Cesare Previti. The lawyer who had got Berlusconi his Arcore mansion on the cheap and delivered the Mondadori publishing house by bribing a judge was to be justice minister. Vittorio Dotti subsequently gave the lowdown on his former colleague's politics: Previti claimed to be a Craxi supporter, but when his guard was down, he sang the praises of Chilean dictator and mass murderer Augusto Pinochet, even affording him the affectionate nickname "Pinochietto."[2] Thankfully, throwing dissidents out of helicopters wasn't the done thing in Italy, not even with the say-so of corruptible judges.

Nonetheless, apart from making Al Capone attorney general, it seems hard to imagine a more worrying appointment for the head of a country's justice system. Previti's double-dealing and corruption weren't public knowledge at that stage, but he already had something of a reputation. According to Dotti's girlfriend, Stefania Ariosto, her partner was "in charge of legal affairs; Cesare Previti was in charge of illegal ones."[3]

In 2014, Dotti spilt the beans on his time as a top Fininvest lawyer and subsequent Forza Italia politico, evidently trying to put clear blue sky between his activities and those of Previti. Dotti claimed that he had asked Berlusconi for the job of justice minister. The mogul refused. Soon after, Dotti was taken aside by Previti, who mockingly asked him in his guttural Roman accent whether he was prepared "to smash the magistrates." Dotti said "no." "That's the reason why you can't be minister," Previti told him.[4]

As it turned out, making Previti justice minister was a step too far for the head of state, President Oscar Luigi Scalfaro, who refused to sanction the appointment. The president cited the conflict of interests inherent in having the prime minister's personal lawyer as justice minister.[5] Berlusconi gave Previti the defense ministry instead, which meant this crook was in charge of the nation's *carabinieri* police force—the law enforcement division responsible for some of the most important criminal investigations, such as those into mafia crimes. And as defense minister, Previti would, of course, be in the cabinet. It was soon obvious that Berlusconi's adviser for "illegal affairs" was sticking his nose into justice matters at every opportunity, to the extent that he earned the additional soubriquet "the Real Minister of Justice."[6]

The prime minister was certainly going to need all the legal help he could muster. Just before his interrogation in November 1994, the legal portents were already looking grim. On May 4, Milan prosecutors had announced they wanted to arrest Marcello Dell'Utri on suspicion of having faked Publitalia receipts in order to divert funds into secret accounts. In July, with reports circulating that Berlusconi's brother, Paolo, might be arrested for corruption-related offenses, the government announced the infamous decree, swiftly dubbed the Salvaladri (save a thief) law, that would prevent the judiciary from issuing arrest warrants for most crimes relating to political corruption and fraud. Suspects already being held in relation to such crimes were released; journalists who published reports on ongoing probes were threatened with jail.

Berlusconi said the extraordinary measure had nothing to do with his personal interests. But political scientist Gianfranco Miglio later revealed that the mogul had told him the exact opposite was true: "We had to pass that decree. The magistrates were after me and my friends . . . I have to stop them before they become the bosses of Italy, perhaps with [Clean Hands magistrate] Di Pietro in my place."[7] It appeared that the decree was designed to be sneaked out under the cover of the final rounds of football's World Cup, in which football-mad Italy had reached the semifinals. But when Brazil beat Italy in the final, the public's attention soon refocused on Berlusconi's brazen attempt to get his friends out of jail.

Marcello Maddalena, the head of the Associazione Nazionale Magistrati, spelled out the essence of the save-a-thief decree. "Someone who steals a few lire goes to prison; someone who steals billions from the till of a company, leaving others penniless, so they can live it up in the Caribbean, can't even be arrested." Ex-ministers, 49 finance police and political party officials with millions hidden in Swiss bank accounts were free to walk. Overnight, a total of 2,764 suspects walked, including 300 or so caught up in the Mani Pulite probe.[8]

Indro Montanelli, by now well and truly in the anti-Berlusconi camp, used the pages of his new paper, *La Voce*, to urge the public to bombard the justice ministry with protests. When the size of the public backlash became apparent, the interior minister, Roberto Maroni, a member of Berlusconi's coalition partner the Northern League, denounced the measure, claiming he hadn't known that serious Tangentopoli suspects would be released just like that.

Berlusconi's TV poodle Emilio Fede treated his master to a 22-minute interview in which the mogul attempted to justify the Salvaladri law. Over on Canale 5, the mogul's attack dog Vittorio Sgarbi frothed at the mouth, calling Antonio Di Pietro and the rest of the Clean Hands magistrates "murderers," in an attempt to undermine their investigations. "They should go to church and pray for the all the people they've killed," he said in a reference to those caught up in the probe who had taken their own lives.[9] The mogul's ever-active pollsters revealed the public was appalled by the save-a-thief decree, however, and within weeks Berlusconi had rescinded it.

Just days after, judges issued arrest warrants for two more Fininvest officials: Salvatore Sciascia, the group's chief finance officer, and Gianmarco Rizzi, a former tax inspector who had decided to cash in and work for Berlusconi rather than the state. Neither man turned himself in. Incredibly, it emerged that on July 24, the defense lawyer for the fugitive Sciascia met Prime Minister Berlusconi and Cesare Previti, the defense-cum-justice minister (and Fininvest executive), for dinner at Arcore, before the pair were finally taken into custody.[10] The murky meeting came to light only after a dozy telephone receptionist at Arcore let it slip to a reporter from *La Repubblica* newspaper. Just three months after it was sworn in, Berlusconi's first government was already mired in sleaze.

The mogul's excuse sounded familiar: "It was just a simple dinner among friends."

"That's the problem," said *Corriere della Sera*. "No one can tell where the family business ends and where the business of state begins."[11]

Soon after his government was sworn in on April 23, 1994, Berlusconi had promised a "blind trust" for his business empire, to separate its interests from those of government. But how "blind" could this system be, given that everyone else knew of Berlusconi's twin role of mogul and head of government? "There's only one way to resolve the Fininvest problem," said Montanelli. "Sell it."

The mogul made a big deal of stepping outside of cabinet meetings every time something came up for discussion that might have had an effect on his business empire. This principled neglect of his company affairs didn't appear to harm Fininvest, which grew from being Italy's number two business to the country's largest during Berlusconi's first period in office.[12] Berlusconi had also promised to keep his paws off his TV competition, Rai, the state broadcaster. He stated he would "not even move a potted plant" in the organization's headquarters. But the anti-Berlusconi attitude, particularly that adopted by the Rai 3 channel, infuriated him. Demonstrating his complete inability to comprehend or accept the need for criticism to be aired in a democracy, the mogul declared it was "anomalous that in a democratic system like Italy's that the public broadcasting system should be against the government."

Berlusconi argued that taxpayers' money given to Rai in the form of a license fee should not be used by politically partial program makers—never mind, of course, that he controlled three private national channels that were at least as biased, and probably more so. Within weeks of the election, two employees from Berlusconi media outlets, Carlo Rossella and Clemente Mimun, were made head of news at Rai 1 and Rai 2, respectively—effectively ensuring Berlusconi had influence over news and current affairs on five of the six main TV channels.[13]

Berlusconi the populist was well aware of the stellar poll ratings of prosecutor Antonio Di Pietro, whose popularity seemed impervious to the TV attacks of Sgarbi. So the mogul turned to an old aphorism in an attempt to neutralize this menace: "Keep your friends close and your enemies closer." At the end of April 1994, just days after magistrates announced they intended to arrest Dell'Utri, Berlusconi rang a surprised Di Pietro and offered him the powerful post of interior minister. No doubt intrigued and flattered, the magistrate demonstrated his naïveté by agreeing to fly down to Rome to meet with the prime minister.

Most observers think there was never much chance Di Pietro would accept the offer—his credibility would have been ruined by accepting a job from someone whom most people expected he would be seeking to indict sooner or later—although, in that context, it does perhaps seem a little odd that Di Pietro agreed to meet Berlusconi at all. When he arrived at the given rendezvous the next day, he discovered he had been lured to the home of Cesare Previti. There was a crowd of journalists waiting outside, obviously invited by Berlusconi's PR team.[14] The magistrate declined the offer of work and got on with his real job. Berlusconi tried to entice Di Pietro's colleague, Piercamillo Davigo. He, too, declined a post in government. The Milan pool of magistrates hastily issued a notice stating that none of its members would be accepting ministerial positions so that all could concentrate on the job at hand.[15]

And it was a job given extra urgency just a week earlier when a young officer from the finance police, vice-brigadier Pietro Di Giovanni, told prosecutors that he had been offered a bribe by a colleague, allegedly using money from one of Berlusconi's companies. Antonio Di Pietro took charge of the investigation and uncovered evidence that finance police officers were accepting bribes in order to keep quiet about false tax returns provided by a number of big Milan companies, including Berlusconi's holding company, Fininvest. Some of the firms under investigation accepted plea bargains. Fininvest decided attack was the best form of defense, however, and claimed that it had been the real victim, because the payments were really extortion money, made under duress.

Berlusconi also claimed he knew nothing about the payments, which were relatively small, amounting to 330 million lire—about $300,000. How could he, as prime minister, be aware of the minutiae of a huge company, whose day-to-day management was no longer his concern? This was a defense that he would repeat over the years as investigators probed the finances of his business empire. Di Pietro and colleagues soon established that the Berlusconi family was indeed involved in the financial minutiae, however. In July, under interrogation, the mogul's brother, Paolo Berlusconi, admitted he had known about the payments but claimed finance police officers had turned up the heat on the company with "an unjustified expansion of their enquiries to include a meticulous control of formal irregularities." It's never clear how "formal" irregularities are when Berlusconi is concerned.

Paolo Berlusconi said his brother knew nothing about the payments. "I personally manage all that concerns tactics and strategy while Silvio Berlusconi has responsibility for the overall global strategy of the group."[16] However, two wiretaps and an incriminating visit to the prime minister's office a month earlier seemed to contradict this.

Investigators discovered that on June 8 Berlusconi received Massimo Maria Berruti, the former finance police officer who shelved the probe into Berlusconi's Milano 2 financing back in the 1970s, at his official Rome residence, Palazzo Chigi. The visit came to light only when police discovered Berruti's visitor pass. Upon leaving his meeting with Berlusconi, Berruti had called Marshall Alberto Corrado of the finance police. The next day, Corrado called another colleague, Colonel Angelo Tanco, telling him to say nothing about one of the three alleged bribes made by the Mondadori publishing house, a Fininvest subsidiary. The latter two conversations were recorded by investigators, although, crucially, Berlusconi's discussion with Berruti was not.

But the circumstances were so incriminating, suggesting that Berlusconi directly intervened in an attempt to obstruct the inquiry, that magistrates decided they had enough evidence to formally investigate him. Indeed, the two finance police officers would subsequently admit that they had been promised generous payments if they kept quiet about the source of the bribes.

On November 22, 1994, *Corriere della Sera* splashed its front page with the news that Milan prosecutors had sent Berlusconi an *invito a comparire*—an official request to appear for interrogation. *Corriere*'s exclusive caused a sensation, with the world's media already focused on the prime minister in Naples, as he earnestly led the UN's international conference with other G7 leaders in attendance.

On December 13, still furious that he'd been made an international laughingstock, Berlusconi told his nemesis and Milan's chief prosecutor Borrelli, during their confrontation, that the Berruti visit and subsequent phone calls proved nothing. Borelli asked Berlusconi about Fininvest's "hidden slush funds" and how they were created.

"I prefer to call them 'non-registered funds,' even if they were kept totally hidden from me. I came to know about them only when these events came to light," the prime minister said.[17]

Berlusconi added that the three alleged bribes, totaling 330 million lire, were small beer for a company the size of Fininvest, which "pays a billion lire a day in taxes." The prime minister claimed nothing had emerged from his interrogation to show he had any "direct responsibility" for the three incidents of bribery. "I hope you are now aware of the damage this request for an interrogation has brought to me personally, to me as prime minister and to our country seeing as you sent me notice the exact moment when I was presiding over the UN conference on world crime."

In May the following year, prosecutors requested indictments for Berlusconi and his brother, Paolo, as well as for several finance police officers and Berruti. Berlusconi was eventually convicted—three years later—and sentenced to two years and nine months in prison. Paolo Berlusconi was spared after judges decided that he had assumed guilt to save his brother.

But Silvio Berlusconi, as with all Italian defendants, had the right to two appeals. The court of appeals confirmed the conviction in May 2000. But the second appeal, to the highest court, the Supreme Court of Cassation in Rome, saw the conviction overturned, with judges declaring there was insufficient evidence to show that Berlusconi had ordered the bribes. The Supreme Court cast doubt, however, on Fininvest's defense that the company was the victim of extortion by finance police officers.[18] But the officers were all definitively convicted, as was Berruti. Berlusconi could hardly claim to be running a clean ship.

Back in late 1994, however, the mogul and his minions were already counterattacking against the magistrates. Many of the Mani Pulite suspects had been making noise about the unfairness of the investigations, suggesting left-wing politicians had been spared, and Berlusconi jumped on the bandwagon. The claim about left-wing bias doesn't bear much scrutiny: the prosecutors took out a good number of leftists and ex-communists in Milan, for example. There just happened to be fewer leftists in power. Indeed, Berlusconi's decision to start labeling the prosecutors as "communists" was nonsense given that it was no secret that some in Milan's pool of magistrates, including Antonio Di Pietro himself, were on the center-right.

In November that year, just before the prime minister was called in for interrogation, his justice minister, Alfredo Biondi, sent ministry inspectors up to Milan to investigate woolly claims that the Mani Pulite magistrates had acted improperly by showing "unusual vehemence and decisiveness" in their probes of Berlusconi's business affairs. The inspectors found no evidence but were under political pressure from on high to continue intimidating the prosecutors "until the interrogation of Berlusconi was over," one of the two inspectors later claimed.[19]

These investigations proved fruitless. But the Berlusconi team couldn't believe its luck when Antonio Di Pietro himself encountered legal problems. When an insurance salesman called Giancarlo Gorrini stepped up and told Berlusconi's brother, Paolo, that the magistrate had accepted an interest-free loan from him for 100 million lire, there was much excitement in the prime minister's camp. Might this be evidence the popular prosecutor had taken the generous loan in exchange for legal favors? Soon ministerial investigators were on the case. They found no evidence of graft on Di Pietro's part—only naïveté. The ministerial probe (in which his defense-cum-justice minister Previti appeared to play an inappropriate part) was then quickly shelved.[20]

Rather than work under a cloud, Antonio Di Pietro did a very un-Italian thing and quit, without revealing his reasons, to the shock of his colleagues and the general public. Not satisfied with the result of his dirty work, Berlusconi then exploited this silence on Di Pietro's part by portraying his resignation as evidence that he was at odds with the "communist magistrates," who were on some sort of witch hunt.

Despite Sgarbi denouncing Di Pietro and colleagues as "murderers" for their energetic pursuit of the Tangentopoli criminals, it was Berlusconi and his team who, ironically, found themselves on the side of killers with regard to the coming legal war. Two years earlier, in the spring and summer of 1992, Cosa Nostra had killed the Palermo magistrates Giovanni Falcone and Paolo Borsellino in bomb attacks, even as the Mani Pulite investigations were gathering speed in Milan, 600 miles to the north. With the state's top two anti-Mafia prosecutors murdered in the space of two months, the Sicilian crime syndicate was now looking to strike at magistrates in Milan, the rich northern finance capital in which it had huge financial interests. Important Mafia informants have since revealed that the assassination of Di Pietro was being considered by the upper echelons of Cosa Nostra.[21] As it turned out, the hit wouldn't be necessary; Berlusconi would do them the favor of killing Di Pietro's reputation instead.

While the dirty maneuvers against the corruption investigations were in full swing, Berlusconi's former tax lawyer was changing the rules regarding tax evasion. For the big fish, fines for tax dodging were now up for negotiation rather than set in stone. Antonio Fazio, then governor of Bankitalia, told a parliamentary commission the measure was "an incentive to commit further tax evasion."[22]

But the really bad smell came when tax lawyer turned minister Tremonti announced the government's first legislation—designed with Berlusconi's business interests specifically in mind. On June 10, the economics minister, who appeared to believe he was still looking out for Berlusconi's finances and not those of the Italian treasury, announced decree number 357, which offered huge tax breaks to companies that were investing heavily in the years 1994–1995. By strange coincidence, Fininvest was snapping up US film rights in this period to boost its TV empire. The result: a near 250 billion lire ($150 million) tax break bonanza for you-know-who.[23]

During the first Berlusconi government, even lawmaking that wasn't of direct consequence to Fininvest had a tawdry edge to it. Not for the last time, the mogul showed how his free-market, liberal conservative credentials were just a sham by failing to back labor reforms that would have allowed companies to sack workers who consistently failed to show up for work. A decree to this end introduced by the following caretaker government of Carlo Azeglio Ciampi was allowed to quietly die rather than become law.[24] The reason for this strange antipathy to improved productivity was the Alleanza Nazionale, many of whose voters believed the state owed them jobs for life. Berlusconi had promised a million new jobs. By Christmastime, Italy had lost another 200,000 posts.

The government itself didn't make it to Christmas 1994. Northern League chief Umberto Bossi, who would prove a capricious and highly unreliable ally over the years, pulled the rug from under Berlusconi's shabby first administration at the start of December, calling the mogul a "mafioso" who "was worse than Pinochet." The League's ministers quit the cabinet and Berlusconi resigned on December 21, less than eight months after he was sworn in. In parliament the next day he railed against the rambunctious, cigar-chomping Bossi. He was, said Berlusconi, a "Judas" who had "a double, triple, even quadruple personality," which was rich coming from someone with more faces than a Swiss watch factory.

The League had been increasingly fed up with Berlusconi for months. The Salvaladri decree had gone down badly with its law-and-order-supporting core constituency. Now it appeared Berlusconi himself was being dragged into the Mani Pulite investigations, and League bigwigs feared they would lose large numbers of supporters by being associated with him. The flexible morals of both Berlusconi and Bossi, and the fractured nature of Italian politics, meant they would continue making deals over the years.

But for now, the tycoon-politico's first go at running the country was over. Italy had been warned. What on earth were the chances of anyone ever voting for him again?

CHAPTER 6

JUSTICE FOR SALE

"Who would I be if I couldn't be Berlusconi? The son of Berlusconi," the mogul said candidly, even as his first government was collapsing in ignominy in less than a year. He and some of his closest associates were under investigation for serious crimes including bribery, tax evasion and mafia association. And, as we saw before the election, his business empire was on the ropes. The political obituary writers were sharpening their pencils.

But like a prizefighter who doesn't know when to quit, Berlusconi stood up and fought back with courage and skill. To be fair, he had little choice but to counterattack. What applied back in January 1994 was still true a year later: if he was without political power, hostile left-wing politicians might carve up his TV empire and magistrates would be able to arrest him at will. His remarkable ability to survive and regroup was helped by his planet-sized ego. "I'm a simple businessman. But one that works miracles," he once said, demonstrating the arrogance—and triteness—to which a third of the population has appeared impervious in three general elections.[1]

Thus, not burdened by doubt or self-awareness, the mogul set to work, reviving his companies and reestablishing his political power base. Shrewd appointments played a key role. The tough Mondadori executive Franco "The Kaiser" Tatò was charged with overhauling Berlusconi's Fininvest holding company, to which the various subdivisions belonged. Tatò succeeded in giving more autonomy to the individual groups—Mondadori (publishing), Mediaset (TV), Mediolanum (asset management), Medusa (film) and Pagine Italia (directory listings).[2] The ailing Standa supermarket chain was sold off and, in 1996, Mediaset was quoted on the stock market. Although this ruffled quite a few feathers among Fininvest's management, it had the desired effect. By 2001 Berlusconi's empire was well and truly in the black again. And he was a very wealthy man indeed. *Forbes* magazine estimated that his fortune might now be as high as $14 billion. Not bad for an average Joe who had started his career selling vacuum cleaners.

Berlusconi still had a little legal tidying up to do, however. And, of course, the tycoon was on constant lookout for any attempts by political opponents to legislate against his media business. Things were made a bit easier thanks to the peculiar political situation in which Italy found itself. Because Bossi and the Northern League had parted company with Berlusconi, he no longer had a majority and had to quit the post of PM. But the head of state, President Oscar Luigi Scalfaro, wanted a period of stability rather than the uncertainty brought by fresh elections at a time when the lira was already plummeting on the currency markets. So he chose a Berlusconi minister, Lamberto Dini, to head a caretaker government. This appointment was backed by the Northern League and the center-left. The mogul probably knew there was never that much danger of this hodgepodge of left, right and center agreeing to do anything very radical.

The immediate threat to his TV channels came from public-spirited campaigners outside of parliament. (It's tempting to note that in Italy, the phrase "public-spirited campaigners *in* parliament" might sound like an oxymoron.) These protestors, seeing that deputies and senators had failed to divest Berlusconi of his private TV monopoly, took matters into their own hands by organizing a referendum for June 1995. Under the Italian constitution, the public is allowed a legally binding vote, striking down an existing law, if campaigners can muster a petition of half a million electors.

On this occasion, the public would vote on whether one person should be allowed to own more than one national TV channel. Petition organizers also wanted to place new limits on TV advertising. It sounded like a declaration of war to Berlusconi, and his TV programs set about trashing the campaign at every opportunity—as they'd done with the short-lived attempt to ban presenters' "advertorials" in the middle of quiz and light entertainment shows back in 1993.

The consumer groups organizing the referendum were hopelessly outmatched by Berlusconi's TV clout. And they received no help from state network Rai, which wasn't permitted to broadcast spots of a political nature. Italy's toothless broadcast watchdog said the campaigners deserved a decent right to reply on Berlusconi's channels, which of course they didn't get. In the referendum, 57 percent of the public voted against the proposals.[3] Berlusconi said the result was "the declaration of God," although it wasn't clear which God he was referring to.

The billionaire tycoon's biggest legal problem remained the magistrates in Milan, who were intent on wrecking his plan to remain at liberty and acquire vast power and wealth for himself, and quite a lot for his close friends. The evidence that Fininvest—and possibly the prime minister himself—had been involved in the bribery of finance police officers was bad, but there would be much worse to come: revelations of much bigger bribes, hundreds of millions of dollars discovered in foreign slush funds, and—perhaps the Berlusconi empire's most sordid achievement to date—the corruption of Rome's judiciary.

The mogul's TV henchmen, led by Sgarbi, continued to denounce Mani Pulite prosecutors at every opportunity. Meanwhile, behind the scenes, Berlusconi's cronies made sure that Antonio Di Pietro, the Italian who had come to personify the hard-fought war on corruption, was taken out of the game for good. The popular magistrate had already resigned as a result of the free loan he'd unwisely accepted from the insurance broker. But when Berlusconi upped the ante by claiming that Di Pietro had opposed hauling him in for interrogation in November 1994, the ex-magistrate publicly dismissed Berlusconi's claims as nonsense. High-profile public speeches that followed this denunciation suggested Di Pietro was seriously considering entering politics, too. Here was a rival Berlusconi could do without.

The tool Berlusconi used to dismantle Di Pietro's political ambitions was one of the former magistrate's own "friends." Like Di Pietro's other nemesis, the insurance broker Gorrini, the person to whom Berlusconi turned, Antonio D'Adamo, had a company facing bankruptcy.[4] D'Adamo claimed that Di Pietro had taken a $2.5 million bribe from a banker, Pierfrancesco Pacini Battaglia, in exchange for lenient treatment during the Clean Hands investigations.[5] Wiretaps recorded D'Adamo making calls to find the highest bidder for his story. But it was Berlusconi's legal vulture, Previti, who just happened to be there when D'Adamo called around with his information, and who then helped D'Adamo compile a "dossier" on Di Pietro.[6] Berlusconi-owned companies went on to make purchases from D'Adamo and provide credit for his ailing real-estate business. Altogether the assistance was worth around $12 million. Berlusconi's forces also appeared to exert pressure on other creditors to act in D'Adamo's favor.[7]

Given that the allegations against Italy's most famous former prosecutor were so grave, the former prime minister of Italy might have been expected to present the evidence to the police. Instead, cynically, he sat on the file—only to present it to the authorities in May 1997, when it would do the most damage to Di Pietro, who was then considering his political future after a brief spell as a public works minister in a center-left government.

As with the Gorrini allegations, the charges made by D'Adamo were ultimately shown to be without foundation. The Berlusconi family rag *Il Giornale* eventually made a big payout for the outrageous stories it had printed about the former magistrate. But the constant attacks on Di Pietro's reputation had had the desired effect: the former prosecutor was now yesterday's man in terms of popularity and political potential. Di Pietro would become a senator in 1998 in the small anti-corruption party, Italy of Values (Idv), which he launched himself. From hero, he hadn't exactly gone to zero, but he was destined to remain a minnow in Italian politics—albeit a virtuous one.

Italy's favorite prosecutor might have begun fading from the scene as early as 1995, but his former colleagues kept on digging for dirt. Some of them might even have had in mind Berlusconi's promise that he would quit politics were it ever proven that he had bribed Craxi. This explosive information now appeared to be within their grasp. Delving into the exiled former prime minister's secret offshore accounts, the magistrates discovered that Craxi had received payments totaling 22 billion lire (around $14 million) between 1990 and 1991 from something or someone called All Iberian, a shadowy, Swiss-registered account.[8] Berlusconi denied All Iberian had anything to do with him or his Fininvest group.

Investigators began probing a London-based lawyer, David Mills, who, it turned out, helped administer Fininvest's secret funds. By sifting through hundreds of documents from Mills' office, magistrates learned that All Iberian was one of these secret accounts—and a very important one: a channel for vast amounts of money used for mostly nefarious purposes. In just six years around a trillion lire, or $700 million, had flowed from it. Craxi was one recipient. Some of the funds were to secretly maintain investments in Berlusconi's Spanish broadcaster Telecinco—payments that were outlawed by European antitrust laws.[9]

Three years later, in July 1998, Berlusconi was found guilty of having illegally funded a political party (that is, Craxi's Socialist Party). The mogul got two years and four months in prison, but he had the right to two appeals, and incarceration was suspended. Judges added another four years to Craxi's mounting tally—although he would never return from Tunisia to serve the various jail terms. Not for the last time, however, the statute of limitations spared Berlusconi a conviction: ten years on from the alleged crime, the case died before there was time to get the third, definitive conviction at the Supreme Court. Italy's unusual rules, under which the statute of limitations clock continues to tick even after a trial has started, would prove a valuable friend to Berlusconi over the years.

The law wasn't finished with the British lawyer David Mills, though. His dodgy line of work in tax advice wasn't enough to provoke the Italian courts, but he would later be found guilty of accepting a $600,000 bribe from Berlusconi to lie on the mogul's behalf during criminal trials in 1997 and 1998. Prosecutors say he was paid to shield Berlusconi and his Fininvest holding company from charges relating to the exaggerated cost of US film rights. Mills' association with the Teflon Tycoon was so embarrassing that his politician wife, Tessa Jowell, then a minister under Tony Blair, asked for a separation. This prompted the British satirical magazine *Private Eye* to put Jowell on the front cover with the speech bubble: "I have never met my husband."

It's not clear whether Jowell had ever met Berlusconi, but he had certainly thought about her. The lascivious Italian leader was said to refer to Jowell in private as "*il piccolo puntaspilli*" (the little pincushion). That wouldn't have been her nickname of choice, no matter whom it came from. But coming from him it was disturbing.

Mills' own comments certainly seemed incriminating enough. He said: ". . . the B people knew very well that my testimony, to use a euphemism, had spared Mr. B a whole of lot of problems."[10] And as judges would note, Mills declared that the Fininvest slush funds were created on Berlusconi's direct orders.[11]

But the agonizingly slow pace of Italian justice, the legal ruses employed by Berlusconi and the complex nature of the case—involving old accounting trails crossing several continents—meant that the statute of limitations would threaten prosecutors' chance of securing convictions. When the case against Mills timed out in February 2010, Di Pietro hit out at the lucky escape enjoyed by the British adviser: "This is an embarrassment. The crime that Mills and Berlusconi were accused of has been proved but thanks to the usual escapology, justice has elapsed because of time. In any normal country a prime minister involved in such a case would have resigned."

Italy, as everyone with half a brain could see by now, was not a "normal" country. The courts underlined this by ordering Mills to pay €250,000 compensation to the office of the Italian prime minister for "damaging its reputation," something that Berlusconi had already had a fair go at himself.[12]

Back in 1995, while Berlusconi prepared to face the All Iberian/Craxi scandal, something far worse was brewing. Another recipient of money from the All Iberian fund was one of Berlusconi's top lieutenants, Cesare Previti. Berlusconi's slimy lawyer had received the useful sum of €16 billion lire (around $10 million) from the account.[13] Enough money, in fact, to keep the wolf from the door and to bribe a couple of judges.

The latter activity came to light thanks to the Milan high-society figure Stefania Ariosto. This glamorous blonde with a fondness for casinos first came to the attention of the city's law authorities in February 1995 after falling into gambling-related debt—and then into bad company in an attempt to finance it.[14] She eventually agreed to give prosecutors information on loan sharks. But she had something much more explosive up her sleeve: evidence that Rome's judiciary was on the take. Ariosto's partner, Vittorio Dotti, was a senior Fininvest lawyer and the leader of Berlusconi's Forza Italia party in the lower chamber. This gave her access to Berlusconi's inner circle. She revealed to Milan's prosecutors that Roman judges were frequent guests at Previti's Rome residence in the 1980s. Not only that: Previti boasted openly of having judges on his payroll, and he'd declared that the Mondadori takeover battle, which saw the huge publishing house handed to Berlusconi rather than archrival De Benedetti, had really been decided not by Dotti's official legwork, but by the bribes Previti had slipped to a judge.

When Dotti realized what his girlfriend had embarked upon, he told magistrates that it was his "moral duty" to inform his employer

Berlusconi. Prosecutor Piercamillo Davigo threatened him in no uncertain terms: "You won't say a word . . . whoever opens their mouth is aiding and abetting."[15]

Milan's prosecutors wasted no time in squeezing all the juicy information out of Ariosto. Her testimony left them openmouthed: a selection of some of Italy's most powerful judges had passed through Previti's drawing room. She told them that in one such meeting, at the end of 1988 or beginning of 1989, with the company enjoying champagne and lobster, she saw bribery in action. Previti, Judge Renato Squillante and Previti's right-hand man, the lawyer Attilio Pacifico, approached a little table on which were bundles of cash. She heard Squillante (then probably Rome's most powerful judge; the man without whose say-so, no serious criminal in the capital could be arraigned) declare, "Yes, leave it to me." When Previti saw the alarm on Ariosto's face, he told her not to worry.[16] She testified she subsequently saw Previti hand Squillante a partially open envelope stuffed with cash. Ariosto told investigators that on another occasion Previti's wife, Silvana Pompili, confided to her that she felt anxious because she and her husband had on them the money they needed to bribe magistrates.

Ariosto and Dotti went off on vacation soon after her revelations, with Ariosto given a police escort—prosecutors didn't want angry loan sharks interfering with such an important witness. But while the couple was trying to relax on a boat off the Mediterranean island of Sardinia, Dotti received an anxious phone call from Berlusconi himself, demanding to know why Ariosto had been treated to an armed guard. The lawyer told his mogul boss that it was to protect them from menacing moneylenders. Which mole or moles among Milan's law authorities had passed on the confidential information about Ariosto's police escort isn't known. It was clear, though, that Berlusconi and Previti were already worried.

The Milan prosecutors had been joined by a female colleague, the famously dogged Neapolitan magistrate, Ilda Boccassini. It was Boccassini whose unrelenting efforts had ensured that the Cosa Nostra killers responsible for murdering her friend and colleague Giovanni Falcone in the infamous 1992 bomb attack were brought to justice. In the autumn of 1995, Boccassini began to work closely with Ariosto. The magistrate set about spying on Previti and Squillante—with cameras, microphones and wiretaps—demonstrating a diligence that Berlusconi would become very familiar with over the years.

At 11:42 p.m. on New Year's Eve 1995, Judge Squillante picked up the phone to ring Silvio Berlusconi at Arcore. The tycoon wasn't there, so in quick succession he rang Berlusconi's brother, Paolo, the mogul's senior Fininvest executive Gianni Letta and then finally Cesare Previti (who did pick up).[17] Why was this pillar of the judiciary phoning four top figures in the Fininvest empire, all of whom were under investigation for criminal activities? To wish them "Happy New Year," he told magistrates. We can assume Previti at least reciprocated his wishes. But 1996 wouldn't be a happy year for either of them.

Squillante soon got the first powerful hint of this. On January 21 he met other judges and lawyers at the Tombini bar, in Rome's Via Ferrari, not far from the court complex. Among those present was Vittorio Virga, the defender of Paolo Berlusconi, Gianni Letta and Davide Giacalone, who had drafted the 1990 broadcast law in Berlusconi's favor. After 20 minutes of intriguing conversation that touched on slush funds (*fondi neri*) and various mysterious "operations," Squillante spotted a hidden microphone. Only then did the judge realize that he was in investigators' sights.

In March, Squillante, the head of Rome's preliminary investigations section, was himself arrested. Berlusconi told Dotti to declare that his girlfriend was a liar and a fantasist. The lawyer replied that he wasn't in a position to confirm or deny her incendiary claims. The lawyer refused to alter his statement, even when Berlusconi promised to make him mayor of Milan in return.[18]

For her trouble, on December 31, Ariosto had received a mangled, blood-drenched rabbit in the post, mafia-style, with the message: "Happy New Year." But now that her role in the investigation was out in the open, the tycoon's cronies, in the media and beyond, were swift to launch a barrage of vitriolic abuse at her, with Sgarbi and Fede leading the way. In once choice example, the Berlusconi-friendly lawyer Domenico Contestabile claimed that Ariosto had invented a tragic personal story about suffering the loss of three children. It was true: she had lost all three to cystic fibrosis.[19] Contestabile was later forced to pay her damages.

Ariosto fired back by pulling out photos of the sleazy lawyers, judges and Fininvest businessmen together, and sending them off to the weekly news magazine of Berlusconi's archrival, Carlo De Benedetti. Dotti, the lawyer who had supped with the devil, saw his legal work dry up and realized that falling out with Italy's most powerful man was not without consequences.

Naturally, Previti, as the immediate supplier of the judicial bribes, and Berlusconi as their original source were under threat too. Help was at hand, though, from an unlikely source.

Berlusconi was not on speaking terms with the Northern League, after its leader Bossi had stabbed him in the front only seven months into his first term in office. For his part, Bossi still referred to the mogul as the "Mafioso of Arcore." But without the populist party's substantial 10 percent of the electorate to boost his coalition, the tycoon would lose the 1996 general election. The percentage of the vote obtained by Berlusconi and his center-right coalition was, at 43.3 percent, a fraction up on the 1994 result. But the center-left, led by Romano Prodi, had managed to form a bigger alliance. Calling itself The Olive Tree, the group took 45.4 percent of the vote. It wasn't lost on Berlusconi friends and foes alike that had the mogul still had the League's support, he'd have won by a landslide.

As it was, the series of center-left coalitions that followed over the next four to five years proved themselves almost as useful to Berlusconi as his own administrations. When prosecutors attempted to convict Previti, Berlusconi's legal fixer was suddenly loath to drag himself away from parliament, thus making it difficult to organize his trial dates. When, in 1997, magistrates asked parliament to waive Previti's immunity in order to arrest him and force his appearance, lawmakers on the right—and even some on the left—rallied around to block the request.[20] The sordid spectacle was just one example of how center-left governments between 1996 and 2001 would fail to curb Berlusconi's grotesque power.

In the run-up to Christmas 1997 the mogul reminded Italy of his spiritual standing and attempted to put a little distance between himself and his crooked lawyer. "To accuse me of corruption is like arresting Mother Teresa of Calcutta because a child in her institute has stolen an apple," he declared.[21] Had Berlusconi read anything other than fan mail, girly mags or balance sheets, he might have been aware that Mother Teresa was probably not the saint she would have had us believe. In the mid-1990s journalist Christopher Hitchens described her as "the most successful confidence trickster of the last century." Canadian academics, referring to the missing millions donated to her cause, appeared to agree with him.[22]

The center-left coalition led by Romano Prodi, a mumbling economics professor, had won the 1996 election. But Berlusconi, helped by the predictable TV blitz, did better than he might have expected given that the Fininvest boardroom was starting to resemble a rogues' gallery. Shamelessly, the mogul ensured that the most egregious suspects (apart from himself)—i.e., Dell'Utri, Previti and Berruti, the crooked former finance police official—were candidates. In parliament they would enjoy some immunity.

As usual, the best campaign barbs came from one of his former allies: the Northern League whipped up a fake electoral campaign poster of Berruti's face with the words: "Vote for me: I don't want to go to jail."[23]

The new center-left government could have attacked the mogul from the outset. But it didn't. There would be no new laws combating conflicts of interest or excessive media domination, no new media watchdog to replace the toothless "Guarantor of Telecommunications." Neither did center-left leaders appear too bothered that the opposition leader showed no intention of quitting, despite being under investigation for a series of possible crimes.

Prodi lasted two years as leader. The next center-left prime minister, Massimo D'Alema, who was in office from May 1998 to May 2000, assumed that Berlusconi was finished as a serious political force, and instead of attacking Berlusconi tried to recruit the tycoon in his mission to revamp Italy's chaotic electoral system.

Berlusconi played ball until it became clear that D'Alema wouldn't revamp the justice system in order protect him from corruption charges. At which point, the mogul let the electoral reform proposals collapse.[24] Milan's chief prosecutor, Borrelli, later remarked, "Perhaps he [D'Alema] wanted to control the situation, trap Berlusconi. He was kidding himself."[25] Berlusconi's charade of appearing to work with the incumbent prime minister on important constitutional changes for 18 months also had the effect of shoring up his status as the leader of the center-right—at a time when some colleagues had begun calling for the mogul to step down.

Although Berlusconi didn't get the justice changes he might have liked for his own benefit, the center-left coalitions adopted an ambiguous attitude to the ongoing Mani Pulite investigations. Some pundits noted that D'Alema had also tussled with the law—he was briefly put under investigation by a magistrate from Venice in relation to illegal political funding. All the charges were dropped, but prosecutors had probably not endeared themselves to him. It's possible, too, that the more pragmatic or timid sections of the center-left were wary of Berlusconi's media power. The 1995 referendum appeared to show that the public wanted Berlusconi's Coca-Cola TV. Attempts to dismantle the mogul's TV empire would be sure to see his Mediaset channels unleash their fire. But if that was the case, cynics might ask, why didn't these lawmakers simply surrender their seats and get jobs with the Fininvest/Forza Italia juggernaut? As we'll see, some of them did.

The magistrates had yet to find the smoking gun, and the political opposition had proven toothless. But another unexpected menace appeared to confront the 60-year-old mogul in 1997: cancer. Surgeons removed a tumor from his prostate in May that year. There were many rumors then concerning his health. It was not until three years later, however, in a July 2000 interview with *La Repubblica*, that he discussed the ordeal and how he'd reacted with typical fortitude.[26] "I went through a nightmare lasting months. I am cured. I managed to come out of the tunnel," he told the interviewer in the same simple, dramatic language used in his political campaigns. Berlusconi said he'd kept his illness secret so as not to appear weak to his opponents. "A political leader has opponents, and many are ready to take advantage of every weakness." The mogul revealed, too, that his brush with death had proved a life-changing event.

"After the illness I went back to work with greater intensity, but there was another change. Today I give less importance to material things, to money and property," he said. This Damascene conversion would surely preclude him, then, from snapping up fabulous multimillion-dollar homes around the world, including villas in Bermuda, Antigua, Sardinia and Lake Como, and from buying things like luxury yachts. More fool those who believed him.

CHAPTER 7

THE GORY YEARS

The noughties or perhaps the naughties were Berlusconi's glory years—make that gory years if you were an Italian with a shred of dignity or an ounce of good taste. Foreign observers no doubt remember the whoring, the clowning and the embarrassing gaffes: a bandana-clad Berlusconi hosting Tony Blair and his wife, Cherie, in his luxury Sardinian seaside villa; the mogul's toe-curling attempt to ingratiate himself with President George W. Bush at Camp David with a few fawning compliments in pidgin English. But the ridiculous impression he created abroad was at odds with his success in ensuring domestic policies and the priorities of his business empire converged. Italy became Berlusconi PLC.

In the spring of 2001, Italy's fragmented, backbiting center-left was weaker than ever. So, at the start of the new millennium, Berlusconi's time had come again. After winning the general election on May 13, the mogul and his right-wing coalition would remain in power for five years—practically an eternity in the helter-skelter world of Italian politics, and ample time for an unscrupulous mogul–prime minister to abuse the law-making process for his own ends.

The Italian public might not have entirely believed the hype during the election campaign, but some of them liked the sound of it and bought it anyway. Thanks to their leader's bottomless pockets, Team Berlusconi was able to send an extravagant 125-page booklet to 15 million Italian homes before the elections. Titled *Una Storia Italiana*, the book illustrated the mogul's aspirational lifestyle and documented his achievements—entrepreneurial, political, social and even sporting—in a series of fables showing how industry, courage, loyalty and intelligence had enabled the magnate to triumph over the forces of evil, represented by Milan's communist magistrates. Berlusconi was determined that people recognize he was the victim of vindictive prosecutors, not the rogue who'd got away.

The booklet purported to show the "character and passions: the life of Silvio Berlusconi, childhood, adolescence, school friends," and, intriguingly, "the little secrets of Silvio." Readers hoping for dirt on his supposed links with the Mafia, or on how his company had bribed politicians and judges, were to be sorely disappointed, however.

Even the well-documented sins and peccadillos of Berlusconi, part superman, part guy next door, were airbrushed to oblivion. For example, his decision to see a topless actress behind his wife's back for two years, which resulted in the couple's divorce, is described very differently. According to *Una Storia Italiana*, Berlusconi's professional life was becoming "ever fuller, with days and nights dedicated only to work. Something in the relationship with Carla [his wife] changes at the start of the 1980s and love is transformed into sincere friendship." God help Italy should Berlusconi ever write history books. Italians were told of the trash-TV mogul's passion for the works of Dante, Plato and Erasmus, and his predilection for collecting fine art—in addition to that he'd acquired so dubiously with the purchase of Villa San Martino.

How effective this extravagant PR was at winning votes is unclear. The Berlusconi-friendly pollster Luigi Crespi said the mawkish pamphlet might have gained Forza Italia an extra 3 percent of the vote on election day.[1] Crespi's Datamedia (owned by Berlusconi) predicted a landslide for the mogul. Some pundits have wondered whether these vastly inaccurate predictions convinced some left-wing voters that it was game over, and not worth voting.[2]

But of more importance was the mogul's domination of Italian television. His three Mediaset channels gave him more airtime than the opposition. The Rai channels (apart from the left-wing bastion Rai 3), on the other hand, were more or less fair to everyone. Berlusconi's manifesto was also simple, populist—and cynical. Tax cuts figured prominently in the program and, significantly, nearly two-thirds (64.3 percent) of the country's notoriously tax-shy self-employed voted for the center-right. Berlusconi also promised less immigration and more jobs, particularly for the south of Italy. He never explained how squandering more state funds on public works in the corrupt, Mafia-plagued south was compatible with his crusade for economic liberalism. But he didn't have to.

The 64-year-old was practically bald on top by now, but in good health four years after his cancer scare, and as of yet untouched by the plastic surgeons. Berlusconi's belief in his own appeal was such that he allowed only his own grinning, perma-tanned mug on the electoral posters the length and breadth of the country. Local candidates were just faceless conduits for the mogul himself. It wasn't supposed to be, but the 2001 vote became Italy's first presidential-style general election.

He hardly won by a landslide. But by laboriously reforging links with the Northern League and getting the right-wing National Alliance on board again, Berlusconi had sufficient seats to lead a new coalition, which went by the name House of Freedoms. It won 45.4 percent of the vote—only just beating the left-wing Olive Tree coalition, which took 43.8 percent. Under Italy's complex system of proportional representation, it was enough to deliver Berlusconi secure majorities in both chambers of parliament.

Berlusconi found himself in a considerably stronger position than in his first, unhappy experience of government. His Northern League allies were the same belligerent bunch, but their share of the vote had collapsed from 10 percent in the 1994 general election to less than 4 percent. The prime minister knew they weren't in a position to be too unruly. The post-fascist National Alliance had also seen its support slide, from 16 percent to 12 percent, while Berlusconi's Forza Italia had surged from 21 percent to 30 percent. Berlusconi was in the driver's seat this time around. From his opulent Arcore mansion, Italy's new CEO announced: "Italy has turned a page." He added that he intended "to win the respect of people who did not vote for me."

We can assume that Indro Montanelli, Berlusconi's old nemesis/idol, was among the nonbelievers. The grand old man of Italian journalism passed away in July 2001 at the age of 92. Enunciating the sort of passionate half-truth that only he is capable of, the prime minister lamented his former editor's passing: "I weep for the friend with whom I shared so many battles, and to whom I felt bound even when he disagreed with my stance with the spirit of freedom that always animated his work and that I always respected." Years earlier, Berlusconi had offered Montanelli a permanent resting place in the tacky Egyptian-style mausoleum the mogul had built at Arcore for himself, his family and his closest friends, including the Mafioso Dell'Utri, the bent lawyer Previti and the babbling newsreader Fede. Montanelli declined that offer, responding with his inimitable wit: "*Domine non sum dignus*" (Lord, I'm not worthy).[3]

Berlusconi hoped to win over less-skeptical members of the public, however, by looking to the US for inspiration, as he had done when building his TV empire. On becoming prime minister for the second time he made a "Contract with the Italians"—an idea pilfered from Newt Gingrich's 1994 "Contract with America." Berlusconi publicized the stunt on the popular *Porta a Porta* TV show hosted by Bruno Vespa, an old-school Christian Democrat–style figure who made no bones about being in the Berlusconi camp. The Contract consisted of five key pledges: a raft of tax cuts, a reduction in crime, a rise in the state pension, halving unemployment and a massive boost in the number of public works. It sounded like Berlusconi had written it down on the back of an envelope after a boozy dinner at Arcore.

But to show he meant it, the mogul told the toadying Vespa that if he didn't succeed in meeting at least four of his five pledges, he would never again run for parliament. The Italian academic and *La Stampa* journalist Luca Ricolfi detailed how, by the end of his term in office, Berlusconi had failed on at least four of the five counts.[4] Of course, that didn't stop him from standing for election again.

While some ministers were charged with enacting their leader's financially illiterate but vote-catching polices, senior cronies in government and parliament were pursuing Berlusconi's personal interests. His tax adviser–cum–economics minister Giulio Tremonti weighed in early, with an amnesty for tax dodgers that enabled the company's Mediaset TV division to avoid paying the €120 million it owed the Italian state after hiding vast sums in overseas slush funds.

The government's other priority was keeping The Boss out of jail. This was no easy task. Berlusconi's choice of justice minister, Roberto Castelli, raised eyebrows. Reporters demanded to know what the former sound engineer knew about the law. "Absolutely nothing. Zero," he told them.[5] Berlusconi calculated that giving one of his personal lawyers the top job in the justice department would probably be vetoed by the president of the republic (as his attempt to appoint Previti to the post had been in 1994). So, with a mix of cynicism and shamelessness never before seen in a modern Western democracy, the mogul chose a legal novice as justice supremo and placed his own lawyers in all the other key roles—and had them rewrite the law to keep the courts at bay. Thus, the grotesque situation arose in which Berlusconi's associates spent half their time drafting justice legislation, which they intended to exploit during the course of their other job—defending the prime minister in the courts. They were paid handsomely by the state and Berlusconi, respectively, for their roles. And with their help, from 2001 onward, the billionaire declared war on Italy's penal code.

By September 2001, there were proposals to do away with the crime of false accounting, which would save Berlusconi from charges relating to the creation of secret overseas accounts. When this disgraceful legislation was finally passed in February 2002, it had been slightly watered down. But Milan University law professor Alberto Crespi said the measure still amounted to the legalization of slush funds. The new law killed the false accounting charges against the prime minister relating to the $18 million bribe sent to Craxi from All Iberian and also those relating to the creation of the accounts used by Previti to bribe judges. Berlusconi's brother, Paolo, and the mogul's close friend Confalonieri also benefitted from the legislation.[6]

Berlusconi's apparatchiks didn't forget to keep up the pressure on Milan's magistrates. Government inspectors continued to harass them and, in September 2001, led by Berlusconi's interior minister, Claudio "Sky-ola" Scajola—so nicknamed due to his alleged fondness for organizing Alitalia, Italy's national airline, routes for personal benefit—withdrew bodyguards from high-profile prosecutors, including Boccassini and Colombo in Milan, as well as anti-mafia magistrates elsewhere.[7] Nearly 13 years later, in May 2014, Scajola would be arrested as part of a mafia probe.[8]

The Supreme Court even threw Berlusconi a bone in the dangerous Mondadori takeover trial—and rather a large one. It declared that the bribery charges he faced relating to incidents before 1991 had expired in November that year under the ten-year statute of limitations. In addition, it said there was insufficient evidence to support charges relating to alleged offenses committed from 1991 onward.

Previti wasn't so lucky. The lawyer was starting to get wind of a long jail sentence. This wouldn't look good for Berlusconi. And he might have feared that Previti would attempt to drag his boss down with him.

An attempt to buy Previti time came in October 2001, with new proposals from Gaetano Pecorella, a Berlusconi lawyer whom the mogul had appointed president of the Justice Commission in the lower house of parliament. These said that only original versions of foreign documents could be used in criminal trials—thus further impeding proceedings that centered on Fininvest's overseas slush funds. Bernard Bertossa, the chief prosecutor of Geneva in Switzerland (where Berlusconi held accounts that were used to bribe judges), noted that it would not be possible to send original bank statements because the original documents existed on a computer disk; anything else sent to the Italian courts would therefore be a copy. Bertossa described the law as "a catastrophe for international justice."[9] Other international legal figures joined in the criticism, including Guido Calabresi, the head of New York's Court of Appeals.

Two months later in Brussels, on December 6, Italy vetoed European Commission (EC) proposals for European arrest warrants for those suspected of financial crime. The move was backed by Berlusconi, who was well aware that the gung ho Spanish judge Baltasar Garzón wanted to press charges against him for alleged tax fraud and anti-competition breaches by Fininvest's Spanish TV station, Telecinco.[10] In addition, the EC's intention that the warrant also apply to the offense of "racism and xenophobia" didn't endear it to Northern League bigots in Berlusconi's coalition.

The United Nations dispatched its justice observer, Dato Param Cumaraswamy, to Italy on March 11, 2002, to investigate what on earth was going on. His highly critical report on Berlusconi's attack on the Italian legal system appeared on April 3. The UN official also hit out at the conflict of interests inherent in having a prime minister use his personal lawyers to rewrite the penal code.[11]

Justice minister and legal ingénue Castelli protested, though no one listened. In fact, undeterred by the UN censure, Berlusconi's team were busy preparing another *ad personam* (bespoke) legal scam for their master and his emerging weak link, Previti (who'd suffered another setback when judges insisted on using copies of Swiss bank details). This new tactic was the November 2002 Cirami Law, named after the backbencher who'd thought it up. Suspects who thought a particular court was biased against them would be allowed to request a trial elsewhere. The law would give Berlusconi and his associates the chance to move cases away from Milan's Palace of Justice—where Berlusconi was convinced that magistrates and their colleagues on the judging bench were out to get him—and over to neighboring cities such as Brescia. The delays might also prove invaluable. The glacial speed of Italian justice meant that time was already of the essence: the statute of limitations was always threatening to come to the mogul's rescue, and on many occasions it did.

Following the UN criticism, and just 18 months into Berlusconi's second term, the European Union, which prided (or some might say deluded) itself on being the most enlightened regional power on the planet, was beginning to twitch as a banana republic emerged in its midst. The EU demanded that Italy repeal the Cirami Law. The Council of Europe said in its 2004 resolution that the cynical scam "slows down the course of justice . . . and tarnishes the reputation of the entire court system."

Italy's Supreme Court of Cassation was able to overrule the law's application on a case-by-case basis—as it finally did in January 2003, blocking the request by Berlusconi and Previti to have their cases moved from Milan to Brescia. Upon this rare fight back by the courts, Berlusconi flew into a rage and released one of his polemical videos. The billionaire prime minister railed against the "incredible judicial persecution" he was suffering. He listed the extent of his contact with the criminal justice system, including, he said, 1,561 interrogations and court appearances and 871 visits from the police. He obviously felt confident the public would see this as proof of the investigators' vindictiveness, rather than an indication of the mountain of incriminating evidence that had piled up against him.

On April 29, 2003, Previti was convicted of, among other things, bribing the judge Vittorio Metta with hundreds of thousands of dollars from Fininvest slush funds. Metta, who'd ruled in favor of Berlusconi in the 1991 Mondadori takeover battle, was handed a jail sentence. "The final picture is that this was certainly the biggest case of corruption in the history of the Italian republic," the judges said in their 600-page report, explaining why they had sentenced Previti to a total of 11 years in prison for the Metta bribe and an unrelated corruption conviction.[12] Some of his many enemies cheered. Of course, he still had his second and final appeal at the Supreme Court. But in July 2007, he lost that too and spent a (very) brief time behind bars. Berlusconi, the big fish, had got away, however.

While Previti was heading for a definitive conviction, the prime minister had made his position considerably more secure by introducing a law that gave immunity from prosecution to the holders of the five highest offices of state—those of prime minister, president, the speakers of the

Senate and the Chamber of Deputies, and the president of the Constitutional Court. The timing—in June 2003—was perfect, allowing the mogul to walk away from the SME bribery case, in which he and Previti were accused of corrupting a judge to win control of the state-owned food company (See Chapter 3). Berlusconi sought to justify the law but made a fool of himself by paraphrasing Orwell: "All citizens are equal but maybe this one is slightly more equal than the others, given that 50 percent of the Italians have given him the responsibility of governing the country."[13] It was a lot less than 50 percent. And this supposed economic liberal sounded like a Soviet dictator with his snout in the trough.

Berlusconi's immunity kicked in just as judges were beginning their summing up. Previti was convicted—but eventually freed on appeal when the process timed out. Although the Constitutional Court struck down the immunity law, it was too late. By then the case against Berlusconi was a lost cause for the SME investigators. And so the mogul remained one step ahead.

While it's true he had a lot of legal maneuvering to do, Berlusconi also enjoyed being prime minister. It flattered his (very large) ego. In addition to gifting Italy with his vision and entrepreneurial skills, Il Cavaliere fancied himself an international statesman. But while his self-serving abuse of power in Italy was at least performed with a certain élan, on the world stage Berlusconi revealed himself as a buffoon and vulgarian.

Italy's international relations seemed to get off to a promising start in Berlusconi's second government, thanks to the appointment of Renato Ruggiero as foreign minister. This former head of the World Trade Organization had the right international experience as well as the pro-European credentials to reassure Berlusconi's important EU neighbors that Italy's basket-case reputation was unjustified.

Unfortunately, when Ruggiero objected to the xenophobic and EU-baiting outbursts from various goons in Berlusconi's right-wing coalition, The Boss made it clear to his foreign minister that he was there to do as he was told, not to do as he thought best. Ruggiero quit in January 2002, after just six months in the job. Clearly, Italy needed a foreign minister more in tune with the mogul's way of thinking. There was only one person up to the task: declaring his international affairs expertise, Berlusconi appointed himself Italy's interim chief diplomat.

Officials in Brussels choked on their long, Michelin-starred lunches on hearing the news. One senior European Commission figure noted "the prospect of double doses of Berlusconi is not seen as an attractive one. People here have made it pretty clear what they think of his conduct in office so far. It's not just his flunkies, his tan and his stream of limousines. It's his lack of political skills."[14]

Following the September 11, 2001, atrocity in New York, what the Western world needed were shrewd and steady hands on the tiller. Berlusconi swiftly signaled his diplomatic skills by declaring European civilization superior to that of the Islamic world, thus alienating potential allies against Islamic extremism, such as Turkey.[15] He claimed he'd been misquoted. He hadn't. Berlusconi would continue to put his foot in his mouth for the next ten years, always promptly denying the latest gaffe. It seems to have taken him that long to realize that TV cameras and YouTube were there to record his pearls of wisdom for eternity.

In the months after he took over as foreign minister, Berlusconi stuck two fingers behind the head of the Spanish foreign minister while diplomats posed for a group photo, in a witless and inexplicable indication of a cuckold. Berlusconi laughed, even if no one else did. On Wall Street he told potential investors that "another reason to invest in Italy is that we have beautiful secretaries . . . superb girls."[16]

The mogul saw a golden opportunity to cement his international standing by signing up to US president George W. Bush's obtuse but headline-grabbing War on Terror. Silvio Berlusconi could certainly do obtuse and headline-grabbing. He rocked up to Camp David in September 2002 but was humiliated by Bush—himself no Noam Chomsky—when he attempted a few fawning lines of pidgin English in a comedic Italian accent: "I consider that flag of United States not only a flag of a country but is a universal message of freedom . . . and democracy."[17]

"Thank you, sir. His English is very good," said Bush with a smirk. Those present tittered. No doubt the US president was relieved he hadn't had to speak Italian.

It was, though, a spiteful and stupid attack on a German member of the European Parliament (MEP) that really indicated how unfit Berlusconi was to represent his country abroad. In July 2003, Italy had just assumed the rotating presidency of the Council of Europe. As Italy's leader, Berlusconi addressed the EC parliament, only to find himself facing some provocative questions from Martin Schulz, the vice president of the German social democrat MEPs. Schulz focused on Berlusconi's apparent attempt to dismantle half of Italy's penal code for his own benefit.

Berlusconi didn't respond directly to Schulz's questions but said he knew someone who was making a film about the Nazi concentration camps and declared: "I will recommend you, Signor Schulz, for the role of Camp Guard."[18] Politicians and journalists, sometimes irritated but more often than not bored in interminable European Union meetings, woke with a start and emitted astounded "tuts" and "ooohs" as translators delivered through their headphones the latest wit and wisdom of the new president of the Council of Europe. Berlusconi's coalition colleague Gianfranco Fini appeared to be looking for a hole in the floor to swallow him up.

If Berlusconi doesn't always reflect long and hard before opening his mouth, he has always placed a premium on personal appearance: from the ban on beards among his parliamentarians to the importance of his immaculate navy suits and clean fingernails. In December 2003, the tycoon decided it was time for his first face-lift. Italian plastic surgeon Angelo Villa, who shared his patient's aversion to false modesty, said he was proud of the result. "A politician's face is a valuable asset, and when someone decides to undergo an operation that is so important for his image, he must choose the best person to do it," Dr. Villa told the daily *La Repubblica*, adding, "I am one of the best."

Villa, a friend of Berlusconi's daughter Marina, described the delicate balancing act he'd had to achieve, i.e., taking years off the 67-year-old mogul, while still allowing him to perform the famous saccharine grin. "Whatever you are supposed to put right, you must not change the expression of the face, and that takes a lot of experience," he said. During the two-week recuperation period, Berlusconi kept an unusually low public profile, although he felt able to chair a cabinet meeting, in which he asked one of his colleagues: "Don't you find me handsome?"[19] He'd also undergone liposuction and a crash diet to lose 10 kilos ahead of the June EU elections. An understandably hungry prime minister told a reporter from the enemy *La Repubblica* newspaper: "Don't come too close or I might bite you."

Despite the outrage he generates, some of Berlusconi's antics—at home and abroad—have shown, conversely, why a lot of people, including many Italians, like him. He's often very funny, even if you laugh at him rather than with him.

Britain's freeloading first couple Tony and Cherie Blair paid Berlusconi a visit, or rather jumped at the chance of a free weekend, in August 2004, at the mogul's Villa Certosa on Sardinia's glamorous Costa Smeralda. Cherie Blair, an extremely wealthy lawyer, later gushed about their host. "I've never had such a night as the one we spent with him in Sardinia," she told an Italian magazine. "We all found ourselves singing 'Summertime' together. Silvio even interrupted the singer and made me sing." Demonstrating her own keen awareness of international affairs, she added: "Silvio has a very large personality, and he is not the same as other world leaders."[20] The British visitors were even treated to fireworks that spelt out "Viva Tony!" The previous summer Berlusconi had wowed guests by igniting a mini volcano in his garden, launching a cascade of lava into the sea. Alarmed neighbors called the fire brigade.

Best of all, while the Blairs were chowing down on *spaghetti allo scoglio* and lobster and drinking fine Sardinian Vermentino, Berlusconi was sporting a white bandana to cover up the unfinished results from a hair transplant. With the Blairs due to go on a boat ride with their host, Cherie Blair revealed that her husband was desperately hoping Berlusconi would remove the handkerchief from his head.

"[W]e went out with him simply putting another bandanna on his head which matched the color of the shirt he was wearing. As we went out, Tony said to me: 'Whatever happens, make sure I am not photographed next to Silvio wearing a bandanna. Make sure you are in the middle, otherwise the British press will kill us,'" she said.[21]

Britain's malevolent tabloids, of course, murdered both of them. The bandana at least drew attention away from Berlusconi's new face.

But Berlusconi's informal style more often than not went down like a lead balloon. Toward the end of his six-month presidency of Europe, in December 2003, Berlusconi was in Brussels hoping to end his train-wreck tenure on a high note by persuading all of the EU's notoriously fractious member nations to sign up to a new European constitution. At one stage, in an attempt to lighten the mood, Berlusconi declared: "Let's talk about football and women." And turning with a nudge and a wink to the four-times-married German chancellor Gerhard Schroeder, he said: "Gerhard, why don't you start?"

Berlusconi was—and is—a one-trick pony. Whether he's leading delicate diplomatic negotiations or hosting a rowdy dinner with friends, he treats everyone—and every situation—as if he were doing a stand-up routine for package holidaymakers in Rimini. The routines usually go down well at home. But judging by his frosty response, Chancellor Schroeder doesn't take his holidays on the Adriatic's version of Coney Island.

Back at base, Berlusconi's TV empire had a problem that needed fixing. As long ago as 1994, the courts had said that in order to encourage competition, Berlusconi was obliged to give up the terrestrial broadcast slot occupied by his Rete 4 channel, that dread dimension of the worst American repeats and Emilio Fede's sycophantic prattling.

Older viewers (mostly Berlusconi voters) liked the channel, though, and it brought in useful advertising money. Following another delay in 1998 by the vacillating center-left Prodi government in enacting the courts' orders, the deadline for action—i.e., the displacement of Rete 4 from terrestrial to satellite—was due to fall on December 31, 2003. Berlusconi's unsavory communications minister, Maurizio Gasparri, was ready, however, with legislation to help his boss. The notorious broadcast media reform bill, known simply as the Gasparri Law, was supposed to open up the market. But, as Vienna-based ethics watchdog the Organization for Security and Co-operation in Europe noted, it simply maintained the status quo—a duopoly of Rai and Mediaset.[22] And, of course, Mediaset got to keep the terrestrial slot of Rete 4. Gasparri rewrote the rules, citing the explosion in digital TV (which hadn't yet happened) as evidence there was no need to make Mediaset concede one of its terrestrial slots. Gasparri then stacked the odds even further in Berlusconi's favor. The measure of the media controlled by one person would now also include ownership of other media, such as videos, books, DVDs, and billboard advertising. As a result the proportion of Italy's media controlled by Berlusconi fell overnight from 30 percent to 20 percent.[23]

In December 2003 the Italian president, Carlo Azeglio Ciampi, refused to sign the first version of the Gasparri Law, saying there was too little digital coverage in Italy to justify allowing Rete 4 to keep its terrestrial slot. Gasparri responded by promising that 50 percent of Italian homes would be able to receive digital programming by April 30, 2004. The government failed on this promise too—only 18 percent of homes had complete digital TV coverage by the end of April. But still, Rete 4 kept its broadcast frequency. The law was passed in May 2004, to fierce criticism from domestic and international observers.

There was also fierce criticism of the Frattini Law of July 2004, which ostensibly set out to tackle concerns over conflicts of interest in public life but did nothing to resolve issues relating to Berlusconi's dominance of Italy's private media. Crucially, the legislation said owning a company was not incompatible with public office as long as the individual was not closely involved in its management. Berlusconi declared that all his time was devoted to being prime minister.[24] The media freedom representative of OSCE (Organization for Security and Co-operation in Europe) described the Frattini Law as "a source of concern from the point of view of the quality of democracy."[25]

Perhaps even more pernicious, as the Berlusconi government's media blitz continued, was Gasparri's move to stop Mediaset's archrival Rai from privatizing some of its assets, including broadcast towers. With the sale, the state broadcaster had hoped to generate around $500 million to invest in content and new media.[26] Here was a supposedly liberal, free-market government, behaving like a Soviet satellite state. And to top it all there was a huge subsidy available to help Mediaset as it launched into digital TV. The Berlusconi government generously offered to pay viewers 75 percent of the cost for the digital decoders they would need to watch Berlusconi's digital TV programming—and that of other broadcasters—in a €220 million ($350 million) state giveaway. But Mediaset was seen as the big winner because the funding allowed it to launch its lucrative Premium Gallery service—sparking complaints from competitor Rupert Murdoch's Sky Italia and an investigation by the European Commission (EC).[27]

In 2008, the EC ordered the Italian government to retrieve millions of euros in illegal subsidies from Berlusconi's Mediaset broadcasting empire. The EC order illustrated more clearly than ever the grotesque farce inherent in Berlusconi's control of Italy's government and its private media. The EC's competition office said "it would be for the Italian state [i.e., Silvio Berlusconi, the prime minister] to decide the exact amount of aid to be recovered from Silvio Berlusconi [media magnate]."[28]

When, after five long years, Italy returned to the polls in 2006, Il Cavaliere lost to his old adversary, Romano Prodi. Berlusconi's enthusiastic participation in the invasion of Iraq had played very badly with the Italian public, which, since the days of Craxi and before, had adopted an ambivalent or even hostile attitude to America's foreign policy initiatives.

More important, though, was the stagnant state of the economy. Berlusconi's talk of liberalism, dynamism and competition was just hot air. He was too concerned with opinion polls to attempt anything as bold as dismantling the ubiquitous castes and vested interests that stifled growth and jobs.

The Economist, the international house journal for the center-right, declared Berlusconi's second administration an "abject failure."[29] In 2006, Italy was the slowest-growing large economy in Europe. "The Berlusconi government has also undone much of the improvement to the public finances made by its predecessor: the budget deficit and the public debt, the world's third-biggest, are both rising once more," *The Economist* noted in its list of charges.

Berlusconi could hardly consider his time in office a letdown, however. In 2006, *Forbes* magazine estimated his personal wealth to be $11 billion. Not only that, the magistrates had yet to deal him a serious blow. And this was the real achievement of the second Berlusconi regime. Marco Travaglio, a protégé of Indro Montanelli, and the most tireless chronicler of Berlusconi's crimes and misdemeanors over the last two decades, told me: "It's simple. If it hadn't been for this deluge of personalized laws, Berlusconi would have been in jail since 2006–7."[30]

But it didn't occur to the mogul's friends or foes that some of his legal scams, in addition to their immediate benefits, might also come back to haunt him.

On December 5, 2005, just months before Berlusconi was kicked out of power, his government passed the cynical Law 251—better known as the Save-Previti law. This piece of legislation drastically revised the statute of limitations (thus reducing the window of opportunity prosecutors had to gain a conviction once a crime had been committed), apparently in an attempt to ensure that some of Previti's bribery charges timed out. The collateral damage was massive: the law also killed hundreds of trials for corruption, assault and even manslaughter.[31] The Save-Previti law also contained an amendment that meant convicts aged 70 or over would no longer go to prison. Thanks to this legislation, Berlusconi's crooked 70-year-old lawyer would spend only three days in jail following his definitive conviction in May 2006 for passing a huge bribe from chemicals company SIR to another firm (activity unrelated to Berlusconi's business empire), and his definitive conviction in July 2007 for bribing Judge Vittorio Metta to hand Berlusconi the Mondadori publishing house. The shortened statute of limitations would also save Berlusconi in later trials, including the one in which he was charged with bribing British lawyer David Mills with $600,000.[32]

But in order to appease the law-and-order lobby among his right-wing supporters, Berlusconi ensured that the Save-Previti law toughened penalties for mafia-related crimes, terrorism and sex offenses; and there would be no age limit for incarcerating such criminals. After all, what were the chances that the mogul would be accused in the coming years of, say, paying for sex with an underage prostitute? The answer, of course, was much greater than anyone then imagined.

CHAPTER 8

GETTING AWAY WITH IT

Fact and Fiction

Some of the most dramatic episodes in Berlusconi's career have taken place at his tub-thumping political rallies. One such incident occurred on the evening of Sunday, November 26, 2006, when the mogul was taken off the stage, not in handcuffs—as most of Italy would have liked to have seen—but by aides who'd called an ambulance.

The 70-year-old mogul was in the Tuscan town of Montecatini Terme telling young supporters of his plan to merge his Forza Italia and the old former-fascist National Alliance into one party (to be controlled by him, naturally). "That is what I plan to leave as a bequest of my political activities," he said. "Now excuse me, emotion is getting the better of me and I . . ." His voice trailed away and he gripped the podium for support, before collapsing backward with his eyes closed into the arms of staff, who carried him away.[1]

A short time later he had recovered sufficiently to salute fans who were shouting, "Silvio! Silvio!" before staff whisked him off to Milan's San Raffaele Hospital in a helicopter. Berlusconi's personal doctor, Umberto Scapagnini, inventor of a special elixir that supposedly provided the mogul with his exceptional physical stamina, said the tycoon had suffered "a loss of consciousness for a few seconds, caused by extreme tiredness and the very great heat" inside the hall.

It soon emerged, however, that doctors had detected a minor heart problem. Despite Berlusconi's attempts to keep a lid on things, within weeks the papers were reporting that he'd flown to the Cleveland Clinic in the US to have a pacemaker fitted.[2] Earlier in November, the septuagenarian's physical limits and his reluctance to accept them were highlighted when he injured his right knee after joining in the warm-up before a football game. The injury required surgery and the mogul had to walk with a crutch. Another enemy, Old Father Time, was announcing his presence.

Advisers—even Scapagnini, whom Berlusconi nicknamed "Dr. Scopagnini" (Dr. Fuck-agnini) on account of the sexual prowess allegedly provided by the medic's elixir—told the tycoon to take things a bit easier. Naturally, Berlusconi ignored their advice and got on with what he was probably best at: fighting back when everyone had written him off, pursuing his own interests and offending good taste with abandon.

In 2006, many Italians were still trying to make sense of Silvio Berlusconi. Some might have been justified in saying his political success had been exaggerated. Although he had come from nowhere, politically speaking, to win two general elections, he hadn't won—and he never would win—anything like 50 percent of the vote in a national election. In fact, by themselves, his Forza Italia, and the People of Freedom (PDL) party that followed it, would never poll as much as 40 percent. Clearly, two-thirds of Italians were suspicious of, or had an aversion to, the tycoon-premier.

During Berlusconi's two decades in politics, there was never a charismatic, or even interesting, center-left leader to oppose him and put up a good fight. But given Berlusconi's legal problems and endless gaffes, the $64,000 question remained: Why would *anyone* vote for him? The political vacuum created by the Clean Hands investigations (outlined in Chapter 4) paved the way for his successful election bid the first time around, in 1994. The public then had seven months of Berlusconi, prime minister, to judge what he was, or wasn't, capable of. Critics imagined that was enough to doom him to the opposition benches forever. But the fallout from Tangentopoli has been much longer-lasting than anyone could have imagined at the time: with the political establishment dispatched in a stroke in 1993–1994, the only center-right Italy has had all these years is Berlusconi and his minor collaborators from the Northern League and the National Alliance. Some Italians, often pensioners and the self-employed, will never vote for the center-left. Even those unimpressed by his antics have held their noses and voted for him anyway. He certainly appeals to the most tax-averse citizens in a country where the sense of civic duty is sometimes undetectable.

But this is the tricky bit: many Italians—millions of them—actually *like* him. He's a strong, larger-than-life national leader in the tradition of Mussolini and Craxi. Much of his clowning and lowbrow jokes, which raise eyebrows abroad, chimes with the provincial outlook of his Italian supporters.

Many Italians see themselves in Berlusconi. As cultural commentator Beppe Severgnini has noted: "He loves his children, talks about his mother, likes football, knows how to make money, loves new homes, hates rules, tells jokes, says bad words, adores women, partying and good company. He's a man with a long memory that's capable of tactical amnesia . . ."[3]

His immense wealth has bought him associates who are willing to go to almost any lengths for him. And even those on the center or right, who view him with distaste, will vote for him if it means giving the left a bloody nose in a country where politics is as fiercely tribal as football.

And for the millions with little interest in, or even an aversion to, politics (or at least politicians), Berlusconi's attitude—and stardom—gets their vote. To them, he represents anti-politics and, above all, celebrity. In November 2009, the Italian edition of *Rolling Stone* crowned him "rock star of the year." I recall a reader's comment on the website of *The Sun*, Britain's biggest-selling daily paper, during the height of Berlusconi's sex scandals: "I wish he was our Prime Minister."

Berlusconi's womanizing and ostentatious wealth give many middle-aged male Italians a vicarious thrill. He's also been able to build up, subconsciously perhaps, a fan base among the millions, particularly women, who watch his anodyne and pro-Berlusconi TV channels.

And then we come to the "Truman" factor. The theory goes that for the past two decades Joe Public in Italy has been living the part of Truman Burbank in Peter Weir's dark comic masterpiece, *The Truman Show*, in which the protagonist unwittingly lives his life in a carefully constructed TV reality show. Relatively few Italians read national newspapers: those on sale are all arid and highbrow. So when *La Repubblica* or *Corriere della Sera* publishes embarrassing new information about Berlusconi, the vast majority of Italians never read it. There are no mass-market tabloids, no Murdoch *Suns* or *New York Posts*, to keep the masses entertained and vaguely informed. The best-selling paper, the sports daily *Gazzetta dello Sport*, carries just a page on news and current affairs. Instead, more than nine out of ten Italians turn to the television to learn what's happening in the world. And with Berlusconi owning three of the six major national channels and with him helping decide who runs the other three (state) channels, what viewers generally get to see is carefully doctored.

But where Berlusconi and his electoral success are concerned, crafty spin, cynical populism and black comedy are never far away from something darker still. Il Cavaliere has always polled remarkably well in key parts of the Italian south. The suspicion was—and still is—that mafia clans trade block votes for political favors, more often than not from center-right politicians in some parts of Sicily, Campania and Calabria. Berlusconi's suspected ties to Cosa Nostra—via the activities of his mafioso lieutenant Marcello Dell'Utri and the presence of the gangster Vittorio Mangano at the mogul's Arcore Villa, near Milan—are on record. In April 2008, after being elected prime minister for a third time, Berlusconi reminded us of these ties when he declared convicted Mafia killer Vittorio Mangano "a hero" for never having said anything incriminating about him to prosecutors.[4]

But evidence of links between the center-right and the mob dates back 20 years. During the 1994 general election, hundreds of miles south, far from the official seats of power in Rome and Milan, Giuseppe Mandalari, the accountant of Cosa Nostra's former boss of bosses Salvatore "Totò" Riina, was wiretapped in Palermo talking up Berlusconi and Forza Italia.[5] His efforts apparently worked: the 1994 Berlusconi coalition claimed a remarkably high proportion—54 out of 61—of parliamentary seats in Sicily. Three of the newly elected members of Berlusconi's coalition even phoned Mandalari to thank him for his help.[6]

In the 2001 general election, the center-right's success in Sicily was even more startling; it won all of the 61 seats contested.[7] Many Mafia trial witnesses and informants say that an agreement existed between Forza Italia and the Sicilian Mafia, under which the party would soften the penal code in exchange for votes in clan-dominated areas. Even when Forza Italia was out of power, between 1996 and 2001, it promoted legislation that saw the notoriously tough island prisons of Pianosa and Asinara (off the coasts of Tuscany and Sardinia, respectively) closed down, in line with the wishes of mobsters.

The center-right's worryingly ambivalent attitude to organized crime was demonstrated in August 2001, just months into Berlusconi's second administration. Pietro Lunardi, the minister for infrastructure, who ought to have been urging all-out war on the clans who skimmed billions of euros a year from public construction projects, appeared to advocate a live-and-let-steal approach. "Mafia and Camorra (the Naples crime syndicate) have always existed so we should just learn to live with them," he said.[8] Once again the head of state, President Carlo Azeglio Ciampi, awoke with a snort and issued an ineffective censure.

In September 2003, Berlusconi and Renato Schifani, the Sicilian lawyer leading his Forza Italia party in the Senate, railed against magistrates for charging suspects with mafia association (*concorso estermo in associazione mafioso*). The gist of their argument seemed to be that any number of innocent politicians or businessmen might unknowingly find themselves innocently doing deals with mobsters. When the widows of murdered Palermo magistrates Falcone and Borsellino hit out at Schifani, he was unrepentant, dismissing them as "militant leftists" who "deliberately misunderstood" the argument he and Berlusconi were making.[9]

Murkier, but more unsettling still, was the extraordinary event that occurred on July 12, 2002, during a mafia maxi-trial in the Sicilian town of Trapani. There were 40 mobsters in the giant cage at the back of the courtroom. They were joined, via video link, by magistrate-killer Totò "The Beast" Riina and his brother-in-law Leoluca Bagarella, from prisons in Aquila and Ascoli, respectively. To the surprise of court officials, Bagarella suddenly made a long declaration to the court, berating politicians for not maintaining their promises to soften the hated "41-bis" solitary confinement regime for those convicted of serious mafia offenses.

Bagarella said he was "speaking out in the name of all prisoners enduring the 41-bis regime, who were used, abused and humiliated like trading goods by the various political forces."[10] The same day, the governor of Ascoli prison sent a message to the prosecutor's office in Palermo that conveyed threats of "big trouble" from Sicilian, Campanian and Calabrian crime clans if authorities failed to water down 41-bis.

Palermo prosecutor Guido Lo Forte was in no doubt what the messages meant. "We can tell from Bagarella's words that what Cosa Nostra had been expecting regarding 41-bis has been disregarded."[11] In other words, it was a message to politicians. Shortly after this, in December 2009, 41-bis was transformed from a special measure that isolated mob bosses to a permanent part of the penal code—albeit in a slightly less severe form (prisoners would now, for example, be allowed to socialize with a maximum of five other convicts for up to four hours a day). Berlusconi's government could claim credit for the revision. But if the admittedly unreliable claims of Mafia informants were in any way grounded in fact, the question remains: should politicians have been negotiating with the Mafia in the first place? Although the full details have yet to come to light (perhaps they never will), it's generally accepted that state officials held secret talks with senior Cosa Nostra figures in the early 1990s after the Sicilian Mafia launched a wave of deadly bomb attacks in reaction to the success of maxi-trials and the use of solitary confinement for convicts.

The center-right party of Berlusconi is not the only political force tainted by links to organized crime. Figures in the center-left Democratic Party, and above all the Machiavellian seven-time Christian Democrat prime minister, Giulio Andreotti, have been on the receiving end of mafia accusations. But in the past 20 years, the whiff of something rotten appears to have come largely from the center-right; this would be highlighted later in the decade as journalists and investigators shone a spotlight on the activities of Naples' Camorra crime families.

Occasional broadcasts have broken Italian TV's eerie silence regarding the serious claims that Forza Italia and Berlusconi have links to the mob. The most clamorous of these episodes occurred on March 14, 2001, on the *Satyricon* talk show on Rai 2. The campaigning journalist Marco Travaglio appeared on the live TV program to present evidence about the dubious provenance of the money Berlusconi used to kick-start his real-estate empire, the links his right-hand man Dell'Utri had with Cosa Nostra convict Vittorio Mangano, and even the chilling final interview that the murdered anti-mafia magistrate Paolo Borsellino gave to two French journalists. In that testament, filmed just two months before he was killed by a Cosa Nostra bomb, Borsellino referred to Palermo investigators' interest in the links between Berlusconi, Dell'Utri and the Mafia. Remarkably, the magistrate's interview was never deemed important enough to merit prime-time broadcast on any of the major channels.

The studio audience for the *Satyricon* show listened in stunned silence. The program's presenter, Daniele Luttazzi, appeared equally amazed by the list of incriminating evidence reeled off by the then relatively unknown Travaglio, as he quoted the juiciest bits from his new book *L'Odore dei Soldi* (*The Smell of Money*), written with politician Elio Veltri. He relayed the information in the style that he would become famous for: he was cool, arch and articulate and possessed an encyclopedic knowledge of the facts.

"The terrible thing—or maybe the good thing," Travaglio said at the end of the interview, "is that these are not revelations that I've had to go out of my way to discover. They've all been said in court. But no one talks about them."

Luttazzi closed the interview with these words: "I'd like to thank you. You're an independent man and it's not easy to find independent people in this shitty country." For the first time, a mass TV audience, which continued to acquire viewers rapidly as the 26-minute interview progressed, was shown the black marks on the career of Silvio Berlusconi.

In the mogul's camp all hell broke loose. Berlusconi announced he was suing the book's authors for €10 million. The courts eventually dismissed the defamation claims and made Berlusconi pay the legal costs.[12]

More significant was the reaction from Berlusconi friends and foes immediately after the program aired. His supporters called for Rai's entire management to be axed; supposedly independent newspapers such as *Corriere della Sera*, instead of getting sucked in, dithered in their coverage. The London-based *Economist*, and its sister publication the *Financial Times*, did what the Italian papers ought to have been doing, and spelled out that Berlusconi, a man suspected of a raft of serious offenses and whose media power meant conflicts of interest were inevitable, was unfit for high office. There was—and is—the suspicion that these British publications have a particular beef with Berlusconi, more so than with other crooked or disreputable European leaders, such as Turkey's Recep Tayyip Erdoğan or Spain's Mariano Rajoy, because the Italian leader has failed to adhere to their liberal economic philosophy. These journals had only a tiny fraction of the Italian readers enjoyed by Italian papers, and in making swinging political pronouncements on a foreign country, they also sounded overbearing. In any case, Berlusconi's TV programs and publications counterattacked, while Rai offered accommodating interviews to the mogul and his key associates.

Despite the damage wrought by Travaglio's "revelations," Berlusconi went on to win the 2001 general election just weeks later, albeit with smaller majorities than he'd been expecting.

Why did the grave allegations against Berlusconi over the years have so little effect? "Because the people who were saying this stuff were so few in number and so isolated," Travaglio told me.

> Everyone just thought: 'Oh it's just Travaglio, Santoro or Gomez; just that lot making a noise again.'
>
> Berlusconi once said to me: 'I'm your core business.' And that I should be grateful, which is like a doctor being told that he should be grateful for cancer.

It's not possible for a human being to be as rich and as powerful as Berlusconi without experiencing side effects. In the mid-2000s there was the inevitable transition from crafty sleazeball to hubris-filled dictator. The eminent psychotherapist Luigi Cancrini, interviewed for the Articolo21 website in July 2009, described Berlusconi as "a personality with unlimited ego-centricity."

> Up until the point he was a businessman, things were OK. The problems started with his acquisition of political power. And when a normal narcissism is strongly stoked by and combined with too much power, the result is a pathology—a genuine personality disturbance. He [Berlusconi] has an image of himself that is very grandiose, I would say ridiculously and dangerously grandiose, as often happens to someone who has around him people who only say "yes." This is how people lose contact with reality.[13]

On his blog in 2011, Beppe Grillo, the leader of the anti-establishment Five Star Movement, noted: "We are being governed by a man whose psychological and physical condition is extremely suspect, a man who would undoubtedly be impeached if this were any other country."[14]

The egotistical mogul had to keep up appearances. To do this, he made return visits to the plastic surgeon, touched up his hair transplant and turned his face a preternatural shade of orange. And his libido, never lacking at the best of times, appeared to grow with his advancing years. With opulent villas all over the world, billions of euros in the bank and who knows where else, he decided it was time to party a little. Paparazzi were among the first to learn of Berlusconi's sleazy social events. From 2007 to

2008 the Italian snapper Antonello Zappadu took 5,000 pictures of Berlusconi's parties in Sardinia.

From 2006 onward rumors had been mounting about the goings-on at Villa Certosa, his fabulous property set in 60 hectares of landscaped grounds on Sardinia's VIP-laden Costa Smeralda. Berlusconi was reported to have given the property a €12 million upgrade since the Blairs' celebrated visit in 2004. There were now artificial lakes, guesthouses, an amphitheater, and supposedly even a secret underground canal connecting the villa to the turquoise sea—inspired by James Bond films. If fun was to be had, Villa Certosa seemed the ideal spot. And so it was that an endless parade of young women, starlets and even foreign politicians would come to enjoy—and in some cases regret—Berlusconi's hospitality on the beautiful Mediterranean island.

In April 2006, the weekly gossip magazine *Oggi* published a cover story entitled "Berlusconi's Harem." It included shots of Berlusconi slipping his hand inside the shirt of one of the women. But the privacy watchdog banned *Oggi* from publishing the rest of the photographs. Gossips said there were far juicier photos doing the rounds, and it wouldn't be long before they were published as well.

Back in Rome, Berlusconi hadn't given up on his intention to move back into Palazzo Chigi, the prime minister's office. Officially, he wanted the top job to save Italy from the supposed Red Peril. More importantly, he needed to introduce more media legislation to boost Mediaset at the expense of Rupert Murdoch's fast-growing Sky Italia satellite TV service. And once he returned to power, he'd be able to resume the raft of self-serving justice legislation he needed to combat the magistrates.

Like his idol Margaret Thatcher, who served as British prime minister for over a decade, and morphed from shrewish housewife to fur-clad international stateswoman, the mogul who collects criminal indictments like parking tickets began to think it was his right to hold high office and hobnob with powerful friends abroad. Thatcher, though, schmoozed President Mikhail Gorbachev as part of her effective campaign to end the Cold War. And, as we've seen, while the formidable British leader was meeting Gorbachev at every opportunity in 1988 to argue her case for Western-style democracy, Berlusconi was earning money from the Soviet state with a joint advertising venture.

Even worse, with the Berlin Wall already dust by 2007, Berlusconi was still denouncing the Red Peril. At every opportunity he told Italy he was on the side of "freedom"—freedom, that is, to do what he liked. The historian Paul Ginsborg called it "negative freedom," that is, "the sense of putting [his] acquisitive instincts and interests first," ahead of civic concerns.[15]

Of course, Berlusconi never demonstrated the politics of conviction that allowed Thatcher, for good or for ill, to radically overhaul the British economy. Ironically, during the two years he was out of power, from 2006 to 2008, the center-left government of Prodi actually introduced a modest degree of liberalization to the Italian economy; Thatcher would have approved.

The tycoon probably didn't notice, but his legal travails were endless. In 2007, prosecutors in Milan specified new tax fraud charges against the mogul, saying he had exaggerated the cost of buying film rights in order to divert money to overseas slush funds.[16] It would be interesting to know how seriously Berlusconi took this particular charge: it was one among dozens, but one that would turn out to be so very fateful.

He knew, however, that Prime Minister Prodi's parliamentary majorities were slim, particularly in the Senate. And so he decided to get his wallet out again. In one of the most exquisitely tawdry incidents in the two decades of Berlusconi's grubby grip on Italian politics, he appeared to give an anti-corruption campaigner in the Senate €3 million ($3.9 million) to change sides and vote down Prodi's wafer-thin majority.[17]

Sergio De Gregorio, the senator who has since admitted taking the bribe, is of an unfortunate porcine appearance: jowly and as big as a house, he looks like he ate the money. Certainly he's never given it back. This single act of corruption—and who knows how many more politicians may have accepted bribes over the years—came as a particularly depressing blow to the millions of honest Italians. De Gregorio was a parliamentary representative of Italy of Values (Idv), created by none other than former magistrate Antonio Di Pietro, with the aim of campaigning *against* corruption. Idv was a small but important part of Prodi's center-left coalition in 2006.

Shortly after the elections, however, De Gregorio mysteriously quit the party and founded his own party—Italians in the World—which aligned itself with Berlusconi's People of Freedom party. The defection proved a crucial blow to Prodi's government, which had been clinging on to power with a three-seat majority in the Senate. It finally collapsed in May 2008.

Five years later, in October 2013, De Gregorio was sentenced to 20 months for accepting the bribe at a plea bargain hearing in Naples. Berlusconi was on trial, accused of bribing De Gregorio, as this book went to press. He denies the charge. After his conviction De Gregorio was contrite. "I now believe I behaved in an absolutely reprehensible way and was aiming to bring down the Prodi government as part of a sort of holy war being waged by Berlusconi."[18] He added: "I urge Silvio Berlusconi to leave the political scene, which would free Italy from a lot of dirt."

By the end of 2013, the three-time prime minister was already fading fast as a political force. But in the Berlusconi universe the seven years between 2006 and 2013 proved a very long time. And, as it turned out, a spectacularly tawdry one.

President George W. Bush and his father, former President George Bush, look on as Italian Prime Minister Silvio Berlusconi and former President Bill Clinton shake hands Thursday, April 7, 2005, prior to dinner at the prime minister's Rome residence. The visit came on the eve of the funeral for Pope John Paul II.

White House Photo by Eric Draper

Silvio Berlusconi with his second wife, Veronica Lario, in October 2007.

www.raucci.net

Noemi Letizia, September 2009, at the 66th Venice Film Festival.

Nicolas Genin

President Barack Obama meets with Italian Prime Minister Silvio Berlusconi in the Oval Office of the White House, June 15, 2009.

Official White House Photo by Pete Souza

Nicole Minetti in September 2014.

Hot Gossip Italia

Russian President Vladimir Putin with the prime minister of Italy, Silvio Berlusconi, in Bocharov Ruchei, Sochi in 2005.

http://www.kremlin.ru Photo by the Presidential Press Service

Silvio Berlusconi at the European Peoples Party Summit, March 2006.

European People's Party

PART II

THE FALL

CHAPTER 9

FIDDLING WHILE ROME BURNS

Italy's relationship with Berlusconi seems weird enough when you read about it in the foreign pages of your newspaper. But experiencing the country's democracy in action, particularly when it's in the process of reelecting the media mogul, is stranger still.

On April 14, 2008, at the Foreign Press Association in Milan, I watched as a political train wreck unfolded on the TV screen. There had been no rehabilitation of Berlusconi's reputation, but he was heading for victory again. Together with his right-wing allies, he polled almost 47 percent—a bigger share of the vote than he had received in 2001. It was enough for majorities in both chambers of parliament. Later that evening, over a couple of *negroni sbagliati* in Porta Venezia, I asked a writer friend of mine, Fabio, how Berlusconi did it. He glared at me briefly before declaring: "He's a genius—like Hitler."

As the final counts came in the next day I recalled an incident at my last staff job with a British newspaper, a few years earlier: the news editor was crowing because the publication's reporting had forced the interior minister in the Blair government to quit. And the story that consigned Home Secretary David Blunkett to political oblivion? The nanny of Blunkett's ex-lover appeared to have had her visa application processed more quickly than usual. I tried to imagine what the British press would make of a prime ministerial candidate whose closest associates hung out with mafia bosses and bribed judges and who had himself been charged with, and convicted of, serious crimes, only to be saved by his own manipulation of the criminal justice system.

But in Italy, it was, as some Anglo-Saxon papers noted, a case of "Mamma Mia, here we go again." It became apparent quite quickly, however, that things were different this time around. Berlusconi's third term in office will be best remembered not for its self-serving legislation, nor even the corruption charges, but for the prime minister's sleazy private life and the sense that Italy's most powerful man was going deliriously off the rails. From 2008 onward we saw the sexual excesses and "planetary" gaffes that would make Berlusconi a household name around the world—and mark his irreversible decline as a political force. His association with young prostitutes and drug dealers, his racist and obscene remarks about world leaders, nutty off-the-cuff lawmaking and murky deals with overseas dictators all imbued his government with the decadent feel of ancient Rome. And Berlusconi was Emperor Tiberius.

Of course, Italy should have guessed what was coming. But the old Berlusconi chutzpah and the tacit (but widely understood) message that he regarded taxes as optional helped at the ballot box. Voters were fearful that his center-left rival Prodi would send the revenue inspectors around. When Italy signed up to use the euro, the single European currency, it had promised to keep its national deficit in check. Berlusconi hadn't bothered to do this because spending cuts and tax increases weren't popular. This practice, which continued from 2001 to 2006, had alarmed the rest of Europe. From 2006 onward, Prodi did the right thing—and paid the price on election day.

And sure enough, with the tax-averse tycoon back in charge, fiscal receipts plummeted, as documented by Italian writer Curzio Maltese. In his 2010 book *La Bolla: La Pericolosa Fine del Sogno Berlusconianio* (*The Bubble: The Dangerous End of the Berlusconian Dream*), Maltese quotes an antique dealer in Verona: " 'Here, from the day Berlusconi won the election, people stopped issuing receipts . . . Artisans, plumbers, medical consultants, shopkeepers, all of them. Restaurateurs and hotel owners issue fake ones.' "[1]

"Anti-communism, the church and the other things, even the question of television channel ownership, none of them matter," said Maltese. "The essential point is that with him, you can evade serenely. They voted Berlusconi out of fear that Prodi would send in the Revenue."

Maltese isn't alone in arguing that Berlusconi had allowed fear of tax collectors to supplant Italians' dwindling fear of communism. Shop owners, small businessmen, professionals and the self-employed tend to vote for the anti-tax candidate. And as the owner of any number of overseas slush funds, and indeed a convicted fiscal cheat, Berlusconi's tax-dodging credentials are impeccable.

Two years after Berlusconi dislodged Prodi in 2008, tax revenue fell sharply, swelling Italy's national debt by €14 billion a year.

As he prepared to party hard in his 27 luxury homes around the globe, Berlusconi wanted those annoying magistrates off his back. Within two months of being sworn in on May 8, 2008, parliament had approved another immunity law giving the top four state officials, including the prime minister, immunity from prosecution.[2] Berlusconi justified the legislation (which would, like its predecessor, eventually be struck down by the Constitutional Court) by saying he had to defend himself from vindictive prosecutors: he had already made 2,500 court appearances and spent €174 million on legal fees. In case we didn't get the idea, he revealed: "I'm the universal record-holder for the number of trials in the entire history of man—and also of other creatures who live on other planets."

On Planet Italia, Berlusconi sounded uncharacteristically gracious in victory. He told a chat show host that his government would be open to suggestions from the opposition on measures that affected the "well-being" of Italy. "I feel a great responsibility, because the months and years ahead will be difficult ones." They would, he said, be "decisive for the modernization of the country."

With modernization uppermost in his mind, the tycoon announced there would be at least four women in his new cabinet. They weren't handed any of the top posts, such as finance or foreign affairs. Given their résumés, that was probably for the best.

Mara Carfagna was the quintessential female appointment in Berlusconi's third government. This strikingly attractive brunette from Naples had been a topless model and a dancer on one of Berlusconi's tacky TV shows; she was a shoo-in for equal opportunities minister. Just a year before, while she was flashing the flesh to the admiring male population, the mogul told her: "If I weren't already married, I would marry you immediately." The pair denied rumors of an affair. This new humiliation for Berlusconi's wife, Veronica Lario, followed TV footage of her husband telling buxom Venezuelan model Aida Yespica that he'd "follow her anywhere, even to a desert island."[3]

Lario railed against her husband in an open letter published in the anti-Berlusconi newspaper *La Repubblica*. This prompted a public apology from her husband. By now, though, no one was in any doubt that the marriage was over in all but name. And as the next chapter will show, Berlusconi's creepy dalliance with an 18-year-old would, more than any of the myriad sexual scandals of 2008–2009, prove the final straw for Lario—and herald the unraveling of his reputation.

But on a post-election high, the prime minister was not going to write off political talent simply because it was easy on the eye or for fear that cynics might jump to the wrong conclusion. Underlining his commitment to equal opportunities, the other three female ministers were also young and attractive. Mariastella Gelmini, Stefania Prestigiacomo and Michela Vittoria Brambilla, his education minister, environment minister and tourism minister, respectively, had all risen without trace, too—and were suitably grateful. Even before the election, the writing was on the wall for any politically experienced but dowdy female members of Berlusconi's party who'd been hoping for a cabinet seat: the ageing Lothario stressed the importance of good looks for female politicians. Casting a roving eye around parliament, Berlusconi, 71, declared that female politicians from the right were "more beautiful" than those on the left. "The left has no taste, even when it comes to women," he declared.[4] Some people probably wondered how much taste some young right-wing female politicians had when it came to men.

But the evident influence of Berlusconi's libido in his choice of ministers showed the rot was setting in. This was the period in which the mogul's cronies took to the limelight themselves. The Bettino Craxis, Cesare Previtis, Sergio De Gregorios, Marcello Dell'Utris, and even the mob had all helped him acquire his enormous power and wealth, but—while brilliantly effective—these characters had remained, at least notionally, in the shadows.

In his third and final government, a decadent and deluded Berlusconi mixed with a new bunch of friends and hangers-on: a parade of starlets, political lightweights, impresarios, pimps and floozies were always ready to flatter him and—in the words of one dear "friend," the inept and babbling Mediaset news anchor Emilio Fede—to use the billionaire mogul as a *bancomat* (ATM), while taking center stage themselves.

Berlusconi more or less gave up the pretense that he cared much about governing the country. He just wanted to enjoy himself. Referring to her husband's life up until the early 2000s, second wife Veronica Lario once said that Berlusconi didn't have any hobbies "apart from the one that it's best not to mention." She added: "Among his friends, Marcello [Dell'Utri] has his old books, Fedele [Confalonieri] has his music. Silvio no; it's as if he's developed only one part of himself. He works the whole time, all year long. His life is entirely dictated by the rhythm of work." For Berlusconi back then, even a holiday to a luxury villa in Bermuda amounted to "moving from one office to another."[5]

But in the second half of the 2000s, it seems the hobby that "it's best not to mention" began displacing legal, business and political planning as the billionaire-playboy's main occupation. The hints of tabloid fodder that had emerged from Sardinia in 2007–2008 became a reality in June 2009, as hundreds of embarrassing pictures of Berlusconi's racy soirees on the Mediterranean island hit the newsstands.

The Spanish newspaper *El País* printed Italian snapper Zappadu's photos of Berlusconi's seedy parties at Villa Certosa. One of the pictures, published under the headline "The photos vetoed by Berlusconi," featured two topless women in the garden. Another showed a naked man by the swimming pool. I recall squinting at the grainy image of the semi-aroused man, with a pixilated face, as he leaned over toward a woman in a red bikini. "Is that Berlusconi?" I asked Nick Vivarelli, *Variety*'s Rome bureau chief. "No, but he'd like everyone to think it was," he said drily. The man swinging by the pool was actually Mirek Topolanek, the former prime minister of the Czech Republic, a gaffe-prone right-winger, who would quit politics a year later following slurs against Jews and gays.

Silvio Berlusconi was furious at what he saw as a breach of his privacy and called in the lawyers. He succeeded in blocking the photos' publication in Italy but not abroad. The Spanish newspaper's justification for printing the smutty pics did sound a bit sanctimonious. "Silvio Berlusconi should not get things wrong. The publication of the photographs of his private parties aims to show how, as prime minister, he is trying to turn the realm of democratic politics into a simple continuation of his friendships and entertainment," it said.

Other images snapped by Zappadu showed that Berlusconi, like many over-sexed males, appreciated a little light lesbian action. In one picture, he was sitting with five young women in a gazebo. Two of them were on his lap. He's seen grinning approvingly as Angela Sozio, 36, a red-headed former *Big Brother* contestant, sits on the knees of another young woman and kisses her on the lips.[6] Further photos then show the group walking through the Villa Certosa estate and Sozio and her gal pal stage a fake wedding ceremony. Senior figures in the Vatican were already beginning to have palpitations.

Some of the pictures showed friends, entertainers and starlets arriving on a government plane in Sardinia for parties at Berlusconi's home. Roman prosecutors launched an investigation to see whether the prime minister had abused his office by winging guests over using public funds. Perhaps that Spanish newspaper had a point after all. Soon reports were emerging that the mogul had been regularly flying whole squadrons of starlets and floozies over to Sardinia for his bacchanalias.

Berlusconi's libidinous extracurricular activity wasn't confined to Villa Certosa. His stately Roman residence, Palazzo Grazioli, just 400 yards from the Senate, was also a thriving fleshpot. Just how thriving would be revealed in a toe-curling kiss-and-tell tome by call girl Patrizia D'Addario, from the southern port of Bari, who'd recorded intimate chats with the prime minister.

In June 2009, the papers published embarrassing transcripts of her conversations with Berlusconi that left little doubt that they'd been having a sexual relationship. D'Addario, then 42, told the press she was promised $2,800 to attend two gatherings the previous year, and stay the night on one of these occasions, November 4, 2008. She claimed she'd recorded the conversations with her mobile phone.

Prosecutors were also on the case. They were interested in the activity of Giampaolo Tarantini, a seedy businessman from Bari, whom they suspected of procuring prostitutes—pimping—for the prime minister's anything-goes soirees. Bizarre and often unsavory bits of information began to appear in the press. In one of the investigators' wiretaps Tarantini is heard telling D'Addario about the then 72-year-old prime minister's predilection for unprotected sex, while one of D'Addario's recordings showed Berlusconi telling the call girl that he is waiting for her on what he described enigmatically as "Putin's bed."

Emilio Marzano, the chief prosecutor in the southern city of Bari, who was leading investigations into Tarantini's suspected drug dealing and pimping, denied his office had leaked information. It was not the first time a magistrate was forced to deny such accusations. But suspicions over the provenance of the transcripts, and the motivation behind them, hardly mitigated the damage and embarrassment suffered by the prime minister.

Ironically, in order to party with the call girl on a king-sized bed named after the Russian leader, the Americanophile Berlusconi had snubbed an invitation by the US ambassador to Rome to a soiree to mark Barack Obama's election as US president. The mogul had claimed he felt feverish.[7]

A year later, in November 2009, the inevitable memoir by D'Addario, *Gradisca, Presidente* (*Take Your Pleasure, Prime Minister*), hit the bookshops. And only then did the size of the 72-year-old's libido become clear. Berlusconi, it emerged, demanded sex in industrial quantities. Even for Patrizia D'Addario, with many years of experience practicing the world's oldest profession, the number of women Il Cavaliere liked to have on tap came as a shock.

> Having been an escort, I thought I'd seen a fair few things, but I'd never seen 20 women for one man . . . Normally in an orgy you have roughly the same number of men and women, otherwise people get upset. But here the other men had no say. There was just one man with the right to copulate, and that was the prime minister.

In addition to the embarrassment, the mogul may have felt a twinge of satisfaction as the call girl put paid to rumors that his brush with prostate cancer in 1997 had ruined his ability to perform. But D'Addario didn't get much satisfaction, at least at the time. Indeed, women readers probably raised their eyebrows or nodded in agreement as her testimony confirmed suspicions that libidinous Italian men tend to confuse exuberance with genuine skill or ability. Describing the night they spent together in Palazzo Grazioli in Rome, she wrote:

> After the first assault, in which he achieved complete satisfaction, we started all over again . . . He never even appeared slightly tired . . . I'd

> never seen such passion for sex with a woman . . . I was honest when he asked me if I'd enjoyed myself. It didn't seem right to lie. He obviously took this as [a] challenge and began again . . . Then more sex . . . He goes down on my intimate parts and stays there for a long time, such that I thought that he might be sleeping. But no, of course not. He starts up again with more energy than before. He didn't let up until eight in the morning.

Berlusconi raised the possibility of another meeting, but suggested how things might be improved. "Next time we'll need other women," he told her.

Like all Berlusconi's female guests over the years, D'Addario didn't leave without a present: a tortoise, covered in precious stones. "I had to admit it was lovely," she said.

D'Addario's brutal account of her relationship with Berlusconi scotched some of the more elaborate defenses constructed by the mogul's supporters—particularly the claims of Vittorio Feltri, the editor of the right-wing newspaper *Libero*, who'd said that, ever since Berlusconi's operation for prostate cancer in 1996, the mogul was no longer able to have sex. Apparently he was, at least with the help of a penile prosthesis, according to some rumors. This might explain his staying power, and the suggestion he never achieves full satisfaction himself. Although, for Berlusconi, it's probably more about having his ego stroked than about orgasms.

Meanwhile, Niccolò Ghedini, Berlusconi's chief legal adviser, used the old ruse of painting his client as merely a cog in a bigger system: Berlusconi was simply the "end user" of the women. Ghedini added that "Berlusconi could have them [women] in large numbers for free" if he wanted.[8]

The prime minister's sexual appetite invited comparison with that other short, charismatic Italian leader, Benito Mussolini, who was said to have had sex with over 5,000 women, often enjoying the company of three or four different women in an evening.

According to Nicholas Farrell, Mussolini's biographer, the wild promiscuity of Mussolini and Berlusconi reflects the sexist culture from which they both emerged. "If you look at Italian TV it illustrates clearly what men like, and Italian women are prepared to play ball with it." He points out that even Italy's most respected satirical current affairs show still has (in 2014) half-naked girls dancing on the desk of middle-aged male presenters. Farrell correlates sexual charisma with political success:

"Mussolini and Berlusconi achieved far more than, say, Giulio Andreotti or Romano Prodi. And there is a connection between the lackluster sex lives of those men and their lack of effectiveness in office."[9]

But there *was* a political price to pay for Berlusconi. Even his allies were twitching at the tide of sleaze hitting the newspaper headlines. Gianfranco Fini, the parliamentary speaker and one of the most senior figures in Berlusconi's People of Freedom coalition, feared the scandals could dent "the public's faith in politics and government institutions"—faith that was already on the low-to-undetectable side. Another staunch conservative ally, Giuliano Ferrara, editor of the Berlusconi family newspaper *Il Foglio*, said the prime minister had to decide whether he wanted to "drown in a happy ending made up of parties and beautiful girls" or restore some dignity to "a great political adventure."[10]

Not surprisingly, the Catholic Church was even less impressed with Berlusconi's libertine lifestyle. Key Church institutions got on their high horse, even though the mogul's sexual transgressions couldn't hold a candle to the Vatican's obscene indifference to the mounting evidence that hundreds or thousands of its priests were sexually abusing young children.

At the end of June 2009, *L'Avvenire*, the official newspaper of the powerful Italian Conference of Bishops, said that Berlusconi should clarify his involvement in recent scandals "as quickly as possible." It laced its pious editorial with a clear political threat, noting that an explanation was demanded, not only by Berlusconi's political rivals, but also by "a section of the public who are not, in principle, opposed to him."[11]

At least Berlusconi's attack-dog editor Vittorio Feltri, Montanelli's somewhat less refined replacement at *Il Giornale*, got *L'Avvenire* off the mogul's back. *Il Giornale* dished dirt on the private life of the Catholic paper's editor, Dino Boffo. Boffo, it said, was a "prominent homosexual" who had been fined for harassing the wife of a man he was pursuing. Boffo quit soon after.[12]

The president of the republic was now Giorgio Napolitano. There were doubts at first whether this communist turned establishment figure would play the role of avuncular arbiter/referee in Italian politics with the same forcefulness as his predecessors. Napolitano would go on to surprise many—and anger some—in proving to be one of the most important, if more Machiavellian, architects of Berlusconi's downfall.

Just before the July 2009 G8 meeting of the world's wealthiest nations, however, Napolitano told the media to stop publishing dirt on Berlusconi's private life.[13] He said it was making Italy an international laughingstock—something the prime minister didn't need as he prepared to chair the high-level meeting with Barack Obama and Angela Merkel et al. in the symbolic venue of L'Aquila, the mountain city devastated by an earthquake just three months earlier.

But Berlusconi had already cemented Italy's reputation as an international gong show eight months before with his jaw-dropping "joke" about the newly elected US president. Revealing his subtle appreciation of Afro-American history, the Italian prime minister hailed America's first black president as "young, handsome and suntanned."[14] For maximum effect, he made his comments at a joint news conference with Russian president Dmitry Medvedev in Moscow.

As many Italians wondered how hard it would be to change their passports, Berlusconi dismissed his critics as "humorless imbeciles." The impression left by this insult to the US president, and indeed by many of Berlusconi's most famous gaffes, is not that he set out to offend, but simply that he is a crass, provincial clod, *un cafone* in Italian. Alluding simultaneously to suspected mob links, wags began referring to Il Cavaliere as "Al Cafone."

But the Obama incident also highlights how, in his third attempt at government, Berlusconi matched his attacks on Italy's penal code with a raft of crimes in the diplomatic sphere. Even Queen Elizabeth expressed her irritation at Berlusconi's childish behavior when he yelled to catch Barack Obama's attention during a G20 photo call at Buckingham Palace. "Why does he have to shout?" she tutted.[15] But if the Queen and Obama were unimpressed, Berlusconi still enjoyed strong relations with other overseas leaders. Unfortunately, these tended to be despots.

On June 13, 2013, eighteen months after Berlusconi had been booted out of office, the investigative paper *Il Fatto Quotidiano* quoted "well placed diplomatic sources" as saying Il Cavaliere had called on the secret service in the spring of 2011 to assassinate his old partner in crime, the human rights abuser and soon-to-be ex–Libyan leader, Muammar Gaddafi. Reasons for Berlusconi wishing to see the back of the dictator weren't hard to find. Few people can be said to have humiliated the tycoon-premier with such casual abandon.

Italy's most powerful man was rarely if ever made to look so servile and ridiculous as during Gaddafi's first visit to Rome in 2009. Berlusconi greeted the Libyan despot with open arms, but Gaddafi, ever conscious of the former colonists' reliance on his vast energy reserves, felt free to rub the Italian prime minister's nose in the reversal of the two countries' fortunes. He stuck a large photo on his lapel of Omar al-Mukhtar, the Libyan resistance hero who was executed by the Italians after leading a guerrilla war against the European occupiers in the 1930s.[16]

Roman authorities allowed Gaddafi, complete with 300-strong entourage, to pitch his Bedouin tent in the grounds of the seventeenth-century Villa Doria Pamphilj palace. Even as he bit his lip, Berlusconi probably allowed himself an approving glance at the capricious Libyan's lifestyle—his disregard for the rules and piquant, quasi-sexual details such as his fierce but wholly subservient female bodyguards, ready to serve day or night in their khaki uniforms and red berets. But it wasn't just about Gaddafi's ego or libido.

The visit followed a treaty in which Italy agreed to pay $8 billion over 20 years as compensation for its colonization of the North African country. But business ties were flourishing—hence Berlusconi's willingness to bend over backward to accommodate Gaddafi, who for decades was largely seen as a terrorist-sponsoring international pariah. The Libyan civil war changed things considerably, however. According to *Il Fatto*'s front page on June 13, 2013, Berlusconi's unusual request in 2011 to Italy's then spy chief Gianni De Gennaro came shortly after the start of the NATO-backed rebellion that saw Gaddafi ousted and eventually killed by one of his own countrymen. According to the *Il Fatto* report, with Gaddafi's star waning, the tycoon-premier decided it was time to switch sides.

On December 23, 2010, only months before his alleged request to take out the Libyan leader, Berlusconi referred to Gaddafi as "my friend" in a prime ministerial press conference. Three months later, with Gaddafi on the ropes, Berlusconi told guests at a dinner in Turin: "I'm saddened for Gaddafi and I'm sorry. What's happening in Libya hits me personally." But with the mogul's international standing already plummeting, thanks to a succession of gaffes and scandals, he was keen to end his perceived closeness to Gaddafi, especially as the dictator appeared to be on the way out.

Berlusconi's chief spokesman, Paolo Bonaiuti, dismissed the *Il Fatto* claims. They were "totally false, incredible, absurd and unacceptable," he said. "How could you think that Mr. Berlusconi could even dream of such a dreadful thing?" I put the *Il Fatto* claims to a Mediaset journalist I knew. "Yeah, why wouldn't he?" was the response. Others were doubtful, however, and suggested that the "assassination" request, if it had been made, was more likely a case of Berlusconi thinking wishfully—and out loud.

The story served to remind the world, however, of Berlusconi's crimes on the foreign stage. His formerly friendly relationship with Gaddafi had been sealed several years earlier in 2004, with the inauguration of the 323-mile pipeline carrying gas from Libya to Sicily. By the late 2000s, the North African country was supplying a third of Italy's energy requirements.[17] Italy was well placed to push for democratic reforms and improvements in human rights in Libya, given its hugely important business ties. Instead, with the cheap oil pouring in, Gaddafi was lauded and given a seat at the table during the G8 Summit in Italy. Berlusconi was too busy kissing the dictator's hand—a gesture usually reserved for popes—to raise the subject of torture and extra-judicial killing.

Naturally, when Gaddafi's police state collapsed, Italy was left looking like one of its collaborators. Italy's diplomats and its terrified energy companies scrambled to repair the damage. The Berlusconi government, certainly, wasn't the only Western administration that sucked up to dodgy regimes and turned a blind eye to how they operated. It may well have been one of the worst examples of such toadying, however. And given Il Cavaliere's friendships with Vladimir Putin, and the Eastern European despots Nursultan Nazarbayev and Alexander Lukashenko, we can safely say his friendship with Gaddafi was part of a pattern.

"Belarussians love you, as shown by the elections," Berlusconi told Belarus president Lukashenko—who had regularly been accused of election rigging—after the pair firmed up energy deals in 2009. Belarus was kicked out of the Council of Europe in 1997 over human rights violations.

The mogul's friendship with Putin, in particular, has caused concern among Western allies. His disconcertingly slavish attitude to the Russian hard man was highlighted at a press conference in Sardinia in April 2008, when a Russian journalist confronted Putin with rumors of an affair. "Not one word of truth," said Putin. Berlusconi, who stood next to the ex-KGB despot grinning like an idiot, made the shape of a pistol with his hands and pretended to take aim and fire at the female reporter. She is said to have left the room in tears—perhaps not surprising, given that journalists are routinely threatened, assaulted and sometimes killed for doing their job in Putin's Russia: excluding reporters working in war zones, 38 have been murdered there since 1992.[18]

Berlusconi next tried to lighten the tone with a dud joke about the attractiveness of Russian and Italian women. Putin returned the favor in 2011 declaring "however much they nag Signor Berlusconi for his special attitude to the beautiful sex . . . he has shown himself as a responsible statesman."

WikiLeaks documents suggest that American diplomats felt otherwise. In December 2010, US secretary of state Hillary Clinton was forced to stick a diplomatic Band-Aid on American-Italian relations when leaked papers showed that her diplomats considered the Italian leader "politically weak," "vain" and "feckless." But her attempts at damage limitation had hardly hit newsstands when fresh accusations appeared—accusations that were far more damaging to the Italian prime minister. According to WikiLeaks, the former US ambassador to Rome Ronald Spogli believed that Putin had bought the political compliance of Silvio Berlusconi by allowing the tycoon a cut from major energy deals. The startling allegations formed the basis of US diplomats' concern that Putin's hold over Berlusconi was becoming a threat to political and economic stability in the region.

A report dated January 26, 2009, quoted US embassy sources from within the Italian prime minister's People of Freedom party as believing "that Berlusconi and his cronies are profiting personally and handsomely from many of the energy deals between Italy and Russia." The report added: "The Georgian ambassador in Rome has told us that the [government of Georgia] believes Putin has promised Berlusconi a percentage of profits from any pipelines developed by Gazprom in co-ordination with ENI." Berlusconi strenuously denied the accusations, although it was certainly true that the Italian government still owned a large stake in ENI, the energy giant that works closely with Russian state-controlled energy giant Gazprom, a major exporter of gas to Europe.[19]

There were reports, too, that senior colleagues were reluctant to confront Berlusconi over his worrying closeness to Putin. Even Foreign Minister Franco Frattini appeared to have little influence on policy toward Russia.

The late James Walston, a political scientist from the American University in Rome and an eminent international relations expert, said the US was not the only country that was alarmed:

> I bet if we saw the WikiLeaks from European embassies in Rome they'd be even more distressed than the Americans. There are real concerns that Europe will come to rely too much on Russian gas. The fear is that Berlusconi is giving Putin rope with which he might hang Europe.

Walston said the writing was on the wall when Berlusconi made a visit to Putin's country home in October 2009, accompanied only by his shadowy Russian-speaking go-between Valentino Valentini: "There were no ministers, no civil servants present. No records of what was said—or what personal deals were cut," he said. "That should have set alarm bells ringing."[20]

Berlusconi's relationship with ex-KGB figure Putin, apart from its financial aspects, also hints at something more instinctive. Berlusconi, the ostentatious playboy and go-getter, finally meets someone to whom he's prepared to play second fiddle, but also someone whose company he enjoys. That someone is, perhaps predictably, a person even more powerful, more bullying and less scrupulous than he is.

Berlusconi's TV empire didn't appear averse to a bit of Soviet-style authoritarianism. In October 2009, Berlusconi's Canale 5 TV channel was accused of an extraordinary attempt to harass the judge who earlier that month had ruled against the mogul's business empire in a bribery case. Judge Raimondo Mesiano ordered Berlusconi's Fininvest holding company to pay old adversary Carlo De Benedetti a potentially crippling sum of €750 million ($1 billion). This was compensation for the corrupt takeover of the Mondadori publishing house back in 1992.

Within weeks of the verdict, the prime minister's flagship Canale 5 channel began secretly filming the magistrate in the streets of Milan as he went about his business. The results were beamed to millions on the *Mattino 5* program, accompanied by a voice-over that ridiculed Mesiano for his "extravagant" and "eccentric behavior," his "impatience" and, most bizarrely, the fact that he wore turquoise socks. Mesiano appeared to have done nothing stranger than go for a shave and smoke cigarettes outside the barbershop while awaiting his turn.[21] The *Mattino 5* journalists' antics were hardly menacing—and might simply have reflected the desire of Mediaset executives to ingratiate themselves with their Dear Leader. But it set a worrying precedent. "The worst thing—the thing that really gives you the shivers—is the shadowing, the spying, the violation of privacy, the public ridicule, with the implied warning: look out, we're watching you," one journalist wrote in the politically moderate *La Stampa* newspaper.

But more concerns regarding the prime minister's malign influence on current affairs surfaced in May 2010 when news anchor Maria Luisa Busi dramatically quit the flagship *TG1* news show on the state Rai 1 channel, saying she was sick of the interference and bias brought by *TG1* director and Berlusconi stooge Augusto Minzolini. She told bosses what she thought of the program's editorial line in a frank letter pinned to a notice board.[22]

Minzolini's *TG1* show, along with its main rival on Berlusconi's own Mediaset network, *TG5*, was fined by broadcast watchdog Agcom for under-reporting the opposition Democratic Party in favor of Berlusconi's People of Freedom party before regional elections in March 2010. But the fine was too little, too late. *TG1* hardly touched the explosive Sardinian and Palazzo Grazioli sex scandals that engulfed Berlusconi in the summer of 2009. The small independent station La7 and Rupert Murdoch's Sky Italia made hay with the juicy story.

Berlusconi must have considered 2009 his *annus horribilis*. Or perhaps one that encapsulated his career in just 12 months.

The year began well. The prime minister showed the populist touch by marching into Naples and apparently resolving the garbage crisis that had turned the southern port into a giant, festering trash can. He won plaudits for his high-profile response to the terrible L'Aquila earthquake—even if he briefly hit the wrong note by telling homeless survivors of the disaster to treat the aftereffects of the calamity as if it were a camping holiday.[23] But by early summer the avalanche of sex scandals was under way and his final term as prime minister was already in trouble. In June, Berlusconi traveled to the Tuscan seaside resort of Viareggio after a freight train carrying liquid gas derailed and exploded near the town's station, leaving 13 dead and dozens seriously injured. Berlusconi said he'd come to the scene "to take charge," but he was greeted by boos, cries of "go home" and insults about his private life.[24]

October brought the enormous fine for the corrupt takeover of Mondadori. And, in the same month, the Constitutional Court threw out his second go at an immunity law, which he'd introduced the year earlier. This meant his criminal trials for bribing lawyer David Mills and evading taxes would resume. In the first week in December, a mafia informer told a court in Turin that Berlusconi had helped the mob. And to cap it all, there was the bloody episode in his hometown, Milan, in the run-up to Christmas.

For Berlusconi it seemed like business as usual when, in the early evening of December 13, 2009, he climbed down from the podium after a rabble-rousing political rally. After a dreadful six months, he felt buoyed by the home crowd of die-hard conservative fans and the extra help, who had been paid €10 a head to turn up and cheer. He launched himself into the crowd in the shadow of Il Duomo, Milan's famous gothic cathedral, as his mawkish theme song "Meno Male Che Silvio C'é" ("Thank Goodness for Silvio") ground away in the piazza. But as he shook hands and drank in the applause, he failed to notice the shadow of another Duomo rising in an ominous arc three feet from his head.

A second later the heavy marble statuette replica of the cathedral swung down and smashed into the face of the 73-year-old tycoon. Berlusconi staggered backward, blood spattered, with two teeth missing and his nose broken. Security managed to bundle him into his car and away from his attacker. Most politicians would have fled the scene there and then. Almost immediately, however, Berlusconi climbed back out onto the roof of his limo; his mouth hanging open in shock and his lips caked in blood, he was determined to have the last word after suffering such a vicious assault. A stunned Berlusconi probably couldn't imagine why anyone would attempt such a thing. Why on earth would they? Where the mogul was concerned, self-awareness was never a forte.

In the hospital the day after the Duomo attack, Berlusconi spoke of his amazement that anyone would wish ill of him. He told the priest and founder of Milan's San Raffaele clinic, Don Luigi Verzè, of his bafflement. "I wish everyone well, everyone," he said. "I can't understand why they hate me now."

For a man of 73 he made a surprisingly swift recovery from the Duomo assault—he had lost a pint of blood and needed surgery on his mouth. Ever the pro, he managed to wring some PR out of it. Saint Silvio of Arcore declared on his website: "Heartfelt thanks to the very many who have sent me messages of closeness and affection. I urge all to remain calm and safe. Love always wins over envy and hatred."

Even opposition figures rushed to condemn the violence. "The bloodied, stunned, scared face of Silvio Berlusconi will remain an icon in the history of this republic," intoned Mario Calabresi, editor of the center-left *La Stampa* paper. The attacker, Massimo Tartaglia, a 42-year-old man with a history of mental health problems, was arrested at the scene. Within a few days it was reported that he'd written to Berlusconi apologizing for his "superficial, cowardly and uncontrolled" act.[25]

More significant were the 300 or so groups that sprung up on Facebook celebrating the attack. The febrile atmosphere in Italy was starting to feel a little like that of the bad old days of the 1970s and 1980s, thanks to the mogul's use and abuse of the country, repelling large sections of society. The mainstream newspaper of record, *Corriere della Sera*, said politics in Italy had come to resemble a "civil war."

Evidence of this antagonism was also apparent in the hours before the assault. During the rally, in which the prime minister railed against the "communist judges" out to get him, protesters hurled abuse at the mogul's plans to make criminal trials expire even more rapidly under a revamped statute of limitations—a move that would extricate the tycoon from yet another bribery charge. Within 24 hours of the attack, prices on Milan's souvenir stalls for the offending marble replica had doubled from €6 to €12, and some traders said they'd sold out.

Even the get-well cards by his hospital bed recalled some of the black marks against him. The macho Russian tyrant Vladimir Putin praised his Italian friend for behaving "like a real man," and Libya's Colonel Gaddafi, the dictator and mass murderer, described the aggression suffered by the Italian prime minister as "deplorable." The German chancellor, Angela Merkel, Europe's *de facto* ruler, also sent her best wishes; but this was before it emerged from a wiretap that Silvio Berlusconi, the continent's least reconstructed leader, as well at its richest, had described Merkel as an "unfuckable lardarse."[26]

CHAPTER 10

BERLUSCONI'S NOT WELL

If the sympathy aroused in most quarters by the Duomo assault provided Berlusconi with breathing space, there was one attack in 2009 that he has yet to recover from. He finally pushed his long-suffering wife a step too far. It started in the spring of that year, with what ought to have been some routine political appointments. Just as his predecessor Caligula made his favorite horse a senator, Emperor Berlusca decided in April to make a clutch of clueless TV starlets members of the European Parliament. Justifying his unusual choice of candidates, the prime minister said he wanted "young faces, new faces, to give People of Freedom a fresh image in Europe."[1]

The political debutantes made Berlusconi's earlier appointee, the topless model–cum–equal opportunity minister Mara Carfagna seem like Franklin Roosevelt. Among the four would-be Euro-politicos was Angela Sozio, the busty *Big Brother* contestant who'd been photographed carousing with Berlusconi and four other young women at Villa Certosa in 2007. "Berlusconi's harem," a cover feature in the weekly magazine *Oggi*, was Sozio's first contribution to the national news and current affairs debate. The mogul's other chosen candidates were Eleonora Giaggioli, an actress; Camilla Ferranti, a former daytime chat show presenter who had appeared in lingerie calendars; and Barbara Matera, a former contender for Miss Italy.[2]

Veronica Lario described her husband's ploy of choosing sexy young women candidates as "shameless trash" in an open letter sent to the press. Faced with a full-on assault from Lario, Berlusconi initially decided that attack was the best form of defense. "I will carry out the election campaign with these so-called showgirls at my side," he declared, "and they will talk as well as me and I will spell out their qualifications and what they have done in life up to now."

Putting up unqualified showgirls as European candidates was, he said, a way "to revitalize our political class with people who are cultured, well-prepared and who can guarantee that they will be present at every vote." He didn't want "the evil-smelling, badly-dressed people" that other parties put up.

But as the row grew, Berlusconi soon backed down and chose alternative candidates. And as usual, when the tycoon made a U-turn, he denied ever having made the plans in the first place. It was the next outburst from the 52-year-old Lario, on May 3, that really floored the prime minister, however.

"I can no longer stay with a man who hangs around with minors," she said, a statement that etched itself like acid on Berlusconi's memory. In the next breath, Lario announced she was divorcing her 73-year-old husband, having learned that he'd gone out of his way to attend the eighteenth birthday party of Noemi Letizia, a Barbie-like blonde who dreamed of being an underwear model—and who called her septuagenarian benefactor "Papi." Lario said that her estranged husband was "not well." Immediately, people began wondering what she meant. Certainly, the creepy relationship between Noemi Letizia and her Papi ratcheted up the "yuck" factor, as far as Berlusconi's private life was concerned. A messy alimony battle was now on the way. Lario's icy put-down of her husband as someone "who hangs around with minors" was also the harbinger of a relentless tide of sex scandals and sleaze-filled headlines that haven't let up to this day.

On the evening of Sunday, April 26, 2009, Prime Minister Silvio Berlusconi turned up at Letizia's eighteenth birthday party just north of Naples. He received a polite applause from the other guests before embracing the birthday girl, who was dressed in a miniskirt. Papi handed her a present—a $7,000 Damiani choker. In an interview with the *Corriere del Mezziogiorno* newspaper two days later, Letizia revealed that Papi Silvio had bought her jewelry at previous meetings.

> He's never deprived me of attention. One year, I remember, he bought me a little diamond; another time he bought me a little necklace. In other words, every time he gave me loads of attention.

Was her father jealous of the attention from another man?

"No, he's really devoted to Papi Silvio."

Berlusconi told the press he was simply participating in the birthday party of a family he'd known for ages. Letizia's father was an "old driver of Craxi," the tycoon's former friend and political patron. Within hours, Craxi's son Bobo told reporters his father had never had a Neapolitan chauffeur, and certainly not one called Elio Letizia. Other people confirmed Bobo Craxi's comments. Twenty hours later, the prime minister's press office, in a forlorn attempt to undo the damage, declared that Berlusconi had never said Elio Letizia had been Craxi's driver.[3]

The newspapers, led by his most relentless critics, *L'Espresso* and *La Repubblica*, had a field day, reporting on the appearance of the 73-year-old at the celebrations. In his defense Berlusconi noted that he'd hardly made the visit secretly, in the dead of night. "If it had been something saucy, do you think I'd have done it with so many photographers there?"

But this merely gave grounds for more charges—of hubris and narcissism. Pictures and videos of the party gave the impression that the event was as much about Berlusconi as it was about the young object of his affection. The highly organized reception, with guests lined up to shake the tycoon's hands, and the gushing comments from the 18-year-old's parents, suggested an event in part organized to massage his ego.

While arguments raged over the origins of Berlusconi's friendship with the birthday girl's father, there were revealing comments about the nature of the Letizia-Berlusconi bond in an interview the young woman gave to *La Repubblica* on April 29. Letizia said that her mother was also a beautiful woman and had been a TV assistant on the local Naples Canale 21 channel. And her daughter dreamed of going one better—of being a showgirl. But her ambitions didn't stop there. In Berlusconi's Italy, it took only a pert young body and a seductive smile to make the short hop from starlet to lawmaker, and Letizia appeared to be aware of this.

"I am also interested in politics," she declared. "I'm ready to take advantage of any opportunity at any of the 360 degrees of the circle." An interviewer asked her if she planned to start off in local politics. "I'd rather have a place in parliament," she replied confidently, noting that "Papi Silvio will decide."

And Letizia's parents were right behind her. The situation brought to mind the naïve or venal parents who encouraged their children to have sleepovers with Michael Jackson. Certainly, Letizia's parents were more than happy about the billionaire's interest in their pride and joy.

On hearing the news of her husband's attendance at the birthday bash, Veronica Lario's response was terse. "The news surprised me," she told the Ansa news agency, "because he's never come to an eighteenth birthday party of any of his own children, despite being invited."

But days later, on May 3, Lario, who knew Berlusconi better than anyone else, unleashed her most devastating salvo. Again in *La Repubblica*, she wrote: "The path of my marriage is now obvious. I cannot stay with a man who frequents minors . . . I've tried to help my husband; I've implored those he's with to change things, as you would with a person who's not well. But it was useless. Now I say 'enough.' "

These comments were echoed in the July 29 diagnosis by the psychiatrist Luigi Cancrini, in which he suggested that Berlusconi had lost contact with reality after being surrounded by sycophants and yes-men:

> Normal [social] contact is assured by the fact that we receive a flow of positive and negative information about ourselves and we continually make adjustments. In Berlusconi's case, rather than change course, he likes to surround himself only with people who sing his praises, and so every criticism of him becomes an attack or a conspiracy.

Lario hit out in another newspaper, *La Stampa*, the same day, with a jibe at Letizia's parents: "Reading in the newspapers that he's frequenting a minor—given that he knew her before she was 18 years old—reading that she calls him Papi, and talks about their meeting in Rome and Milan, with parents who evidently don't appear to object, well this is unacceptable."

The growing scandal was largely ignored by Italian television, raising the metaphysical question of whether a 73-year-old prime minister's suspected dalliance with a teenage girl actually is a scandal if it's not presented to Italians on the TV news. But the opposition newspapers kept at it. And Berlusconi's nemesis *La Repubblica* really put him on the defensive by printing a big interview with Noemi Letizia's ex-boyfriend that appeared to contradict nearly everything the mogul had said.

The young man, Gino Flaminio, wasn't an ideal witness: he had a conviction—but then, so did half a dozen of Berlusconi's lawmakers.

However, Flaminio, having dated Letizia for a year and a half, was able to shed considerable light on the relationship between his 18-year-old ex-girlfriend and the prime minister. It appeared that Berlusconi's story about being a friend of the Letizia family was a tissue of lies. The first step in the events that would draw the lascivious mogul's attention to Letizia occurred after she sent in modeling photos to an agency in Rome. Berlusconi's Rete 4 TV crony and fellow septuagenarian Emilio Fede (who would eventually be convicted of pimping for his master) was a regular at the agency, Letizia told her boyfriend. After poring over pics of young hopefuls one day, he spotted Letizia and drew her to his boss's attention. Four months later, the then 17-year-old got a phone call from the prime minister of a G7 nation. The mystery caller praised the young girl's "angelic face" and her "pureness." Flaminio said he was present when she received some of the calls, and even heard some of the breathy compliments, when she passed him the phone.[4]

The charming caller remained anonymous for some time, saying that Letizia wouldn't believe him if he told her who he was. But his ego soon got the better of him: "But can't you hear who I am?" he asked. When he revealed his identity, both Flaminio and his girlfriend were stunned. Ironically, around the time that the 73-year-old premier was calling a 17-year-old girl he'd never met, using—and some would say abusing—his power to gain her trust, his minister Mara Carfagna was touting her feminist credentials with plans for a new law against stalking.

Based on the telephone calls he overheard, Flaminio said that Berlusconi's comportment seemed paternal. Still—understandably—something about the whole business disturbed him. The biggest bombshell that Letizia's ex dropped, however, was that the then 17-year-old Letizia had spent more than a week over the 2008–2009 New Year period with "between 30 and 40 young girls" at the mogul's Sardinian pleasure palace, Villa Certosa. The female visitors were housed in the various bungalows in the Villa Certosa's extensive grounds. Letizia was allowed to bring a—young female—friend, who revealed that all the young guests were given "little presents, 2,000 euros or sometimes presents like necklaces or bracelets, the usual sorts of presents that an uncle gives a niece."

Berlusconi had no choice but to admit that Letizia had stayed in Sardinia for ten days: "It's true that Noemi was my guest over New Year's Eve, together with many others. I don't understand why it has to constitute a scandal. It's just insinuating things. Such as? Sex? What sex? Oh please, be serious."

Taking its cue from Berlusconi, Italian television all but ignored the revelations. And in a counterattack, Berlusconi supporters launched a fierce campaign to discredit Gino Flaminio. The Berlusconi family rag *Il Giornale* reported that the young man had been accused of punching a policeman; it didn't mention that Berlusconi's interior minister, Roberto Maroni, had been convicted of something similar.[5]

The mogul's forlorn attempts at damage limitation were stopped in their tracks, however, when one of Letizia's aunts weighed in saying she was sick of all the lies and that Flaminio was the only person who'd told the truth in the whole squalid affair.

There was—and is—a widespread belief that Berlusconi's predilection for having at his disposal large numbers of women young enough to be his granddaughters reflects some sort of later-life crisis, or is perhaps a reaction to a failing marriage, or results from having such immense power and wealth for so long. The truth is, he'd been, as the Brits say, playing away from home for as long as his friends could remember.

Almost a quarter of a century earlier, when Berlusconi and Lario were already a couple but had yet to marry, the media and football mogul was already ordering in girls to Arcore like most people phone for pizza. On New Year's Eve 1986, finance police listening in to a phone call between Berlusconi's senior lieutenant, Marcello Del'Utri (who was under investigation at the time in relation to a bankruptcy case), heard more than they'd bargained for regarding the mogul's New Year's Eve plans. Berlusconi was lamenting that his celebrations were ruined because two—presumably young and nubile—participants from his trashy *Drive In* TV show had stood him up. Berlusconi feared it was a grim portent. "If the year starts like this, we won't be fucking anymore."[6] Dell'Utri reassured his boss that he'd manage to "fuck somewhere else," and then sent his best wishes to both Berlusconi and, of course, his fiancée, Veronica.

The tycoon didn't have a monopoly on unreconstructed attitudes to women. In another conversation, recorded a month earlier, Dell'Utri discussed Lario's jealousy in a conversation with Berlusconi's TV lapdog, Emilio Fede. Fede jokingly said he felt "moved" that Berlusconi had been forced to suffer such a tirade. Dell'Utri laughed at the "gratification" his boss must have felt at seeing his partner so jealous.[7]

Nonetheless, Il Cavaliere's libido appears to have stepped up a gear in the late 2000s. One figure who worked closely with Berlusconi for many years told me that bereavement may have pushed the mogul's libido into overdrive—or at least given him the opportunity to indulge it. Like Robert Graves' Emperor Tiberius, who retired to Capri to live for licentious parties after heartbreak, Berlusconi appeared to change abruptly after the deaths, in quick succession, of his beloved mother in February 2008 and then his sister, Maria, just a year later. "There would never have been bunga bunga if they'd been alive. He was very, very close to them. Their esteem was always very important to him. When they died there was definitely a change in his behavior. He seemed less interested in his work, as well."

His business empire was probably a constant source of temptation, as well. After losing the 2006 election, he began paying a lot more attention to television. In particular, he was concerned that attractive young starlets—and even would-be starlets (if they were attractive enough)—should get the break they deserved. The notion of Italy's TV casting couch became proverbial.

Berlusconi actually told the Italian press in January 2008 that "in certain situations to work for Rai, you've got to prostitute yourself or be a left-winger." There was a time when being lefty might have helped you get a job on the Rai 3 channel. Given his easygoing attitude to the flesh trade, only someone with Berlusconi's chutzpah could have made the jibe about prostitution. In September 2007, prosecutors recorded Rai's head of fiction, Agostino Saccà, acquiescing to demands by his patron Berlusconi that he give jobs to the mogul's favorite starlets.[8]

Saccà was the stooge Berlusconi had managed to shove into the director general's office of Rai 3 back in 2003, with orders to clear out the mogul's heavyweight critics, including the journalists Michele Santoro and Enzo Biagi. The servile nature of their relationship was highlighted by the way Berlusconi addressed Saccà with the informal *tu* form of the word "you," while Saccà responded with the formal *lei.* His toadying knew no bounds. Profound observations to his master included the comments: "You are very loved by the people, who'd like to see you as Pope immediately" and "there's a sentimental void in the country and you fill it."[9] Saccà was, in theory at least, the most powerful man in Italian public broadcasting, yet here he was, brownnosing the owner of a rival, private broadcaster who was under investigation for serious criminal offenses.

When they'd finished with the puke bags, investigators sniffing around for evidence of abuse of office slipped the wiretapped endearments to the newspapers, who printed them gleefully. But, yet again, TV viewers—the majority—were left out of the loop.

In 2007, Berlusconi called Saccà urging him to spend—or waste—millions of euros of license payers' money on a film homage to the medieval northern Italian warrior Alberto Da Giussano. The film, "Barbarossa," was a flop. But Berlusconi made the call as a favor to his political ally Umberto Bossi, head of the rowdy Northern League separatists who idolized (the mostly mythical) struggle of Da Giussano against authoritarian Rome.

In June 2007, Saccà was wiretapped bullying one of Rai's directors into giving his partner, Isabella Briganti, a TV part for which she was too old. Criminal investigations for abuse of office were dropped against Saccà when a preliminary investigations judge ruled that as head of Rai Fiction (and thus in charge of film and TV production for Italy's national broadcaster) he was not a public official. Related charges pressed against Berlusconi were also dropped. Saccà, at least, was finally kicked out of the job—which involved managing the biggest slice of the public broadcaster's budget—a year later.

Back in power in 2008, Berlusconi appeared to further undermine the state broadcaster by slashing the license fee. He said this was in line with his low-tax agenda. But his Mediaset TV empire, Rai's direct rival, stood to benefit because the state broadcaster would have less money to invest in new content.[10]

Meanwhile, Berlusconi's entanglements with TV starlets continued. Evelina Manna, a voluptuous blonde he had "recommended" to Saccà, was taped having various tense and convoluted conversations with the mogul. Rumors emerged that plans had been hatched to use Manna to tempt a wavering senator to defect from Prodi's tottering government. This was denied by all parties. Berlusconi might simply have made up the senator story himself to hide the fact he was sleeping with Manna. Prosecutors in Naples wondered whether Manna had tried to blackmail Berlusconi.[11] Once again, no charges were pressed. Manna later admitted that she and Berlusconi had been lovers—and in addition to getting work as an actress, she picked up a handy €700,000 from the billionaire.[12]

By returning to power in 2008, Berlusconi was in a better position to help his TV business as well as promote his dalliances with showgirls. And there was one business rival in particular against whom Berlusconi needed all the political clout he could muster: Rupert Murdoch, the CEO of Newscorp, was no ordinary opponent. The Australian owner of *The Sun*, *The Times*, the *New York Post* and the *Wall Street Journal* and dozens of other publications had launched the Sky TV pay channel in Italy and had watched it grow quickly.

In the late 1990s, when Berlusconi had smoothed the way for Murdoch to enter the Italian television market by allowing him to purchase the small TV outfit Stream from Telecom Italia, all seemed sweetness and light. The moguls were said to have met on their gigantic yachts and enjoyed lunchtime tête-à-têtes in the Italian's Sardinian villa. But in 2007, when Mediaset launched its own pay service, Premium Gallery (despite its name, a sort of poor man's Sky), the growing success of Murdoch's pay TV service seemed more like an obstacle to Mediaset's own profits. So Prime Minister Berlusconi sought to redress the balance. In December 2008, the Berlusconi III government introduced a tax hike on pay TV channels. That meant the value-added tax (VAT) payments on Murdoch's Sky satellite channel doubled to 20 percent at a stroke.

Berlusconi's Premium Gallery would also have to pay the higher tax rate, but the pay TV service accounted for only a small fraction of Mediaset earnings. Sky Italia, which accounted for 87 percent of the country's pay TV, would be hit much harder.[13]

Murdoch was so angry about the tax increase, which he saw as a direct assault on his business, that he appeared in person at the Sky Italia headquarters to manage the counteroffensive, ordering advertising spots on Sky channels, lambasting the Berlusconi government and firing off letters to MPs, denouncing the tax rise. Less subtle measures followed. During the Easter break, Sky Italia broadcast the film "Shooting Silvio," which depicts a man's plan to rid Italy of Berlusconi with a bullet. Angry members of Berlusconi's PDL (People of Freedom) party said the film was "an incitement to violence" against the prime minister. It certainly wasn't put on to boost ratings: critics have noted the ponderous film by Berardo Carboni is more like an incitement to doze off.[14]

Next, Sky Italia poached Mediaset's ratings-topping showman, Rosario Fiorello. Berlusconi was so unhappy about Fiorello going to "the enemy," as he reportedly put it, that he summoned the star to his Rome home in an attempt to dissuade him. But his charm offensive failed.

In July 2009, Berlusconi admitted on one of his own TV channels that the two moguls were no longer on good terms. "The episode of VAT on Sky created a rift with Sky and Murdoch which has been followed by a series of highly critical articles about me."[15] Most of the world's press was printing regular updates on the scandals engulfing the Italian prime minister, but the Murdoch-owned *Times* of London appeared to report the Berlusconi sex scandals with particular gusto.

On April 30, 2009, several dolts in the mogul's parliamentary PDL party attempted to raise their boss's spirits by backing a campaign for him to be awarded the 2010 Nobel Peace Prize. This was just two days after Veronica Lario's "shameless trash" outburst to the Ansa news agency, the rant that really brought Berlusconi's sexism to the public's attention and saw Murdoch's *Times* of London with the bit between its teeth.[16] All six parliamentarians signed up to the motion that lauded the billionaire for having "in life, work and action, combined the liberal thinking of Friedman, the economic humanism of Röpke and the desire of Yunus to create inclusive capitalism." Apparently, he'd also helped foster good relations between Russia and the US in 2003 that ended the Cold War. While some pundits noted that the Cold War had ended at least ten years earlier, most people were too busy laughing to care. It's not hard to imagine Berlusconi believing the flattery, though. If his handsome, suntanned, but inexperienced friend Barack Obama had got the Peace Prize in 2009 for having done absolutely nothing, why shouldn't he get one for making love not war?

But many Italian women weren't laughing. Sexism had been around for a long time in Italy before Berlusconi appeared on the scene, and it will be around a long time after he's gone, but by 2009 there was a sense that a limit had been exceeded. Berlusconi shouldn't escape the blame for making a bad situation so much worse, almost single-handedly instigating a system of patronage in which pretty young women or girls must shake their behinds—at the very least—for the gratification of grizzled old TV execs and media moguls in order to gain advancement. The conservative journalist and former Berlusconi supporter Paolo Guzzanti called it a *mignottocrazia* (tartocracy). Veronica Lario, who'd journeyed from topless B-movie actress to feminist sage (and got rather rich in the process), had it right: "In this country we need to look at ourselves in the mirror. To see things as they really are. A country in which mothers offer their under-age daughters for an illusion of fame; a country in which nobody wants to make sacrifices because fame, money and fortune come via the TV, with *Big Brother.* What sort of future is there for a country like this?"

The future for women doesn't look bright in Berlusconi's Italy. For a time in the 1970s, things seemed to be improving. Women's earnings rose, and they gained important political rights with the legalization of contraception and divorce in 1970 and then abortion in 1978. But thanks, in part, to the medieval attitudes of the Vatican and the emergence of Berlusconi's crass, populist TV, the fight for equality quickly came unstuck. By the early 1980s, scantily clad young women were part of the furniture on the mogul's burgeoning TV shows, and Italy very quickly became the land that feminism forgot.

A feminist's idea of hell might be having to watch Italian light-entertainment shows, with their relentless parade of busty six-foot blondes twirling in scanty costumes, at the beck and call of irritating sixty-year-old, five-foot-nothing male hosts—the lowbrow formula pioneered by Berlusconi.

Even the program seen as Italy's top TV political satire, *Striscia la Notizia* (*Hot off the Press*) on the mogul's Canale 5 channel, is not immune. In fact, the program revels in showgirl culture, having coined the term *veline* to describe the scantily clad dancers—always one blonde and one brunette—who pole dance in miniskirts during musical interludes, before draping themselves over the desks of the middle-aged male presenters. In Britain or the US, feminists would have put paid to such spectacles back in the 1970s.

But in Italy it's par for the course. Illustrating how all-pervasive the culture of sexism is, every two years or so thousands of young female hopefuls compete in heats around the country for the prestigious assignment as *veline* on *Striscia la Notizia*—to be seen, but not heard. In Berlusconi's Italy, exploiting their physical attraction has become one of the most effective—perhaps one of the few—ways for Italian women to get on. Official figures show how disadvantaged women are in the workplace. According to the OECD, the percentage of women employed in the labor market is much lower than in other wealthy nations—and declining. Currently, only 46.4 percent of Italian women work—compared with 80 percent of Norwegian women.

There's an even more worrying aspect of a culture that regards women as sex objects: the levels of violence they are subjected to. Of course, you can't prove that a culture of casual paternalism and misogyny is to blame. But does anyone really think it helps? A third of women in Italy report being victims of serious domestic violence, according to a 2012 UN report. It seems that almost every day the Italian papers report a new case of a woman attacked, mutilated or killed by a jealous husband or ex-partner.[17]

In May 2013, with Berlusconi out of power, Italy's lower chamber of parliament was virtually empty when Mara Carfagna, Berlusconi's former equal opportunities minister, reported back after attending a UN conference on domestic violence in Istanbul. A bitter row ensued between Carfagna and the anti-establishment Five Star Movement's Carla Ruocco, one of the few parliamentarians who bothered to turn up. Ruocco made the provocative, but not entirely groundless, remark that the empty chamber could be explained by Carfagna's lack of credibility—the former topless model owed her place in government to having caught the ex-premier's eye.[18] Carfagna has surprised some people by turning out to be one of the less ghastly parliamentarians in Berlusconi's gang. But many still see the nature of her career progression as an ugly indictment of how Italian society regards women.

"I don't want to judge individual women and how they have made their careers," said Anna Costanza Baldry, a psychology professor and adviser to the anti-stalking organization Differenza Donna. "But it all suggests that for women it's not about their brains or talent but about how they look. And on TV and in magazines there's an impression of women as objects."

James Walston, the late political pundit at the American University of Rome, said Berlusconi would "leave behind a toxic legacy, in which women have largely been robbed of their dignity in public and private life."[19] With the climate of sexism he nurtured, crimes against women could be added to Berlusconi's growing charge sheet. In 2009, his casual misogyny hadn't yet got him into trouble with the law. But even that was about to change.

CHAPTER 11

RUBYGATE AND BUNGA BUNGA

Reporters in Italy looking for an amusing quote to liven up a story don't usually consider the country's dour judiciary as the first port of call. But for Milan's juvenile crime magistrate, Annamaria Fiorillo, they might make an exception. On the fateful night of May 27 to 28, 2010, a 17-year-old exotic nightclub dancer, *nome d'arte* Ruby the Heart Stealer, left police custody in Milan after Prime Minister Silvio Berlusconi had called surprised officials to say that Ruby, née Karima El Mahroug, should be released because she was none other than the granddaughter of the Egyptian president.

"If she's the granddaughter of President [Hosni] Mubarak then I'm Queen Nefertiti," scoffed Fiorillo. The magistrate already had Berlusconi's number. But before Fiorillo was able to take charge, the belly-dancing "Egyptian" runaway, held for suspected theft, was released into the care of one of the prime minister's associates. This upstanding pillar of the community was the regional councilor Nicole Minetti, a member of Berlusconi's PDL party, who also pimped for the mogul and performed explicit lesbian floorshows in a nun's costume. She took the 17-year-old El Mahroug back to a flat she shared with a rowdy Brazilian prostitute for safekeeping.

With magistrates' interest understandably piqued, the probe that would become the Rubygate affair began.

El Mahroug was not born in the upper echelons of Egyptian society, but to a poor family in Morocco in 1992. When she was nine years old they moved to Messina, in Sicily. At the age of 14, she fled what she said was a very unhappy home, where she suffered beatings from her father and rigid Islamic restrictions on her dress and lifestyle.

After she'd run away, her existence seemed to be a depressing and unrelenting participation in the flesh trade, in which she flaunted her precocious physical assets in order to get what she wanted. But by the time she'd worked her charms on Italy's most powerful man, she would be a very rich woman indeed.

Her first port of call after leaving home was a disco in Sicily's second city, Catania. The establishment's owner offered to put her up—but she didn't like the price that came with it and fled again. This pattern of short stays with strangers continued until September 2009, when, still aged 16, she participated in a beauty contest near Messina. In the jury was none other than Silvio Berlusconi's "talent spotter," Emilio Fede, the Sicily-born crony and newsreader who had brought Noemi Letizia to the mogul's attention. Fede said he was moved by her story and longed to help her. The fact that Fede was a judge was to be important in the eventual prosecution: as one of the judges, prosecutors say that Fede would have known her age then—and almost certainly would have revealed it not long after to Berlusconi.[1]

Not long after being discovered by Fede, El Mahroug moved to Milan. Many reports said she was already in the game—she certainly never appeared short of cash.[2] When the then unknown El Mahroug was mugged in the Corso Buenos Aires shopping district in 2010, officers who recovered her stolen handbag reported it contained the equivalent of $5,000. The cash was probably a handout from the prime minister.

It was an accusation of theft leveled against El Mahroug that brought the whole squalid theater of what would be called Berlusconi's "bunga bunga" parties into the open. Katia Pasquino, a young woman who'd put El Mahroug up for a few weeks, said the young Moroccan had stolen €3,000 ($4,000) from her apartment. At around 6 p.m. on May 27, two weeks after the alleged theft, Pasquino spotted El Mahroug by chance, again in Corso Buenos Aires, and called the police. El Mahroug finished up at the city's main police station in Via Fatebenefratelli. Magistrate Fiorillo gave arresting officer Ermes Cafaro clear instructions for her to be taken to a safe unit for juvenile suspects.[3] But then, out of the blue at 11:49 p.m., Silvio Berlusconi, who was on an overseas trip in Paris, called the police station. The prime minister spoke to the duty officer in charge, Pietro Ostuni, telling him that the young suspect was actually the granddaughter of the Egyptian president, and he would send around one of his associates, Nicole Minetti, to collect her. To make this story sound legitimate, he described Minetti as his "ministerial adviser"—a job title he'd made up on the spot.[4] Minetti had been a go-go dancer, but retrained as a dental hygienist. The mogul had spotted her political talents while she was tending his gums after the Duomo attack a year earlier. Comic turned populist politico Beppe Grillo later joked that given the way Berlusconi was careering off the rails, she was probably his psychologist, too.

Minetti was certainly the prime minister's chief madam. Appropriately, she was accompanied at the jailbreak by a Brazilian hooker, Michelle Conceicao. After seeing her charge released from police custody, Minetti left 17-year-old El Mahroug in Conceicao's safe hands in a dingy flat in Milan's canal district. A week later, the police were called again when the young Moroccan needed hospital treatment after a fight with the 32-year-old Brazilian.

Milan's magistrates were becoming ever more interested in the young runaway and, above all, the nature of her links to the prime minister. It couldn't have helped that the seedy, bankrupt impresario Lele Mora, who'd often benefitted from Berlusconi's generosity, offered to adopt the wayward El Mahroug.

Why were Berlusconi and his minions showing such a keen interest in this 17-year-old belly dancer? The answer wasn't long in coming.

In fact the *merda* hit the fan just a few months later, at the end of October, with a tide of eye-popping newspaper reports, led again by *Fatto Quotidiano* and *La Repubblica*. Even non-journalist friends who usually showed little interest in current affairs were ringing and emailing to see if I'd heard the latest developments about a story that was, to use the newspaper cliché, sensational. For reporters, it was like eating a whole box of chocolates at once, with sleaze, prostitution and national security concerns: part *West Wing*, part Caligula and part Benny Hill. The prime minister wasn't laughing, though. Seven months later, on May 31, 2011, he found himself on trial at Milan's Palace of Justice, not for the usual white-collar crimes—but this time charged with paying for sex with a minor and abuse of office for having attempted to cover up the act by getting El Mahroug released from police custody and out of harm's way with the mendacious phone call.

El Mahroug was nominally the victim—in Italy it's a crime to pay for sex with someone under the age of 18. But she didn't look like an ingénue. Magistrates estimate she pocketed hundreds of thousands of dollars, possibly millions, in jewels and cash from Berlusconi. The prime minister has always denied the charges of paying for sex with a minor and of abusing his powers and insists the evenings that El Mahroug attended were in fact "elegant dinners." But participants say they weren't even edible dinners. A couple of girls I spoke to said the food—usually overcooked *pasta tricolore*—was an afterthought, and they learned it was best to eat before they got there. In any case, this time Berlusconi must have known he really was in big trouble.

Investigators were already hot on the trail, thanks to a series of illuminating interviews with El Mahroug herself over the summer of 2010. It was during these four interrogations that El Mahroug told prosecutors that the prime minister regularly held X-rated soirees at his principal home, Villa San Martino in Arcore, just outside Milan. El Mahroug also introduced them to the exotic phrase "bunga bunga," which they learned referred to a sort of extreme lap-dancing competition with added groping, in which the lucky winner or winners got to sleep with Berlusconi. Participants referred to their host as "Papi," the term of endearment used by Noemi Letizia.

Interviewed by prosecutor Antonio Sangermano on August 3, El Mahroug described what she said was her first dinner at Arcore, on February 14, 2010, when Fede sent a limo around for her and whisked her to Villa San Martino.

"That evening Berlusconi explained to me that bunga bunga consisted of a harem that he copied from his friend Gaddafi [the former Libyan dictator], in which the girls take their clothes off and have to provide physical pleasures." She added that she had refused outright to participate and was driven home at 2:30 a.m.

El Mahroug was never going to rank as the most reliable witness in the world. But police wiretaps, including one involving Emilio Fede in August, confirmed the existence of bunga bunga. Other young female participants furnished astonished magistrates with the salacious details. At these events nude girls danced around a giant phallus, chanting Berlusconi's self-aggrandizing theme tune "Meno Male Che Silvio C'é" ("Thank Goodness for Silvio"). Perhaps the prime minister congratulated himself on re-creating the raw carnality and aesthetic sensibilities of the ancient world, but one look at Villa San Martino's interior, with its kitchen-sink, neo-baroque style, mini-discotheque and guests in miniskirts, suggests otherwise.

Some guests—the ones who liked the sound of the cash and a job on TV, but didn't really know what they were letting themselves in for—left in a hurry. One participant roped in by Mora told investigators she was "horrified" by what she'd seen. Another, Melania Tumini, a friend of Madam Minetti, described Berlusconi's Arcore villa as a "whore house."[5] But it was a whorehouse with one difference: there were lots of girls, but usually only one customer. Berlusconi was, said El Mahroug, "the only male protagonist." As ever, it was all about him.

As news of the investigation leaked out to the newspapers between October 26 and 28, 2009, Milan's chief prosecutor, Edmondo Bruti Liberati, called in Berlusconi's old foe, Magistrate Ilda Boccassini, the anti-mafia specialist, to lead the case. Small and olive skinned, with fiery red hair and a temper to match, the 64-year-old Naples-born prosecutor is famous for her methodical approach and has a reputation for toughness that led some Italian crime reporters to dub her "The Terminator."[6] She first came to the public's attention when she moved to Sicily to track down the mob killers of her mentor, Giovanni Falcone, back in 1992.

Unlike some prosecutors, who talk to the press with surprising alacrity, Boccassini keeps a low profile, preferring to slip in and out of Milan's Palace of Justice, surrounded by her armed guard, with the minimum of fuss. Interviews with Boccassini are as rare as hens' teeth. But, in 2007, she spoke candidly of her experiences, and what drives her, to pupils at a Milan high school.[7] She said she had felt compelled to hunt down the killers of her friend Falcone, whom she met while the pair worked together on an investigation into Cosa Nostra's laundering of its criminal assets in Milan. "Fifteen years have passed since Giovanni's death. I still feel resentment and anger," she told the schoolchildren. "That's not nice, but I have to admit that's how it is."

A month before she delved into the El Mahroug case, Boccassini was launching a nationwide crackdown against 'ndrangheta. This is the brutal crime syndicate, based in the southern Calabria region of Italy, that has overtaken Cosa Nostra in terms of size and reach, thanks largely to its dominance of Europe's cocaine trade. In July 2010's "Operation Crime," 3,000 police officers raided houses and hideouts across Italy to capture more than 300 suspected members of the crime group.

Another glimpse at her corruption-busting zeal and the motivation behind it came at the end of November 2011, when she surprised reporters by making an unusual public statement about the threat posed by Italy's "gray economy," the murky area of business and commerce operating at the limits of legality. The gray economy had reached its zenith under the cloudy skies of Milan, Italy's finance capital. A black-and-white view of law and order / good and evil in Italy will always be a bit simplistic. But in this northern City, the gray economy was truly booming. The public officials who turned a blind eye, the politicians who watered down planning legislation, the businessmen who dealt with people they perhaps shouldn't, were all making some people very rich, allowing organized crime to flourish and hastening the city's moral decay.

Boccassini held the press conference after ordering the arrest of fellow magistrate Giuseppe Giglio in a Milan-based probe into the national expansion of the 'ndrangheta. Giglio, a prosecutor in the Calabrian capital, Reggio Calabria, was held on suspicion of tipping off 'ndrangheta members about police activity.[8]

"Ilda the Red" even took a swipe at the Vatican for having lauded a senior 'ndrangheta mobster, Giulio Giuseppe Lampada, who was jailed in 2009. She noted that he had received "important and prestigious recognition from the Vatican" in reference to his being made a member of the Order of St. Sylvester. Nothing, it seems, escapes her notice. Nor are her colleagues spared the odd outburst. Unlike her courtroom prey Berlusconi, Boccassini, the prickly magistrate, doesn't see life as a popularity contest.

In the Rubygate case, Boccassini pushed for wiretaps on everything and everyone possible, and insisted the investigation remain hush-hush for as long as possible. It was Boccassini, along with prosecutor Gherardo Colombo (with whom she briefly fell out), who had finally nailed Berlusconi's former right-hand man, Cesare Previti, for corrupting judges. Berlusconi, however, got away that time. Would this be her chance to nail him?

Boccassini's team swiftly established one of the principal lies told by Ruby. The young woman said she'd been to Arcore on just three occasions; in fact, she had been there, sleeping over, 15 times, beginning around February 2010. Prosecutors would also have to prove that El Mahroug was lying about another pivotal issue: she claimed she had never had sex with Berlusconi. Prosecutors would contend she had sex with Berlusconi on 13 occasions. But proving it would be no easy task.

However, with sufficient evidence that felonies had been committed—including the crime of abuse of office—magistrates began bugging the phones of key protagonists, and the deliriously absurd and tawdry details continued to flow freely into the newspapers. Of the scores of young women who had partied hard at Arcore, a large group came to be known as the Olgettine—after their place of abode, Via Olgettina in the Milano 2 development. Things had come full circle. Berlusconi was housing his harem in the apartments that had made his name and his fortune. The new town built with dubious means was now home to scores of the Emperor Berlusca's shady ladies. The gossip magazine *Oggi* listed 130 young ladies, including El Mahroug, who were on call to satisfy the mogul's lust and ego.[9]

The events around El Mahroug's May 27 arrest and her interviews with the authorities must have set alarm bells ringing for Berlusconi. But the sex-crazed prime minister was having too much fun to stop. On August 22, his talent spotter Fede brought to Arcore two new and beautiful young women, Ambra Battilana and Chiara Danese, whom he had wooed with promises of jobs as *meteorine*—the completely unqualified, but sexy, girls who presented the weather reports on his wretched *TG4* news show. The account Battilana and Danese gave to magistrates of their evening at the mogul's mansion provided some of the most eye-opening and probably most credible descriptions of Berlusconi's "elegant dinners."

> **Ambra:** We entered the house and found ourselves in front of Prime Minister Silvio Berlusconi. He had two trays in his hands. One had rings on it. He said they were Tiffany, but I realized they were just trinkets. He offered them as gifts. Just then loads of girls arrived. They all started to take gifts from the trays. The girls had a very informal attitude with the prime minister. They were excited. The prime minister introduced himself to Chiara and me

and seemed pleased to meet us. He told us we were beautiful. We reciprocated the compliments. Berlusconi clearly found us attractive.

Chiara: The soiree began with the dinner. We were all seated around the table, about 15 of us, with Fede and Berlusconi and me and Ambra I remember Roberta Bonasia, Marysthell Polanco who I'd see on the TV in *Colorado Café* the two Neapolitan twins (Eleonora and Imma De Vivo) from *Celebrity Island* [a reality show]; a girl from Cuba, who called herself Lisa, who swiftly showed a homosexual interest in me; a tall blonde woman, who sang during the dinner; a large-breasted woman; and a fairly tall brunette, whom I later realized was Nicole Minetti; two black girls, who were rather vulgar and dressed indecently—when I saw them I immediately thought they were prostitutes; a rather tall gentleman, who wasn't presented to us; and another guy who played the piano; and another older woman of about 50. Fede sat between Ambra and me and touched our legs the whole time. I felt uncomfortable and embarrassed and exchanged anxious looks with Ambra. The prime minister didn't eat anything and continued to tell obscene jokes—they were so disgusting it put me off my food. But everyone else was laughing out loud and at a certain point, the song "Meno Male Che Silvio C'é" ["Thank Goodness for Silvio"] began and all the girls started to dance around the table.

Ambra: Marysthell said that if Berlusconi noticed me it would make my career. Emilio Fede told me that the twins from Naples had received a payment of €3,000 each to participate in the dinner. Berlusconi kept looking at Chiara and me. He dedicated songs in French and Italian to us. The worst was yet to come. Fifteen minutes after we'd sat down, some of the girls uncovered their breasts, offering them to Berlusconi so he could kiss them. They also touched the prime minister's intimate parts and made him touch theirs. While this was happening, the girls were still singing "thank goodness for Silvio!" and calling the prime minister "Papi" and Berlusconi called all of us "my little girls, my little girls."

Chiara: After the umpteenth obscene joke, Berlusconi brings in a statue, it's in a kind of case. From it emerges a little man with a huge penis. The statuette is the size of a half-liter bottle of water. Its penis is disproportionately big. Berlusconi begins passing it

> around among the girls. And he asks them to kiss the penis. They kiss it and simulate oral sex with it, or they approach him with bared breasts. They all laugh. Ambra and I don't take part in indecent games. The girls, visibly happy, start to approach the prime minister, they make him kiss their breasts and they touch him . . . they do the same with Emilio Fede. At a certain point, the prime minister, visibly content, asks: "Are you ready for bunga bunga?" The girls shout together: "Yessss!!!" Ambra and I didn't know what bunga bunga was, even if the statue gave it away. I felt agitated and unwell.[10]

At that point Chiara asked Emilio Fede for some chamomile tea—although a cab home would have seemed a more obvious request to make. But, in an attempt to reassure them, Berlusconi took the startled guests for a tour of his pleasure dome; the young women noticed that the walls were adorned with placards reading "Long live Silvio." They entered the disco room, equipped, as any reasonably upgraded seventeenth-century villa would be, with a pole-dancing platform. Berlusconi, the perfect host, remained close behind Ambra and Chiara, patting their buttocks.

> **Ambra:** Berlusconi showed us the swimming pool and the gym and said that the next time, he'd organize a party in the pool, so that we could be more intimate and get to know each other better.

Nadia Macrì, 27, a hooker who partied at Arcore, told investigators she had sex with Berlusconi in the swimming pool, in an underwater bunga bunga session. She added the encounter also involved a girl who was "very, very young."[11] But it was the disco room that seemed to be the usual center of the action.

> **Chiara:** In the little discothèque with the pole in the middle and the little sofas, and a DJ in the corner, the girls began to dance in a rather vulgar way. They lifted up the skirts and showed their bottoms. Some were dressed as nurses—like the twins from Naples and Bonasia, who had a whip in her hand. The nurse outfits were very short with little red crosses, caps and breasts exposed and white underwear on view. And the girls without uniforms showed their buttocks and breasts. Dancing, they approached him,

touched him and made him touch them, it was the game that Berlusconi called "bunga bunga."

Ambra: At a certain point, Nicole Minetti put on a performance. She was dressed in one of those outfits that you rip off. She was completely nude and dancing around the pole. Once she was nude she approached Berlusconi, and dancing in a provocative way, put her ass in his face. Then she spun around and put her breasts against his mouth and the prime minister kissed them. The other girls tried to join in this dance started by Fede and Berlusconi. Behind me I heard remarks such as: "What have these two come for?" All the girls came around us, touching us, trying to remove our clothes, they were touching us everywhere.

Chiara: Fede and Berlusconi encouraged the girls to involve us in the game, saying: "Go on, take your clothes off, go, take them off, dance." At this point we were literally terrified. We wanted to leave, but didn't know how to. Our discomfort was obvious. Building up the courage, we said to Fede: "We really want to go."

Fede gave it to them straight: "If you want to go, fine. But don't think you'll be a *meteorina* or Miss Italia." They left anyway.

Before long we found out how the Arcore soirees proceeded after the bunga bunga stage—not that it was difficult to guess. One of the Papi girls, Diana Gonzales, was heard on the magistrates' recordings talking about a particularly rowdy night on October 2. "There was a stack of girls—there was nowhere to sleep. And that scoundrel didn't take me to his room to sleep." The lucky winner of bunga bunga that evening appeared to have been a woman named Aris, whom Gonzales bumped into the next morning. Aris had a smile on her face because she'd "received twice as much as expected." The mountains of recordings and witness statements suggest the dinner guests, who merely pushed their food around the plate before stripping and fondling the prime minister, got an envelope stuffed with €2,000 to €3,000 ($2,600–$4,000) for their trouble. But an overnight stay bagged them at least €5,000 ($6,500).

Any doubts about the grimness of the Arcore bacchanalias were dispelled by other recordings, interviews that spoke of the young guests vomiting, and testimony that described women arguing and fighting to win Berlusconi's lucrative affections. The mogul demonstrated his peculiar mix of rapaciousness and fastidiousness by frequently sending girls off "to wash themselves because they smelt bad." Prosecutors recorded one female guest describing the aftereffects of an orgy: "There were 20-year-old girls there who were worn out, dead." Another, who had taken and passed an HIV test, commented, "When someone goes to bed with 80 women you never know."[12]

As the tawdry details continued to leak out, some of the protagonists saw there was even more money to be made. In particular El Mahroug, as an underage participant in the paid-for sex fests, appeared to realize the prime minister was potentially in calamitous trouble. That might explain why, by September, her phone calls to Spinelli, Berlusconi's trusted accountant and paymaster, asking for more money seemed ever more shrill. In one of these almost daily calls she spoke of the situation becoming "almost critical."

She also told a friend that the billionaire was ready "to cover her with gold" if necessary to keep her quiet. The impression that El Mahroug was already playing her own game was reinforced by her constant contact with lawyers. In a conversation with her nightclub-owner boyfriend Luca Risso, she claimed she had told Berlusconi: "I told the magistrates lots of things because the evidence was there in front of me. But I've hidden lots of other things."[13]

According to Piero Colaprico, the reporter for *La Repubblica* who broke the Rubygate story, Berlusconi's people (it's not sure exactly who) met with El Mahroug on October 6, 2010, in an attempt to win her silence. And as early as July, Berlusconi's associate Lele Mora, a sleazy talent scout, had attempted to calm El Mahroug and ensure she was "on message."

But when the scandal hit the front pages and Berlusconi realized the full gravity of the situation, he instructed a team of lawyers to put the young Moroccan on a leash. She continued to act unpredictably, however. She was also getting greedy. "I spoke to Silvio and I told him that I expect to come out of all this with at least something," she told a friend. "I mean getting €5 million." Berlusconi had already given her €60,000 to help her open a beauty salon, and probably €300,000 worth of gifts, including a diamond necklace. But a when a teen tearaway from a troubled background finds herself with what one of her lawyers would later describe as "the opportunity of a lifetime," what did the prime minister expect?

Berlusconi continued to deny that he'd ever paid for sex. He even attempted to brazen things out and relieve the political pressure with a few lame jokes. It was "better to be passionate about beautiful women than be gay," he said. And before the trial, while on a tour of the island of Lampedusa in the spring of 2011, he exhumed an old gag, in which pollsters supposedly ask women if they would have sex with him: "30 percent said 'yes,'" he said, "while 70 percent replied, 'What, again?'"

Inevitably, he claimed that left-wing investigators were orchestrating a plot against him. His supporters accused prosecutors and the prime minister's critics of interfering in his private life and moralizing when they had no right. The charge of moralizing might have carried more weight if Berlusconi hadn't spent so much of the previous 20 years sucking up to the Catholic Church and making pious pronouncements of his own. In May 2007, even as a game of musical beds was being played in his Sardinian villa, Berlusconi hit out at progressive Catholics who supported civil partnerships for gays and for heterosexuals who didn't wish to marry, describing such partnerships as an attack on the traditional Church and the family. "You can't be a Catholic—and therefore follow the doctrine of the church—and at the same time align yourself with the other side. We say 'no' to this caricature of marriage."[14]

But Berlusconi must have known that revelations about his dissolute private life meant the two-decade war with magistrates was entering dark new territory. Boccassini and company weren't investigating the usual financial crimes; they were looking at the less-salubrious-sounding charges of sex with an underage prostitute and abuse of office—crimes that were punishable by 3- and 12-year jail terms, respectively. And, unlike the tax fraud and bribery allegations against him, this case didn't involve complex, decades-old accounting trails spread over several continents. It was recent, clamorous—and there was no chance of the charges being killed by the statute of limitations.

El Mahroug denied from the outset, and continues to deny, that she ever had sex with the prime minister. But she would present the defense with a particular problem if called to the stand. The mogul's lawyers wanted the court to believe the young woman's declaration that she and Berlusconi had never had sex. At the same time, the defense wanted the court to *dis*believe El Mahroug's description of rampant sexual activity at the bunga bunga parties—it was very important to the defense to prove that the parties were relatively innocent. Due to a key legal technicality, the prosecution could win a conviction on the sex with a minor charge simply by showing that El Mahroug had been present and in the thick of things at the tycoon's bacchanalias.

Berlusconi also had the loyalty of his sidekicks to worry about. By January 2011, the *Corriere della Sera* newspaper was reporting fears in Berlusconi's camp that those accused of pimping for the premier—Fede, Mora and Minetti—were considering plea bargains: organizing and abetting juvenile prostitution were very serious crimes.

Former dental hygienist Minetti was considered the most likely of the three to turn, having been recorded describing Berlusconi as "a piece of shit . . . just out to save his flabby ass." The reams of incriminating wiretaps were making it a little difficult for her to claim to have been at Arcore for polite conversation. In one recording, Minetti was heard telling a friend that there were "five types of women" who went to the bunga bunga parties. "There are the sluts, the South Americans who come from the slums and don't speak a word of Italian, the more serious ones, others who are somewhere in the middle, and then there's me, and I do what I do," she said.

The prosecution, on the other hand, failed to find the smoking gun—or in terms familiar to those who recall the Bill Clinton–Monica Lewinsky affair, a DNA-stained dress—that demonstrated beyond doubt that Berlusconi had had sex with El Mahroug. At one point a British newspaper was preparing to print the claims of one of the Olgettine that she had seen Berlusconi have intercourse with Ruby on three separate occasions at Arcore. But the paper pulled the piece after balking at the woman's demand for a multimillion-dollar payment in exchange for a complete, on-the-record interview.

El Mahroug was recorded saying that Berlusconi *wanted* to have sex with her, and one of her friends was overheard telling someone that El Mahroug had admitted having had sex with the prime minister, but prosecutors would never hear the admission from the young woman herself. Another question mark concerned her age. That she was 17 at the time of the "parties" was not in doubt. But would the prosecution be able to show that Berlusconi knew that she was underage? Failure to do so could mean an acquittal under Italian law. Another complication was that El Mahroug declined to present herself as one of the victims of the scandal and seek civil damages—to do so would have been admitting prostitution, which would have sullied her reputation. She seemed to be receiving a ready supply of cash from somewhere, however. And Berlusconi's camp kindly provided her with a new lawyer.

Prosecutors appeared to have the mogul dead to rights, however, on the abuse of office charge, thanks to the recording of Berlusconi calling the police station with the ridiculous "granddaughter of Mubarak" claim. Or so it seemed. The mogul's roller-coaster ride still had some surprises in store.

After a preliminary hearing in Milan on Valentine's Day in 2011, the prime minister was ordered to stand trial later that spring on charges of paying for sex with an underage girl and abusing his office to cover up his relationship with her. Judge Cristina Di Censo ordered a fast-track trial that did away with the need for lengthy committal proceedings because there was "clear evidence of abuse of office and sex with a minor." Before long, Minetti, Fede and Mora, the friends / sidekicks / leeches / lifestyle gurus who'd egged Berlusconi on and used him like a cash register, would be on trial, too, for pimping.

In October 2010 a comico-tragic video turned up on the website of *Oggi* magazine showing talent scout Mora in action. In the clip, scantily clad young women in high heels assemble at an address in Viale Monza, Milan, before the impresario drives them in his Mercedes to Arcore, straight through the gates of the then prime minister's residence, without so much as a word—let alone a proper security check—from police guarding the entrance. In addition to the legal and ethical questions over Berlusconi's libertine lifestyle, the video raised another and possibly more serious issue: what kind of security risks was this leader of a G7 nation exposing himself and his country to?

Following the release of the video, the head of the parliamentary security committee, Massimo D'Alema, demanded that Berlusconi appear before the panel to answer questions. Berlusconi refused.

And for the mogul, the danger of blackmail was ever present. Some claimed there had already been hints of menace when the Noemi Letizia scandal broke. The threat of blackmail was also whispered through the Rubygate wiretaps and witness statements. "All the girls at Arcore took photos," El Mahroug told investigators. "We all thought one day they might be useful."

What on earth was he doing? The phrase uttered by Berlusconi's estranged wife, Veronica Lario, comes to mind again: *Berlusconi is not well.* It wasn't only his critics who began to say so. Despite the mountain of trouble he was in, the emperor with increasingly few clothes continued to indulge himself. In April 2011, three months after his indictments for Rubygate, two loyal friends were recorded discussing the prime minister's psychological state—and his fitness for running the country.

Flavio Briatore, the Formula One racing tycoon, was on the phone to the right-wing Berlusconi ultra-loyalist and PDL parliamentarian Daniela Santanchè. Briatore told her that Lele Mora had just informed him the prime minister's bunga bunga nights were still going strong.

Briatore: Yes, yes, everything's going on as if nothing has happened; everything as it was before.

Santanchè: But that's madness.

Briatore: Not there—but in the other villa. He's not changed a fucking thing, the same players, the same . . .

A few days later the pair spoke again.

Briatore: We're in God's hands now, no? Because I heard the other night there was a big party.

Santanchè: Really? But what the fuck can we do? Tell me!

Briatore: He's not well. When I spoke to him, I said: "Prime Minister, just forget it." He's ill, Daniela. Veronica's right, he's not well because a normal person doesn't do those sort of things. Lele is still bringing . . . organizing them . . . even he's embarrassed.

Santanchè: Well, everything's going to collapse.

Briatore: Daniela, we're talking about really serious problems in a country that has to be overhauled—a country that risks going under at any moment, even if it [the government] had more MPs. And he's continuing to do that stuff there?

Santanchè: Are you sure he's started again?

Briatore: 100 percent sure. 100 percent.

Santanchè: I'm lost for words, lost for words. But why?

Briatore: Because he's not well. He's ill, Dani. You know he gets his pleasure when he sees these girls tired; when they leave tired. By

> now they know that after a couple of rounds they should say they're tired, that he's left them shattered.[15]

As Piero Colaprico, *La Repubblica*'s chronicler of the Rubygate affair, noted in his book *Le Cene Eleganti* (*The Elegant Dinners*), Berlusconi at the time wasn't superman: he was a 74-year-old survivor of prostate cancer who had a heart problem. Did anyone, apart from Berlusconi himself, really believe he was leaving dozens of 20-year-old girls "shattered"? Having handed out €12 million ($15 million) in cash to his party friends in the space of 12 months, he seemed less like Valentino and more like Europe's richest charity case.[16] But the pathetic figure he cut wasn't the only thing weighing on his friends' minds. Briatore, the conservative businessman, saw a country going to the dogs. To everyone but the distracted and deluded leader of Italy, it was clear the economic collapse that began in the US in 2008 meant that a financial storm was coming, the like of which Italy—and the rest of Europe—had never seen. "If I were in his [Berlusconi's] position, I wouldn't be able to sleep at night," said Briatore. "But not because of the whores. I wouldn't be able to sleep due to the state that Italy is in."[17]

CHAPTER 12

FINAL FLING

Berlusconi is better at winning elections than he is at governing," Guido Crainz, a noted professor of modern Italian history, once said. It's hard to argue with that. After the tub-thumping election rallies are over and the nudge-nudge, wink-wink routines have had the desired effect of making his opponents appear detached and humorless, Berlusconi was required to make hard decisions, and very often, unpopular ones. But he's a salesman, not a doer. So he's always left the dull, day-to-day business of government to his *eminence grise*, Gianni Letta, a trusted former executive in his Fininvest business empire. In addition to skipping the boring bits of prime ministerial work, perhaps Berlusconi hoped he could avoid the blame when the economy collapsed. And make no mistake, Italy Incorporated was heading for the edge of a cliff, and threatening to drag the European Union, the world's biggest economic block, over with it.

But perhaps Berlusconi was simply too distracted to pay attention to the economic peril his country was in. There was the hard partying, and, of course, his endless legal problems. By involving a 17-year-old in his private life and by allegedly abusing his powers to conceal it, he had created a new mountain of trouble. By the start of 2011 Berlusconi was facing criminal charges in three cases: the alleged bribery of British lawyer David Mills; tax fraud relating to his TV empire; and the newest charges, paying for sex with a minor and abuse of office. Unfortunately, in his third term in office, Berlusconi found the old trick of ad hoc lawmaking was not entirely successful.

In 2008, Angelino Alfano, Berlusconi's lackey in the Justice Ministry, had had another go at passing an immunity law to protect the holders of the four highest offices of state from prosecution. Within a year, the Constitutional Court judges quashed the proposed law—just as they'd done with the first immunity law back in 2004.

A year later, in March 2010, Alfano managed to get another bill through parliament, the "legitimate impediment" law. This law allowed ministers to skip any court appearances on the grounds that they had important government business to attend to. Realizing that orgies might not count as official duties, Berlusconi took advantage of the scam by upping his state visits abroad. In January 2011, this legislation was also dismissed as unconstitutional. Senior judges noted that all citizens were supposed to be equal in the eyes of the law, so it would be up to trial judges to excuse ministers from hearings on a case-by-case basis.[1]

These legal maneuvers had one thing in common: they were blatant attempts to keep The Boss out of jail. Their purpose was so blatant, in fact, that critics and opposition MPs could hardly be bothered to voice their disgust and outrage. Berlusconi and his cronies didn't just try to impede the trails: his lawyers planned new rules to prevent charges from being brought in the first place. Beginning in mid-2009, the government touted new limits on wiretaps, which might spare Berlusconi further blushes, but would also, as collateral damage, allow mafia crimes to go undetected.[2]

The 2009 restrictions were not enough. Days after the Rubygate scandal exploded on the front pages of the newspapers, the mogul's parliamentary supporters proposed even tougher rules on wiretapping. These rules would limit a judge's ability to authorize a wiretap and allow for huge fines—of up to €100,000 ($130,000)—on magistrates if material gained from a wiretap was published by the press and the accused was subsequently acquitted of wrongdoing. The punishment would be retroactive for five years.[3] This was Berlusconi's attempt to lash out at the prosecutors who had humiliated him by recording the protagonists of the Rubygate affair, and had then allowed the fruits of their wiretaps to spill into the newspapers.

It's worth noting that Berlusconi's vitriolic attacks on the Italian judiciary, while provoking opprobrium from critics at home and abroad, have probably gone down well with significant sections of the Italian electorate. Everyone in Italy knows that the justice system is a basket case. It moves with glacial speed and seems to victimize those least able to defend themselves. Infamously, the Regional Administrative Tribunal in Catania once took fifteen years to decide the date for the first hearing of a case concerning salary arrears. In Italy, it takes on average 450 days to evict a tenant who has not paid rent—426 days longer than in Holland. Some of this can be blamed on the tardiness of individual judges. The least efficient justices take 50 percent longer to try cases than their most efficient colleagues overseeing comparable trials.

Four of every ten people behind bars are there awaiting trial—very often for months or even years. Rich white-collar criminals such as Berlusconi can afford the legal teams to keep the law at bay. But that probably hasn't stopped the billionaire's attacks on magistrates chiming with thousands of exasperated ordinary citizens.

And Berlusconi could justly feel aggrieved about the endless leaks to the press. How does evidence flow so easily and frequently from prosecutors' offices, and/or from the courts, into the hands of eager journalists before it's presented before a jury? As a reporter from a country (the UK) with strict contempt of court rules (that drastically limit what can be published about a defendant once he or she has been charged), I was astonished by the free-for-all enjoyed by Italian newspapers. In Italy, juries are led by judges who are supposed to be immune to the malign influence of the press. It is their role to guide the lay jurors. But judges are human, too (and why have lay jurors if judges are going to tell them how to vote?).

Italian reporters who cover court cases are understandably reticent about the sources that provide, or in some cases sell, them juicy bits of information. Very often, the evidence is not leaked until it has been lodged with the court. This marks out court officials and defense council as possible culprits.

If Berlusconi's travails leave your sympathy glands (understandably) unresponsive, consider the long, tortuous case of Amanda Knox, the American exchange student from Seattle. As this book went to press, she was preparing her second appeal against her conviction for the murder of British student and housemate Meredith Kercher in Perugia in November 2007.

Before the 2009 trial in the Knox case, a deluge of dodgy claims appeared in the press. I have to confess writing one story myself about a witness who came forward to say he had seen Knox and her then boyfriend and co-defendant, Raffaele Sollecito, in the company of the man already convicted of the murder outside Kercher's house in the hours before the crime. These claims crumbled to nothing and were never presented in court.

The gung ho prosecutor in the original Knox trial, Giuliano Mignini, who gained Amanda Knox's conviction in 2009 on the back of a half-cocked theory about a black-magic-inspired orgy that spiraled out of control, returned to court to prosecute the American for slander in June 2010. He was allowed to resume hostilities against Knox, although he had been convicted in the interim of abuse of office for his alleged campaign of harassment against people he had taken exception to in an earlier unrelated case.[4] His conviction was eventually overturned on appeal for lack of jurisdiction.[5] However, even if the Turin prosecutor who charged Mignini had pushed for a retrial and gained a conviction, such an offense would probably not have been grounds for removing him from office until after he had completed two appeals.[6]

There is no clear division between the careers of judges and those of prosecuting magistrates in Italy. They can flit from one role to the other—and sometimes appear to get the different jobs confused, with the unflinching Mignini seemingly a case in point. It's not just Berlusconi's camp that is critical of the magistrates and their power. One left-leaning lawmaker (and certainly no friend of Berlusconi) said to me recently: "Their power is very great indeed. I think we've created a monster, and we don't know how to dismantle it."

Defenders of the magistrature ask us to consider what Berlusconi would have done without their tireless campaign to make him answer to the law. The argument over the balance of power is one for the constitutionalists.

For his part, Berlusconi has talked for years about limiting magistrates' power and independence, which was granted after World War II to prevent a return to fascism. But his plans for radical reform always sounded like hot air. In the spring of 2011, when he talked up big changes to the justice system by curbing magistrates' power and increasing their accountability, few believed it. Such far-reaching changes would require the country's constitution to be amended, and that would prove nigh on impossible in the two years remaining to a government that was already looking very dog-eared indeed.

More likely, Berlusconi planned to ditch his justice reform proposals in exchange for the re-introduction of immunity from prosecution for the prime minister and other top office holders and for the so-called *processo breve*, or short trial legislation, a bill that caused even his coalition allies to balk.

The short trial scam would have introduced much shorter deadlines for the completion of trials, which would have resulted in extricating Berlusconi from all charges he faced, except those relating to the recent Rubygate scandal. But once again, the hang 'em and flog 'em brigade among his Northern League coalition partners got cold feet when they realized this umpteenth piece of save-Berlusconi legislation would allow thousands of other suspects to walk as well.[7] Magistrates said the cynical *processo breve* proposals would have killed—among other things—trials relating to the Parmalat financial scandal, in which thousands of Italians lost their savings, as well as the manslaughter trial resulting from the Viareggio rail fire of June 2009, which claimed 31 lives. Berlusconi had said back in June 2003 that perhaps some people were more equal than others.[8] Thankfully the Constitutional Court didn't agree.

Crowds gathered at Milan's Palace of Justice on April 7, 2011, a warm spring day, to witness the start of Berlusconi's most humiliating legal battle. But after the breathless buildup, Silvio Berlusconi's "Rubygate" sex trial came to a premature end after just nine minutes—rather less time than it took for one of his bunga bunga sessions. Judge Giulia Turri accepted that the prime minister had official duties to attend, and postponed the trial to May 31. Reporters who had traveled from around the world, hoping for courtroom theatrics from day one, sighed in disappointment. But prosecutors knew they had time on their side.

It's always uppermost in Berlusconi's mind that he has to stay in power because: a) he deserves it, and b) he needs political protection to avoid arrest and prosecution. But in May 2011 his hold on power seemed to be weakening when a war of words broke out between the key parts of his increasingly shaky coalition. The interior minister, Roberto Maroni, a leading figure in the anti-immigrant Northern League, clashed with the defense minister, Ignazio La Russa, a scary, probably not-very-ex-fascist with a voice like the possessed child in *The Exorcist*. La Russa was in favor of Italy joining NATO's bombing campaign in Libya. Maroni opposed it, not on compassionate grounds, but for fear it would send Libyan refugees flooding across the Mediterranean to Italy.[9] Berlusconi did his best to paper over the cracks. But foreign policy arguments were just the start of a series of domestic blows that would push him out of power forever.

On May 30, the day before the Rubygate trial resumed, Berlusconi's right-wing coalition suffered a humiliating defeat when it lost control of Milan. But this wasn't the same Milan in which the tycoon had risen to national prominence a quarter of a century earlier. The mid-1980s stomping ground of Berlusconi and Craxi, Milano *da bere* (drinking Milan), was a boomtown, one big party fueled by endless cash, cocktails and cocaine: the design and finance capital, dressed in Armani prêt-à-porter, the city of yuppies and their spoiled teenage precursors, *i paninari*. By the late 2000s the party was over. Lots of Milanesi still bought cocaine, but most couldn't afford it and it was just chopped-up speed and novocaine, anyway. Rampant consumerism had given way to the city's traditional bourgeois provincialism, and it seemed a grayer, more mean-spirited place.

Milan's substantial conservative constituency, confronted by emerging social and economic problems, looked around for scapegoats. Non-European immigrants, mostly clandestine, were obvious targets. In 2009, Matteo Salvini, a local MP from the Northern League—one of Berlusconi's coalition partners—suggested immigrants should have to use separate carriages on Milan's metro system.[10] He later said it was a joke. The kind of joke Mussolini would have made.

Milan's council, ostensibly led by the high-society figure Mayor Letizia Moratti, was in practice ruled by her reactionary deputy, Riccardo De Corato. He seemed more concerned with closing down left-wing social centers than establishing Milan's reputation as a progressive first-tier European city. By 2011, the petty vindictiveness of the Milan administration proved too much even for mainstream conservative voters, and a left-wing lawyer, Giuliano Pisapia, was elected mayor, even after Berlusconi's PDL had conducted one of the dirtiest election campaigns in recent memory.

Berlusconi still regarded Milan, Italy's business capital, as his home turf. He was so determined not to cede the city to the left that he took personal charge of the campaign to have Moratti reelected. But Berlusconi's involvement backfired in the first major electoral test since he was charged with a sex offense and abuse of office after the Rubygate investigation.[11]

But the loss could not be attributed entirely to the prime minister's legal troubles: the center-right seems to have repelled voters with its squalid campaigning, in which "left-wing" judges were compared to Red Brigade terrorists. Berlusconi himself warned that Milan would become "*zingaropoli*" (gypsyville) if his opponents won, while his Northern League supporters warned that mosques would spring up on every street corner. To some extent Berlusconi had always played the race card, with vote-catching anti-immigration policies, including a spiteful and pointless piece of legislation that made clandestine immigration a criminal offense. But now the failure of this tried-and-tested strategy seemed like another bad omen.

Berlusconi's support in parliament was crumbling, too. Gianfranco Fini, the head of the old post-fascist National Alliance (which had merged with Berlusconi's Forza Italia soon after the 2008 election to form the People of Freedom party), was already semi-divorced from government. In November 2010, Fini, who'd undergone a remarkable political transformation from "post-fascist" to presentable center-right politician, called on Berlusconi to quit, in the face of the mounting Rubygate scandal. Of course, "quit" is a four-letter word in Berlusconi's vocabulary. His press and media cronies turned on Fini, who had attempted to take over the reins of the center-right. Fini soon found himself embroiled in a petty scandal, in which he was accused of selling an apartment owned by his former political party to his brother-in-law below the market price. If Berlusconi had done something this inconsequential, the opposition papers wouldn't have bothered to write about it.

But the Italian public itself gave the mogul a bloody nose in June 2011, when activists collected the half million signatures required to force referendums on key pieces of Berlusconi legislation. One of these was the legitimate impediment law, which allowed the prime minister to avoid trial hearings. The Constitutional Court had already watered the new law down. The electorate killed it completely.

With his political strength fading, Berlusconi was in no position to face the financial hurricane about to engulf the continent. The crisis that would ultimately sink the prime minister can be traced back to white-collar crooks on the other side of the Atlantic. These villains gave huge US financial institutions terminal indigestion by feeding them toxic debt. They were aided and abetted by their accomplices in the ratings agencies who covered it up—until it was too late. Some smug Europeans might have kidded themselves that the effects of the sub-prime financial disaster would be confined to America. But by 2008 there were no longer any real boundaries in global finance: after US taxpayers had footed the emergency repair bill in America, speculators turned their attention to the Old Continent, in their endless quest for the next weak link.

Earlier in the decade, with the world economy booming, investors were prepared to give the Eurozone's weaker members the benefit of the doubt; yoked into a single currency, they were now seen as part of the continent's economic powerhouse, Germany. But with the world on the brink of depression, thanks to events in the US, moneymen took a harder look at the debt-mired economies of Portugal, Ireland, Italy, Greece and Spain, the "PIIGS," and they didn't like what they saw.

With a recession biting, the PIIGS of the Eurozone would be less able to repay their huge national debts. This meant they would be charged higher interest rates on the money they needed to borrow to service the repayments—a vicious circle was under way. For the most part, Italy's banks weren't saddled with toxic debts like their desperate counterparts in Spain and Ireland. But years of political deadlock and low growth meant Italy's national debt was now approaching the €2 trillion mark.

By the summer of 2011 there was already talk that Greece might default on repayments, an event that would be disastrous for the euro. If Italy, then the world's seventh-largest economy, were to go the same way, the euro would almost certainly disintegrate and drag the global economy into a hole from which it might never escape.[12] Once again, the world looked to Silvio Berlusconi to do the right thing. And, in Italy's greatest hour of need, he'd show that his priorities lay elsewhere.

In mid-July 2011 Ireland's credit rating was cut to junk status; Moody's ratings agency predicted the country would need more bailout aid in late 2011 on top of that already received from a special EU fund. The fund had been set up in a hurry to stop the weakest members from tumbling out of the single currency. Italy and Spain insisted their economies were secure from the debt crisis that had seen Greece and Ireland reduced to begging. No one—and certainly no speculator—believed them. Instead, the markets stepped up attacks on both countries. Borrowing costs soared despite pledges from Spanish and Italian finance ministers that they would slash debt levels.

Italy's finance minister, Giulio Tremonti, promised to cut public spending by €47 billion (then the equivalent of around $64 billion) and wipe out Italy's annual deficit by 2014, in a bid to tackle its national debt, which at 120 percent of its annual income was second only to Greece among Western nations.

By August it was clear that the markets weren't satisfied. The European Commission's president, José Manuel Barroso, declared that Spain and Italy were both in the danger zone. In a letter to all 27 members of the European Union, Barroso called for more donations to boost the Continent's bailout fund. Experts agreed the €440 billion ($600 billion) emergency pot wasn't big enough to bail out Rome—and many suspected it never would be.

Berlusconi was keeping a strangely low profile. The flow of leaked wiretaps continued to undermine what little credibility he had left. In mid-September details of his conversations with the seedy Bari businessman Giampaolo Tarantini were splashed in the newspapers. Tarantini, a convicted cocaine dealer, had supplied starlets and hookers for dozens of the mogul's parties. At first, magistrates suspected the drug-dealing pimp had attempted to blackmail the prime minister. Subsequently, their inquiries would focus on the suspicion that Berlusconi had, in fact, bribed Tarantini to lie about the prostitute ring in which they were both involved. The recorded conversations, however, shed considerable light on the prime minister's sexual delusions and the slight regard in which he held his high office. In one conversation the media mogul couldn't resist telling—or attempting to convince—36-year-old Tarantini of his prowess at a party the previous night: "I had a queue outside my door, there were 11 of them. I only managed to do eight of them, I couldn't manage any more. You just can't get round to all of them. But this morning I feel great, I'm pleased with my stamina."[13]

And, demonstrating his priorities, as if we didn't know them already, the mogul was heard in another conversation saying he was only prime minister in his "spare time."[14] His primary interest was to "pass the days with my babes." No doubt he dismissed the comments as jokes. But the joke was on Italy. Even the prime minister's center-right allies were backing off quickly. It was becoming embarrassing to be associated with him. In late 2011, political chaos meant market uncertainty and the arrival of financial ruin that much faster. The country was like a train with no brakes hurtling toward disaster.

On September 29 came the revelation that fatally undermined the prime minister's authority. The European Central Bank (ECB), the continent's equivalent of the US Federal Reserve, issued Berlusconi an uncompromising diktat.[15] Euro-officials wanted further political and economic reforms or they would refuse to prop up Italian government bonds—a last-ditch means to reduce Italy's spiraling borrowing costs. Berlusconi had surrendered Italy's sovereignty to unelected European officials. The ECB's demands, particularly on opening up labor markets, were largely to blame for the crippling national strikes that were subsequently called by Italy's militant left-wing public sector union, the CGIL.

The chaos mounted, even as the mogul tried to celebrate his seventy-fifth birthday on September 29 at Arcore. But there was no respite anywhere. As Berlusconi clocked up three-quarters of a century, he had hoped for a quiet family celebration. Instead, he had to face allegations of more sexual shenanigans. A 20-year-old Montenegrin beauty queen, Katarina Knezevic, appeared in the papers to announce that she had been Berlusconi's live-in lover for the past two years: she claimed they'd met three days after her eighteenth birthday. She didn't say whether she'd been bothered by the competition passing through Villa San Martino's revolving door, but she did deny claims that she had attempted to blackmail him.

Before his birthday the mogul had said the best present he could hope for that year was to see an end to political bickering and to see people "work together to re-launch the economy." Perhaps Knezevic considered herself in with a shot for finance minister.

Everyone knew that Berlusconi's lame-duck administration, weakened by almost daily defections, was adding to the market's jitters. In mid-October, Berlusconi scraped through a parliamentary confidence vote, but the margin of victory served only to highlight the fragility of his right-wing coalition. *La Stampa* newspaper poured scorn on his pre-vote pep talk to parliamentary allies. "Not one new thought was expressed. Absolutely nothing. A complete vacuum. Berlusconi has by now become a factor that is immobilizing and freezing Italian politics," it said.

The barely concealed animosity between the prime minister and Finance Minister Tremonti was adding to investors' fears. Earlier in the month it was widely reported that Tremonti had told Berlusconi, "Silvio, don't you understand? You're the problem," when the premier asked how his government might beat the speculators.[16] The money markets looked at the colossal €400 million ($530 million) debt that Italy had to refinance in the next twelve months. And responded by raising borrowing costs within sight of the levels that had forced Greece and Ireland to seek bailouts. But Italy was too big to bail out. The country was heading for bankruptcy, with no rescue in sight.

On November 4, the prime minister's political humiliation was almost complete when it was reported that inspectors from the International Monetary Fund (IMF) were being sent in to police the promised reforms and spending cuts. World powers led by Germany, France and the US had effectively imposed IMF checks on Italy to stop it from going the way of Greece.

Franco Pavoncello, a political science professor at Rome's John Cabot University, correctly predicted that, thanks to the news leak about the ECB's intervention, the mogul's time in office was about to run out. "Until now, everyone's been asking whether it's a good thing to get rid of Berlusconi in the middle of this financial crisis, even though he's a liability," he said. "Italy is effectively coming under outside control. That's why rebels now feel they can leave Berlusconi's PDL party . . . the government might only last a matter of days."[17] Italy's supposedly neutral head of state, President Giorgio Napolitano, warned that Italy was facing an "unprecedented crisis." Before long we learned that rather than playing the part of referee, he had done everything he could to show Berlusconi the door.

On November 8, 2011, Berlusconi finally bowed to the inevitable and announced he was stepping down. With the lack of good grace we'd come to expect, he had earlier stormed out of parliament after failing to win over rebel MPs. The eight parliamentarians who refused to support him were labeled "traitors" in a scribbled note captured on camera. Once it was clear his parliamentary majority had vanished, the prime minister and the president met for 45 minutes. Soon after, the increasingly hands-on head of state announced that Berlusconi would be quitting in a matter of weeks—once he had passed key economic reforms demanded by the EU.

The prime minister's mawkish side was on show later that evening when he lamented the actions of the MPs who'd rebelled. "I felt not only surprise but also sadness, because the people who didn't vote for me were people with whom I've been close for years, from the start of Forza Italia [his first political party]."[18] Most observers, however, saw rats fleeing a sinking ship.

Italy and the rest of Europe prayed that the prime minister's eleventh-hour forced exit would be enough to restore confidence and prevent a meltdown.

Despite the gravity of Italy's situation, the mogul's longest meeting in the previous 48 hours had not been with the president, the finance minister, or his economic advisers, but with his oldest children, Marina and Pier Silvio, key lieutenants in his business empire, and Fedele Confalonieri, chairman of his Mediaset TV company. "This is a good example of Berlusconi's priorities. The euro is at risk through Italian inaction, but the Italian prime minister is looking after family interests," said James Walston, a respected politics professor at the American University in Rome.[19]

When Berlusconi told President Napolitano that he would quit in just weeks or days to halt the disastrous downward slide of Italy's stock market, the irony of the situation probably wasn't lost on him. The tycoon had entered politics 17 years earlier, in part to save his business interests from left-wing politicians who wanted to dismantle them. Now he was about to quit office in order to save his business interests, only this time it was the markets that threatened his media empire.

In the midst of the sovereign debt crisis, with the speculators singling out Italy, it was Berlusconi's Mediaset that felt the full force of their attack. The company had already lost 20 percent of its value in five days, but on November 8 the fall accelerated. It was reported that Confalonieri, the Mediaset chairman and the mogul's oldest and closest friend, had told his boss at their meeting a day earlier that the game for him as prime minister was up—and that by failing to step down immediately he risked seeing his business empire fall with him.

"He clearly told Mr. Berlusconi: 'Quit now or you'll bring the company down,'" said Alessandro Baj Badino, the Italian media analyst of Deutsche Bank. Remarks later that month by Berlusconi's eldest son, Pier Silvio, seemed to confirm this.[20] Berlusconi junior, Mediaset's vice president, spoke candidly about what he saw as the "climate of hostility" surrounding Mediaset because of its links to the prime minister, hostility that his father was "well aware" of.

Berlusconi's other motive when he first ran for high office in 1994 had been to avoid prison. By quitting now he would make himself more vulnerable to prosecutors attempting to nail him in three criminal cases. He was facing around three dozen trial hearings in the coming six months. Friend and foe alike knew it was dangerous to write off Silvio Berlusconi. But deep down, even he must have known the end game had moved a step closer.

CHAPTER 13

BLAME THE GERMANS

On November 16, 2011, intrigued Italians awoke to find themselves governed by a caretaker cabinet of highly qualified academics and lawyers, rather than Berlusconi's gang of sycophants, suspects/convicts, dolly birds and right-wing rabble-rousers. There hadn't even been an election. Was it a coup? Sort of. The impetus for this remarkable change was the Euro-debt crisis. But the architect of the transition, which had seen the prime minister's office swap libidinous businessman Berlusconi for Euro-egghead Mario Monti, was the head of state, President Giorgio Napolitano. As the details of events gradually filtered out, Napolitano was shown to be less of a figurehead who simply rubber-stamped legislation and more of a wily and determined power broker.

The foreign press—particularly the US papers—always refers to Napolitano as an "ex-communist," as if this far-left political association forever defines him. America's former chief diplomat Henry Kissinger even labeled Napolitano "my favorite communist," which isn't saying much given that the man who carpet bombed half of Southeast Asia was also pals with Mao Zedong and Leonid Brezhnev.

A closer look at Napolitano's long career, however, reveals a politician with a remarkable ability to adapt to, and even embrace, the prevailing political conditions. When appointed interior minister in Romano Prodi's center-left government in 1996, he was, in theory at least, Italy's first true left-winger to run this key ministry. He showed strangely little interest, though, in shedding light on the backlog of unsolved murders and bomb atrocities from preceding decades, linked to shadowy right-wing paramilitaries. He even assured interior ministry staff he would "not go looking for skeletons."[1] This Machiavellian flexibility meant Berlusconi had no problem backing Napolitano's election as head of state in 2006. Napolitano had given up far-left politics decades earlier, and he was never that far left to begin with.

In style and tone Berlusconi and Napolitano are a universe apart: Berlusconi, the real-estate salesman of politics; Napolitano, all calculated sobriety. They did have something in common, however. Both were on good terms with the disgraced former prime minister Bettino Craxi. Although Berlusconi's links were stronger, from the mid-1980s Napolitano and his allies had also made overtures to the champagne socialist. In January 2010, ten years after Craxi's death in exile, Napolitano joined Berlusconi and the rest of Milan's political establishment in celebrating the corrupt ex–prime minister's life and career.[2]

Although few were in any doubt that Napolitano looked discreetly down his long nose at Berlusconi, the president showed little reluctance in signing off on some of the mogul's most controversial legislation. This included the attempts to make the holders of the four highest state offices (which included the posts of prime minister and president) immune to prosecution, and the subsequent "legitimate impediment" law that allowed ministers to skip court hearings—despite the glaring evidence that these legal ruses were self-serving and unconstitutional.[3] The president was even criticized by his predecessor, Carlo Azeglio Ciampi, for the alacrity with which he'd allowed these laws into the statute book. Napolitano might not have thought much of Berlusconi, but the mogul had been elected head of government, and the head of state preferred not to disrupt the status quo.

But things had changed radically by the summer of 2011. The Eurodebt crisis was escalating fast, and Berlusconi's dead-duck government looked set to drift on perilously, possibly into the spring. It seems at this point Napolitano decided the status quo that needed his discreet support was not Italy's parliamentary democracy but the European Union and its ill-conceived, and increasingly precarious, single currency, the euro.

The Italian president already had something of a reputation as an effective behind-the-scenes player. He was now being flattered and cajoled by the European Commission and the European powers in France and Germany to create a road map for Berlusconi's exit. His first task was choosing a successor to Berlusconi. The obvious candidate was Mario

Monti, who had not been shy about speaking out about Italy's economic and political woes, and the drastic action that was needed to deal with them. Monti had appeared to be putting himself forward for the top job when he penned a series of manifesto-type articles in *Corriere della Sera*, setting out his action plan for the country. Napolitano saw Monti, a former European Commissioner for competition and one of Europe's great and good, as a safe pair of hands. By July he was already sounding Monti out for the top job, according to interviews with Monti, printed by journalist Alan Friedman in his 2014 book *Ammazziamo il Gattopardo (Let's Kill the Leopard)*. Around the same time Napolitano also commissioned prominent banker Corrado Passera to produce an emergency economic program to rescue Italy. Passera came up with 196 pages of tough medicine: €100 billion ($130 billion) of state privatization and tax hikes.[4] In October, with the Euro-debt crisis worsening on a daily basis, German chancellor Angela Merkel was on the phone to Napolitano, Italy's supposedly neutral head of state, seeking his help to "nudge Berlusconi off the stage."[5]

Goaded on by Europe's most powerful figures, Napolitano now had the bit between his teeth. On November 9, in a smart move that simultaneously announced his intentions and rendered them virtually unstoppable, he plucked Monti from his then role as president of Milan's Bocconi business school and made him a senator. With the markets preparing for their final assault on Italy—and with the growing expectation that Monti's appointment as prime minister would be the country's last chance at salvation—Berlusconi agreed on November 8 that he would quit, his decision made inevitable by the final, fateful parliamentary defections. Within a week Napolitano swore in neo–prime minister Mario Monti, who began assembling the unelected cabinet of businessmen and academics who would govern the country for the 18 months until the next general election.

Berlusconi and his supporters were outraged when allegations of Napolitano's possibly unconstitutional machinations emerged. One of Berlusconi's MPs, Melania De Nichilo Rizzoli, said: "We are not a German colony. The European treaties do not allow the interference of one state in the political affairs of another European state." These events also forged Berlusconi's animosity toward Berlin, which continues to this day.

In the final weeks of 2011, having hard-nosed bankers in charge of Italy calmed the markets and averted the immediate crisis. But the complete abrogation of the democratic process left a nasty taste in the mouth.

The 2004 heroics of "Super Mario" Monti, who fined Microsoft a record €497 million ($620 million) during his time as Europe's competition commissioner, were soon forgotten. Instead, left-wing conspiracy theorists looked at Monti's links to Goldman Sachs (the "Vampire Squid" that had been mired in the scandal of the falsification of Greece's public accounts that enabled it to join the euro[6]) and had a field day. But to be fair, most Italians I spoke to simply shrugged their shoulders. What choice had there been? Arrange Berlusconi's exit by fair means or foul—or see the euro and the global economy fall off a cliff? Napolitano sought to play down the extent of his involvement in events and denied he'd acted improperly. But he could probably argue, too, that the end justified the means.

Berlusconi was forced to watch and bide his time. His public attitude to Monti was completely ambivalent. He did little to disguise his anger at having his position usurped by an unelected bureaucrat and at the "suspension of democracy" that this entailed. But he was often complimentary about Monti and his caretaker government, especially at the start—when Monti's poll ratings were enviably high.

Just hours after Monti won the necessary parliamentary confidence votes, Berlusconi said that his unelected successor had got off "to a good start." In fact, Italy's elected politicians on both the left and right pledged their support, even when Monti read them—and Italy—the riot act in his maiden speech. Monti told the Senate that Italy had to accept plans by his "government of national engagement" to slash waste, corruption and privilege—or see its economy fail.

He pledged to overhaul archaic employment laws that offered excessive privileges to regular workers in larger firms, while denying rights to those on temporary contracts. He also promised to "gradually" lower tax rates while cracking down on Italy's ruinous levels of tax evasion, and to consider the reintroduction of Imu, the property tax on first homes, which Berlusconi had abolished. Trimming pensions, fighting organized crime and deregulating professional services were also on the agenda.

It sounded like the right medicine, even if the left might have balked at the idea of introducing flexibility to labor markets, and the right, led by villa-collecting mogul Berlusconi, curled its lip at the notion of new property taxes. But with both wings of parliament clearly incapable of leading Italy out of its mess, they had no choice in the short term but to support the caretaker regime. Italy's parliamentarians might have been overpaid, underachieving and in many cases corrupt, but they weren't stupid. Some difficult and very unpopular decisions on spending cuts, tax hikes and dismantling Italy's ubiquitous vested interests were on the cards, and MPs and senators from left and right were glad to let Monti and his technocrats bear the blame from those hit hardest. It was a bit like an 18-month holiday for Italy's politicians, at least until the later stages of Monti's reign, when the wheels began to fall off. Election time—and a resumption of Italian democracy—saw the old caste begin jockeying for power again.

Very soon Monti's all-out war on tax cheats was making many Italians nervous. One strategy was to probe deeper into people's bank accounts with the authorities' new powerful computer system, Serpico. This sowed seeds of distrust in the minds of many voters. Italians' terror of the tax authorities was demonstrated by the reaction of comic and political activist Beppe Grillo. He described the tax collection office Equitalia as the "terror of every Italian" and said he could understand why an anarchist group had that very day sent it a parcel bomb.[7]

There's no doubt that tax evasion is a huge problem in Italy. *La Repubblica* newspaper quoted finance department data that suggested levels of tax evasion had leaped fivefold in the previous three decades, with the treasury losing €275 billion in 2009 alone. The same month that Grillo made his "terror" comments, an 80-strong squad of tax inspectors raided hotels and restaurants in Cortina to intimidate the chic ski resort's high concentration of hard-up yacht and private jet owners, many of whom claimed to earn less than €20,000 ($25,000) a year.

Berlusconi certainly isn't the only Italian who has hidden huge sums overseas. The tales are legion. As Monti was enjoying his first week in office, finance police nabbed an elderly couple in Venice who'd declared only six euros of income in a decade. A 10-year audit performed on the couple found more than €300 million ($400 million) of undeclared wealth, much of it tucked away in foreign accounts. The same month a truck carrying 13 tons of gold was stopped as it attempted to pass over the border to Switzerland. One banking association in the Italian-speaking canton of Switzerland estimated that the banks in that region alone were harboring €130 billion ($170 billion) of Italian assets, stashed out of reach of Rome's tax authorities.

By boosting tax revenues and cutting spending, including the country's colossal pension bill, Monti's technocrats were able to win ECB's support in propping up Italy's bonds, and thus defy financial Armageddon. But apart from this—admittedly crucial—short-term objective, in retrospect his government's achievements appear slight.

One of Monti's key ministers, Elsa Fornero, who was in charge of employment and welfare, told me that the cabinet's collective political naïveté saw it fail to press home the huge advantage it had enjoyed over Berlusconi and the rest of the political establishment in the first few months.[8] Thus, the powerful castes and cabals, from pharmacists and taxi drivers to lawyers and notaries, who stifle Italy's economy, were left untouched. Labor reforms were limited. In addition, Monti's austerity measures made the recession worse and allowed political opponents—including Silvio Berlusconi—to begin campaigning on a pro-growth, anti-austerity ticket by the end of 2012. In February 2013, by which time Monti was already out of office, Fornero admitted: "After a year of a technical government trying to push the country towards a more virtuous way of public life, we are back to the same situation."[9]

After three years of unrelenting bad news, Berlusconi enjoyed some respite in 2012. By the summer, buoyed by the collapse of some of the tax fraud charges against him and his Fininvest executives, including his eldest son, Pier Silvio Berlusconi, the former prime minister sought to re-engage with national politics. He declared that he'd like to return to government as finance minister in a new center-right administration—though no one doubted he wanted to be anything other than prime minister.

But after swapping the company of his old hawkish advisers for that of pimps and starlets, Berlusconi's political judgment was becoming increasingly erratic. At the beginning of June he called on Italy to consider withdrawing from the euro. "The economic crisis can't be solved. We have to go to Europe and say forcefully that the ECB should start printing money," he wrote. "If it doesn't, we should have the strength to say 'ciao, ciao' and leave the euro." Less than 24 hours later, while Italians were still picking their jaws up off the floor, he dismissed his remarks as a "joke."[10]

But blaming the euro and Germany, Europe's dominant economic power, for forcing austerity on the rest of the continent in order to prop up the failing single currency became Berlusconi's new rallying call. Even his most loyal supporters didn't bother to parrot his communist warnings anymore.

In addition to a fixation with 18-year-old Barbies, the mogul appeared also to have a problem with powerful women, and Germany's redoubtable chancellor Angela Merkel in particular. The previous autumn, with the financial crisis spiraling out of control, he'd used the phrase "unfuckable lardarse" (while on the phone to another of his seedy associates, Valter Lavitola) to describe Merkel, one of the European heavy hitters piling on the political pressure to have him removed from power.[11] Was it a coincidence that the Adonis of Arcore, showing remarkable rudeness by even his own standards, had kept a visibly peeved German leader waiting 15 minutes while yapping on his mobile phone as she stood ready to greet him at a NATO conference in 2009?[12]

Monti's honeymoon period was already history by the summer of 2012, with the public exasperated at spiraling unemployment and deteriorating public services. The softly spoken economist, whose working life had oscillated between bureaucracy and high academia (he was taught at Yale by James Tobin, who has given his name to a proposed transaction tax), was finding, after a tough-talking start, that the reality of governing was much harder than simply writing editorials about it in the newspapers.

Monti now tried to be all things to all men. Flaunting his free-market economic credentials, he told me that he was an admirer of Thatcher, but at the same time insisted he was right behind the euro.[13] With the Italian economy as dead as a dodo, he was soon starting to emphasize the need to boost growth. There was a growing feeling among Europe's more indebted nations that the ECB—and by extension Germany—would have to sanction the use of the Eurozone's weapon of last resort against the markets, namely, its ability to print money. Monti therefore stepped up the pressure on the German chancellor, Angela Merkel, to allow the ECB to be used more aggressively, even if that meant fuelling inflation.

Berlusconi took this as his cue to attack Germany in his own crude and offensive style, in order to build a populist anti-austerity platform from which to fight an election. *Il Giornale*, the Berlusconi family newspaper, led the way, comparing Merkel's Germany to the Third Reich.[14] The piece, signed by the paper's editor, Alessandro Sallusti, went on to describe Merkel as the "new Kaiser" and showed a photo of her waving in what was presumably meant to be seen as—but in fact looked nothing like—a Nazi salute.

The attack came just six weeks after *Il Giornale* targeted Merkel after Italy's victory over Germany in the Euro 2012 football semifinals. Taking a cue from Berlusconi's wiretapped remark a year earlier, it printed a picture of Chancellor Merkel below the headline "*Ciao, ciao culona*" which translates as "Bye-bye lardarse." Berlusconi's populist attacks on Germany and Angela Merkel once again undermined his liberal free-market credentials. He was, after all, railing against efficiency measures demanded by a country that was fed up with bankrolling corrupt and inefficient southern European economies—including Italy.

That's not to say the Germans were blameless in the giant euro-shambles. They agreed to France's idea for a single currency in 1989, and pressed ahead with the politically motivated plan a decade later, although it was obvious that none of the participants (not even Germany) had met membership requirements on debt levels. And once the single European currency was in place, the sudden devaluation of the mighty deutsch mark allowed Germany's export trade to swell to a staggering €1 trillion ($1.3 trillion) a year. But Berlusconi the demagogue knew instinctively that a mix of fear and (mostly) envy meant there were always points to be scored by bashing Berlin, though this didn't stop him from being driven around in an Audi limousine.

Berlusconi might have tried to boost his waning political fortunes with demagogue attacks on Germany and the European Union, but there was no disguising that his political enterprise had never seemed so vapid and self-serving. The mogul's criticism of the Monti government alternated with praise, promises and then threats as he sought to secure passage of new justice legislation that he needed in order to get the magistrates off his back. He had nothing useful to say, however, to Italian voters. His remedies for the country were sound bites, perfunctory cures that he had never introduced to good effect despite being in power three times in the past 20 years.

The former prime minister's standing at home and abroad was at an all-time low after his humiliating expulsion from power, the nation's financial meltdown and the endless tales of sleaze. But a remarkable thing about Berlusconi, apart from his resilience and shamelessness, is the loyalty he generates among his hard-core friends and supporters. Despite everything, even as most people were jumping ship, there were—and there still are—the usual suspects ready to support the unsupportable.

To provide a flavor of the moral metal supporting his political effort it's worth mentioning the spotty legal records of Berlusconi's parliamentary PDL party. Of the 19 people with criminal records who served as parliamentarians during Berlusconi's last period in power (2008 to 2011), 13 were members of the PDL and another three were members of the Northern League, his coalition partner.[15] Many more parliamentarians—again mostly from Berlusconi's center-right—were either under investigation, or on trial or had escaped criminal charges thanks to the statute of limitations. More than ever the Italian parliament resembled a delinquents' social club.

And who says crime doesn't pay? Italian MPs enjoyed the highest salaries in Europe: €140,000 and up, and this doesn't include their enormous expense allowances, for which they were not required to supply receipts.[16] And serving just one term in office—turning up when they felt like it, perhaps dining at the heavily subsidized restaurant or having a trim at one of the subsidized hair salons—was enough to guarantee a generous, bulletproof pension. It's no wonder Italians loathe their lawmakers.

Those MPs and senators with the worst legal records tended to keep their heads down. But there were plenty of others, with empty—rather than stained—résumés, who were ready to defend Berlusconi to the last. While his fascination with women has landed him in so much trouble, Berlusconi could—and still can—count on some key female associates to help him out.

The pro-Berlusconi troops leading his defense on the benches of Montecitorio and in the TV studios even had a nickname—"*Le Amazzoni*" (Amazons). Where Muammar Gaddafi had his female security in red berets, Berlusconi has the over-promoted female politicians in high heels who act as his political bodyguard. In Greek mythology the Amazons cut off one of their breasts so they could use a bow and arrow more effectively. Berlusconi would have considered that a terrible waste, and it hasn't been necessary. The barbs from his Amazons have flown thick and fast anyway.

One leading Amazon, the tall, blonde Michaela Biancofiore, 42, published a book in 2013 in which she revealed her feelings of love for Berlusconi. When magistrates finally claimed his scalp later that year, she was straight in front of the TV cameras, telling the BBC: "The Italian people are in love with Berlusconi because he's an innocent." She even declared she would take up Berlusconi's "persecution" at the hands of Italy's "communist" magistrates with the EU Court of Human Rights.

Most of the Amazons, including the ex–equality minister–cum–topless model Mara Carfagna, owe their jobs to Berlusconi's roving eye. Carfagna thanked him again on his seventy-seventh birthday by comparing him to Einstein; compared to some of those around him, he probably is. The pretty but oddly dyspeptic ex–education minister Mariastella Gelmini, who's a constant pro-Berlusconi fixture on the nation's TV screens, is another Amazon and over-promoted figure in the PDL. Her job in Berlusconi's last government was to boost standards in Italy's moribund universities. She certainly can't claim to have led by example. In Italy, higher failure rates often indicate tougher exams and higher standards, and Gelmini, a lawyer, fled Brescia University, where the failure rate for her bar exam was an intimidating 90 percent, and instead slummed it by taking the test at Reggio Calabria University in the south of the country, where the failure rate was just 10 percent.[17]

But there's little doubt who's Queen of the Amazons. The title belongs to the truly formidable Daniela Santanchè. This political beast tears into opponents of The Boss and takes no prisoners. Armed with a dubious claim to a master's degree from Milan's prestigious (and private) Bocconi business school, Santanchè is always ready to defend the indefensible.[18] Her once attractive but strangely ageless face (she was married to a top plastic surgeon for several years) and nasal Milan accent are a constant fixture on news and talk shows. She appears unfazed when she's losing a political argument, which happens regularly. But when all credibility in her point of view has disappeared, she resorts to catty remarks and a sly half grin appears. She is shameless, and she doesn't care if we know it.

The media tycoon is, of course, a genius in the use and abuse of TV; he employs the attractive faces of Carfagna, Gelmini et al. as a foil to the hoary old mugs of both sexes fielded by the center-left. And, above all, Italy is a country where tribal loyalties count. A gang led by someone as rich and influential as Berlusconi, who runs his political party like he runs his AC Milan football club, is, for those without shame, the gang to be in. He built and funded the morally tottering edifice on which they are all perched. They are part of Berlusconi's gang and they'll defend him, and the benefits they get from him, come what may.

The interests of your tribe or your family, rather than the rule of law or civic decency, are paramount. Santanchè articulated the prevailing philosophy a few years ago when it emerged that she'd pulled strings to get her poorly qualified 25-year-old niece a lucrative job with the Lombardy regional government. She didn't deny it but merely said, "that's what everyone else does"—the *Così fan tutte* defense used by Berlusconi's corrupt mentor Bettino Craxi when he was found with his paw in the till, before fleeing the country.

When I first came to Italy, my young and middle-class friend Elena told me about the mafia. "It's not dodgy men in dark glasses and suits hanging around Palermo," she said. "It's the old lady who goes straight to the front of the queue when she goes to the post office because she knows the person who works behind the counter." Bending the rules and benefitting from friendships, acquaintances and associations is endemic in Italy in a way that many Anglo-Saxons probably can't imagine. Rackets are everywhere you look.

The conservative American historian Francis Fukuyama, in his 2011 book *The Origins of Political Order*, talks about the tension in democratic society between the state and its rules and regulations and the fair playing field they provide on the one hand, and, on the other hand, the primordial forces of "tribalism" or "patrimonialism." Fukuyama argued that in the US, the far-right Tea Party loons and neo-cons, by constantly denigrating the state and its institutions, risked taking the country back in time to a savage free-for-all—to a system of patrimonialism that is unfair, undemocratic and economically damaging.

Italy, with its all-pervasive partisanship and cronyism—with family, friends and tribe doing everything in their power to keep their grubby grip on social and financial advantage—serves as a good example of what happens when the state is weak and its institutions are not respected. Patrimonialism is the last thing you want for a thriving, liberal economy. Sclerotic, low-growth, debt-mired Italy is a cautionary tale.

Patrimonialism exists, never far from the surface, like an alternative system of power and governance; cronyism and castes abound. There is the media elite: if you want a good job in a leading national newspaper you'd better know someone or have the right surname; if you want to get elected in some parts of the far south, you'll certainly need an accommodating attitude toward the local mafia clans. If you're after that senior lecturing job at a university, it would help your chances immeasurably if you're a close relative of one of the professors there. The astonishing levels of nepotism in Italy's universities explain their lowly academic standards and dismal world rankings. Roberto Perotti, a professor of economics at the private Bocconi University in Milan and the author of *L'Università Truccata* (*The Rigged University*), told me: "Of course the nepotism is connected to the lower university standards. If a professor at Stanford gave a teaching job to his wife, there would be an outcry. But then in the top [US] universities, people are there on merit."[19]

The worst expression of patrimonialism in Italy is, of course, the mafia itself. In many parts of the south, the state has been replaced by the clans of Cosa Nostra, Camorra and 'ndrangheta. But not far behind the mob in this regard is Berlusconi. His business interests, runaway libido and legal battles—and the friendships and loyalties he needs to sustain them—have replaced the usual function of government: that is, to act in the best interests of the nation. That's not to say patrimonialism wasn't evident in Italy before Berlusconi. But he exploited Italians' adherence to the creed and took its grip on the country to a whole new level. *The Economist* once described Berlusconi as the man "who screwed an entire country." But in reality he simply—and very skillfully—exploited ambivalence toward the rule of law that was already there, as was observed in an article for *The American*.[20] To most Italians Berlusconi is a self-serving crook. For the lucky few, the gift-bearing mogul is Santa Claus.

The Berlusconi aide whose job it has been to deliver the goodies, at least to the mogul's associates lower down the food chain, is his trusty accountant and paymaster general Giuseppe Spinelli. This was the man who dispensed €3,000 bundles of cash in brown envelopes to the call girls and starlets who attended those "elegant" Arcore dinners.

On October 15, 2012, it had been just another day for 71-year-old Spinelli—until he got home and found a gang of low-grade gangsters waiting on his doorstep. The hooded thugs bundled him inside and kept him hostage while he called The Boss and conveyed their demands for a €35 million ransom.[21] The ordeal suffered by Spinelli only came to light a month later when police arrested six suspects: three Albanians and three Italians. The ringleader was named as Francesco Leone, a 51-year-old convicted criminal with links to the Sacra Corona Unita—the mafia group based in the southern Puglia region of Italy. Spinelli said the masked men had ordered him to tell Berlusconi they had documents that they said could extricate his Fininvest holding company from the huge €560 million compensation payment it owed his old enemy De Benedetti for the corrupt takeover of Mondadori back in 1992 (the incident that saw Cesare Previti convicted and jailed).

But within hours of recounting Spinelli's version of events, the Italian press began to ponder the stranger aspects of the case. It was unclear why Spinelli waited 36 hours after his captors had left before calling the police, or why he was then whisked away by Berlusconi's personal bodyguards. Niccolò Ghedini, Berlusconi's lawyer, said he was confident the documents brandished by the bandits were false: "We never saw them, but judging from what they were claiming, I would say we're talking about a complete bluff," he said.

But who was really bluffing? Rumors abounded. The political gossip site *Dagospia* suggested that shady characters in the demimonde of Bari, the capital of the Puglia region, who had supplied prostitutes for the mogul's parties, had acquired an embarrassing video of Berlusconi's nocturnal activities. Could the bandits have gotten hold of a copy?

There may have been a more prosaic explanation for the bizarre episode. Some of the bunga bunga performers even suggested afterward that the "kidnapping" had been staged to get the increasingly greedy and persistent Arcore guests off Berlusconi's back and away from Spinelli, his cash dispenser: after the high-profile abduction, Berlusconi would be able to justify keeping his paymaster off-limits to everyone. This theory isn't without holes, either. Perhaps we'll never know what really happened. But this one murky incident was enough to remind us that Italy had had as its prime minister someone from whom you wouldn't want to buy a secondhand car.

By neglecting his real duties as prime minister during his three periods in office, Berlusconi left Italy to economically stagnate, morally decay and, in some cases, physically fall apart. The trash-TV mogul's criminally negligent policy on the Italian arts and the country's incomparable cultural patrimony—i.e., let it rot—is all too apparent. Some have argued that Berlusconi is not simply indifferent, but actually repelled by the notion of spending state money on culture—in contrast to his willingness to introduce tax breaks that benefit his TV empire. The lack of state financial support for culture and art seems perverse, given that Italy's incomparable cultural patrimony is a cornerstone of the country's multibillion-dollar tourism industry. France, which has rather less to preserve and restore, spends 1 percent of its GDP on culture compared with just 0.2 percent in Italy.

Italy is feeling the effects of this neglect—and of corruption and bad management at every level—to the present day, whether it's Rome's reliance on a handout from upmarket jeweler Bulgari to pay for the restoration of the city's iconic Spanish Steps, or the dismal news last summer that a masterpiece by Raphael in a famous museum had warped because the air-conditioning had been on the blink for six months.[22]

Back in July 2008, the Berlusconi government declared a state of emergency at Pompeii, perhaps the world's greatest archaeological site, which was reclaimed over decades from the volcanic ash of Mount Vesuvius. The archaeological treasure was slowly disappearing before our eyes again. But declaring that Pompeii was falling to bits from neglect was not the same as actually doing something about it, and this unique piece of cultural patrimony continued disintegrating—prompting world condemnation two years later when the ancient city's House of the Gladiators crumbled to the ground after insufficient drainage saw tons of rainwater collect on the 2,000-year-old structure. The master of Coca-Cola TV didn't much care. And neither, then, did his minions.

If France owned these priceless monuments, would it allow walls to collapse at Pompeii or chunks to fall off the Colosseum? Not likely. But any French president you care to name probably wouldn't have snubbed opening night at La Scala as Berlusconi did in 2009—an incident that highlights why the art form that Italy invented was being allowed to wither away. Many critics feel that three decades of trash TV from Berlusconi's Mediaset empire has dumbed down Italy, the birthplace of Puccini and Verdi, and made opera seem less mainstream and less relevant than ever. There isn't a quick buck to be made out of this elaborate art form, no TV advertising, and its female participants are probably choosier about whom they sleep with.

La Prima—or opening night—at La Scala opera house in Milan is the most glittering event in Italy's social calendar. On December 7, 2009, the great and the good, and anyone lucky enough to get a ticket, were there in black tie. But Berlusconi had a prior engagement. It wasn't a pressing matter of state, or even a bunga bunga party. He popped into a cinema multiplex outside Milan, where he took in the FX-laden disaster movie *2012*, in which the human race—Italian politicians included—is threatened by giant solar flares.

At 9:30 p.m., as Italian and foreign dignitaries were thrilling to the Georgian mezzo-soprano Anita Rachvelishvili's take on Bizet, Berlusconi was at the Warner Village Cinema 12 miles away, squeezing into a central row in theater number 10 with his daughter Eleonora, whispering "sorry to bother you" to cinemagoers.[23]

At the point in the story in which the disaster movie's plucky Italian prime minister is seen waiting for the inevitable end in the Vatican's St. Peter's Square, cheers erupted from the cinema audience. It wasn't clear if the applause was meant for the fictional premier or his real-life counterpart. But Berlusconi was in no doubt, and, at roughly the same time Rachvelishvili stood for her 14-minute ovation at La Scala, the mogul rose and took a bow of his own. The embattled prime minister might even have made the trip to the cinema in search of an ego boost, following reports the previous week that cinemagoers had cheered "Silvio, Silvio!" during his fictional alter ego's demise.[24]

Back in the real world three years later, at the close of 2012, the ego boost Berlusconi sought was to be elected prime minister again. He knew that in the next few months he'd have his chance. Deep down, he probably knew, too, that it would be his final bid for power—and that failure to win would leave him fatally exposed to a past that was inexorably catching up to him.

CHAPTER 14

DEMAGOGUES

Prime Minister Monti announced on December 9, 2012, that he'd shortly be stepping down, little more than a year after he succeeded Berlusconi. The sober economist had saved Italy from the worst of the Euro-debt crisis. However, Berlusconi's center-right PDL party was ending its parliamentary cooperation, and Monti's mandate was due to run out by the spring, so the stopgap prime minister decided not to wait till the bitter end. With Berlusconi chomping at the bit to get back into Palazzo Chigi, though, on the money markets the investors' panic attacks returned.

The next day, within hours of opening, Milan's stock exchange had fallen nearly 4 percent and the interest investors charged on Italian bonds shot up as markets digested the implications of Monti's imminent departure. *Lo spread*, the term describing the gap between German and Italian state borrowing costs, had entered the Italian language the year before. And, once again, it was the subject of every news bulletin and newspaper front page.

Various rumors were doing the rounds in Rome. According to some, Monti would launch a new centrist political party in order to continue the reforms he'd started. Others predicted Monti would accept a high-profile job—perhaps finance minister in a center-left government of the Democratic Party. What wasn't in doubt, however, was that the markets' bogeyman, Berlusconi, was marshaling the troops again, more determined than ever to get back into power and use high office to protect himself from the courts. All the signs were there—including numerous meetings with his erstwhile allies/tormentors, the Northern League.

A front-page editorial in the *Corriere della Sera* newspaper fretted that the relative calm brought by Monti had lasted just 13 months, and the battle between pro- and anti-Berlusconi forces was set to resume. "The war continues," the newspaper said. "The world looks at us, incredulous." Or perhaps not. By now, Italy was seen by many as such a basket case that the return of Berlusconi, or at least Berlusconi without his head chopped off and a stake through his heart, had an air of inevitability about it. The deadly serious Germans huffed and puffed a bit. Their newspapers veered between outrage and sarcasm—which rarely hit the mark, reminding us they are better at building washing machines than cracking jokes. But in Britain and much of Europe, no one seemed that surprised.

But by now things had changed. By careering off the rails with his alarming impression of Emperor Nero—or Tiberius, or maybe Caligula (take your pick)—Berlusconi had repelled the powerful Catholic Church, to the extent that it had finally excommunicated him, politically speaking. Millions of pious center-right voters were lost. According to papal biographer and Vatican expert Marco Politi, "Berlusconi's antics had finally repulsed many true Catholic voters, who decided to turn to Monti or even Bersani's Democratic Party, instead."[1]

By the start of 2013, with the Vatican-friendly Monti set to form his own small "Civic Choice" party, the cardinals and bishops were now able to direct votes to center-right, socially conservative candidates, without tacitly endorsing bunga bunga or tartocracy. By the end of the year, Monti's party would be joined by another new group, the New Center-right, a refugee camp for rebels fleeing Berlusconi's sinking PDL. It was led by Berlusconi's former protégé Angelino Alfano, the worm that turned.

The partnership between Berlusconi and the Catholic Church had been long and fruitful: an unholy alliance, if you like, between the sanctimonious powers in Vatican City and the cynical, over-sexed megalomaniac. Until the sex scandals really exploded from 2009 to 2010, Berlusconi's center-right received Catholic votes in exchange for his support in upholding what popes John Paul II and Benedict XVI considered the "non-negotiable principles"—money for Catholic schools and opposition to abortion, living wills and civil unions (for hetero- and homosexual couples).

The cynical nature of Berlusconi's relations with the Church was demonstrated by his truly disgraceful behavior in the Eluana Englaro case.

In February 2009 at the behest of senior figures in the Vatican, Prime Minister Berlusconi issued an emergency decree that forbade hospitals from withholding food and water from patients in a permanent vegetative state whom doctors and relatives had agreed should be allowed to die.[2] Berlusconi's sudden interest in end-of-life issues was prompted by the tragic drama of 38-year-old Eluana Englaro, who had been left brain-dead after a car accident 17 years before, in 1992. After a decade-long court battle, doctors were finally reducing her nutrition and giving her sedatives in preparation for removing her feeding tubes, in accordance with the wishes of her father and consultant physicians—and with the permission of the Supreme Court.

The Vatican, fearing Italy was moving toward legalized euthanasia, took an increasingly vocal interest as the publicity around the case grew. The Vatican's spokesman on health issues, Cardinal Javier Lozano Barragán, said removal of feeding tubes amounted to "monstrous and inhuman murder." *L'Avvenire,* the daily newspaper of the Italian Bishops Conference, accused Italy's highest court of "necrophilia." The anesthetist caring for her, Professor Antonio de Monte, replied: "I'm not an executioner. Eluana died 17 years ago." She had suffered massive brain damage when the car she'd been driving skidded off an icy road and hit a lamppost.[3]

However, after a series of frantic phone calls from the Vatican's lumbering and reactionary number two, Tarcisio Bertone, Berlusconi suddenly acted on his political commitments to the Holy See. On issuing the emergency decree, Berlusconi declared: "This [removing feeding tubes] is murder. I would be failing to rescue her. I'm not a Pontius Pilate." And, with his trademark crassness, he added that this brain-dead woman was, physically at least, "in the condition to have babies."

Eluana's father, Beppe Englaro, said that after the long and agonizing fight to allow his daughter to die, Berlusconi's last-minute intervention on behalf of the Vatican felt like "a grotesque attack on my family." When I met Englaro he told me that, a year and a day before her own accident, a friend of Eluana crashed his motorcycle, suffering serious brain damage. In great distress, Eluana told her father: "If something like that ever happened to me, you have to do something. If I can't be what I am now, I'd prefer to be left to die. I don't want to be resuscitated and left in a condition like that."[4]

Beppe Englaro said that when he looked at his daughter, who had been forced to age lifelessly in a hospital bed for nearly two decades, he saw a "person who has suffered the worst sort of violation that anyone could ever suffer." Where angels feared to tread Berlusconi barged in, trampling over a family that was already in pieces, to promote a controversial cause that previously he'd never appeared to give two hoots about.

Even hospitals that had refused to host Eluana while her feeding tubes were stopped on account of the government's threats were unable to conceal their true sympathies. Giuseppe Galanzino, director of Turin's Molinette hospital, said: "If I was Eluana's father, I'd have died from a broken heart by now." Some of Berlusconi's political allies, including the then Speaker of the lower house of parliament, Gianfranco Fini, said that the Supreme Court ruling allowing Eluana to die should be obeyed. President Napolitano refused to sign Berlusconi's decree, raising the prospect of a constitutional crisis: In the end, the time bought by Beppe Englaro's decision to choose a private clinic—which was to some extent out of the government's clutches—was sufficient for the coma victim to finally pass away in peace: the conflict between state institutions was avoided. But Berlusconi had shown himself willing, and had fulfilled his obligations to the medieval moralists in the Vatican.

Leaving aside his predictable penchant for a little light lipstick-lesbian action, the mogul's attitude to homosexuals also highlights his lip service to the Church. Berlusconi's refusal to do anything to bring Italy in line with the rest of the Western world—and for that matter, South Africa, Brazil and Mexico—in terms of gay equality doesn't mean that he's particularly homophobic. He makes the occasional lame joke—"better to like pretty girls than be gay"—when he wants to deflect charges that he's a dirty old man. But he has lots of gay friends—Lele Mora, the seedy impresario who supplied girls to his "elegant dinners," is one example. Berlusconi is rude and politically incorrect, certainly. But how could such a committed libertine be morally squeamish? There are worse bigots in the centrist Catholic wing of Italian politics, the pious remnants of the Christian Democrats, and even many on the center-left, who happily vote against legislation to deter homophobic violence. These people probably think gays are asking for it. Berlusconi probably doesn't care.

The mogul's split with the Church meant he no longer had enough supporters to win the 2013 general election outright. But we knew he'd have a good go at it anyway.

Before the February election was called, Berlusconi's PDL was languishing at 18 percent in the polls. By the start of February it had shot up to 28 percent, and Europe held its breath. If the mogul knew anything, it was how to run a general election campaign. With three weeks to go before the big day, Silvio Berlusconi resorted to buying voters by promising a cash refund on a tax introduced by outgoing premier Mario Monti. He declared he would scrap the unpopular property tax on first homes and phase out a separate business tax within five years. Payments of the IMU property tax already made would be returned in the post. The plan would cost the economy €4 billion ($5 billion). Berlusconi made some vague remarks about this being recouped by cuts in public spending.

The savvy politician even ensured that the signing of star striker Mario Balotelli for his AC Milan club occurred just at the right time to chime with voters who liked football. And there was a blitz of TV appearances. He knew that the center-left Democratic Party was still favored to win, so he took a giant gamble by appearing in person on *Servizio Pubblico*, the political talk show on the small, independent La7 national channel. The program was hosted by the leftist journalist Michele Santoro, a bruiser who likes the sound of his own voice almost as much as Berlusconi.

During the previous five years, Santoro had led the TV inquisition into Berlusconi's scandals. The TV host, whom Berlusconi had had kicked off Rai in 2002 (along with two other key critics, Enzo Biagi and Daniele Luttazzi), accusing him of a "criminal use of television," had again been accused of bias against the mogul.[5] Berlusconi was aware of this, and that the program's editors were determined to be seen to be as even-handed as possible. The mogul took advantage of this desire to avoid even a hint of bias, and ran rings around everyone.

He began solemnly, saying that were it up to him, he would by now have left politics to establish children's hospitals around the world and open universities. The mogul's "important friends"—Bush (dunce), Clinton (liar), Putin (tyrant) and Chirac (crook)[6]—would supposedly teach young people (goodness knows what) at these institutes of higher learning. But, the mogul sighed, he felt obliged to run for high office again to save Italy from the sorry state it found itself in.

When the questioning got tougher, and interrogators began reminding him of his own complicity in Italy's woes, he starting clowning and broke a pre-program agreement regarding personal attacks on his interrogators. At one point, Marco Travaglio, his most vociferous and persistent media critic, reminded the audience of Berlusconi's "Latin-lover" reputation and the scores of young women he'd had carted into Palazzo Grazioli. In response to this, Berlusconi beamed proudly, and, to audience giggles, took a bow. Santoro lost control of the program. It was a crass, cheap but knowing performance from Berlusconi, and one that probably appealed to his natural supporters and provided another boost in the polls.

Berlusconi won some votes by resuming his populist attacks on Germany and the euro. However, for the first time in a general election, he faced a rival who did populism even better than he did. If Berlusconi peddled non-politics, Beppe Grillo sold a powerful brand of anti-politics.

The incredible rise of Grillo and his nationwide movement of political ingénues reflected a level of disgust with politics and politicians that is hard to imagine if you haven't lived in Italy. Grillo was a popular stand-up comic in the 1970s and '80s. Friends, even those who have little time for him now, tell me how brilliantly and bitingly funny he was. By the 1990s, his routines had assumed an increasingly political edge. Italians, heartily sick of their elected officials, reveled in his lacerating and often profane attacks on Italy's castes and, in particular, its venal politicians, on the left and right. When Grillo started a blog, it soon gained hundreds of thousands of readers and, based on its success, the Five Star Movement (M5S) was born. Grillo launched the online protest group with help from Gianroberto Casaleggio, a frizzy-haired IT expert with John Lennon specs. The movement's "five stars" referred to the five key issues it campaigned on: water (which should not be privatized), the environment, transport, internet access and development.

Because it was an online phenomenon, ordinary people could get involved, and Grillo's blog posts routinely attracted thousands of responses. He continued to use his skills as a stand-up comic to good effect while relentlessly touring the country. At barnstorming rallies he attacked not only politicians but also other castes—journalists (M5S representatives initially eschewed TV appearances), the European Union and bankers. When the movement's internet guru Casaleggio declared that the M5S was pioneering "a new, direct democracy that will see the elimination of all barriers between the citizen and the state," some of the political establishment sniggered.[7] Others predicted that Grillo's political movement would endure only as long as the Euro-debt crisis and Monti's unpopular austerity measures that had been implemented to tackle it.

Berlusconi resorted to rude personal attacks (as opposed to Grillo's rude but very funny personal attacks). "You know why Grillo won't appear on the television?" said the mogul. "It's because his face is too ugly." That remark caused some sniggers, but only because an increasingly puffy and pancaked Berlusconi was starting to resemble a mandarin that had been left in the bowl too long.

Berlusconi and Grillo had some things in common—demagogue tendencies, a dictatorial control over their own parties and legal problems. Grillo was not able to stand for parliament himself due to a 1980 conviction for involuntary manslaughter: a car he'd been driving skidded off an icy road into a ravine, killing three passengers. The M5S appeared confident that it didn't need to have its leader in parliament.

The establishment got the shock of its life when general election results came in on February 25. The M5S had risen from nothing to grab 25 percent of the vote, making this bunch of protesting citizens the biggest single party in terms of the popular vote. This electoral smash-and-grab had effectively ruined the center-left's chances of gaining the majorities in both houses of parliament, which it needed to govern.

Not for the first time, Berlusconi did better than expected. His coalition of right-wing parties came within a whisker of actually being the biggest group in the lower chamber—the criterion that decides who has won an election. The exit polls, which had predicted comfortable victories for the center-left in both chambers, were completely wrong, underestimating the true degree of support for Berlusconi by a scarcely credible degree. The explanation was simple enough. Some people were ashamed to admit they were voting for Berlusconi, but they put an "X" next to his name, anyway. When it comes down to it, an Italian's tax bill takes precedence over national pride in a country that exists more in name than in nature. The exit polls also seriously underestimated Grillo's support; it appeared that some people also felt embarrassed to admit they voted for a party dismissed by establishment figures as an ephemeral rabble.

Under Italy's electoral system, which Berlusconi had tinkered with in 2005 (in an unsuccessful attempt to retain power in 2006), the biggest single grouping was automatically assigned 54 percent of the seats, even if it had not won a majority of the votes. Even Roberto Calderoli, the Berlusconi ally who designed this system, referred to it as the *porcellum*—a pigsty or dog's dinner.

The upshot this time was that the coalition of center-left parties had officially won and was given a bonus number of seats to ensure its majority in the lower house—the Chamber of Deputies. But because it had failed to win a majority in the Senate, it needed the support of another party. Monti's coalition was willing, but too small, to make up the difference. For the amiable but uninspiring center-left leader Pierluigi Bersani, doing a deal with Berlusconi was out of the question, so he turned his attention to M5S.

The protest party had enough senators to prop up a Bersani government, but it steadfastly refused to have anything to do with either of the establishment groupings. Grillo called the increasingly haggard Bersani, the man who'd lost yet another election for the center-left, "a dead man talking." Nonetheless, as the "winner" of the election (his center-left had the most seats in the lower house), Bersani frantically tried to coax the M5S into a deal. He even presented an eight-point plan of reforms in tune with key issues that the M5S had campaigned on, including more growth, less austerity; more social support for the poor; slashing the number and salaries of MPs and fighting corruption and conflicts of interest. "He can insult me all he likes. But now it's up to him to choose," said Bersani. Grillo told Bersani where to stick it.

So with the ever-present threat of a return of financial meltdown, Italy was left with a hung parliament—and, of course, having no stable government just made the markets more jittery. But not only that. President Napolitano's seven-year tenure as head of state and *de facto* referee was due to expire in May. And finally, in a symbolic touch, even the Pope quit in March that year.

Although it couldn't influence events at the Vatican, Italy's shambolic parliament assembled in an attempt to elect a replacement for Napolitano: it would have to be a respected authority figure, someone acceptable to the left and right. After weeks of bickering and inconsequential votes, the parliament failed in even this task. The center-left, in particular, showed itself to be a pathetic, squabbling rabble, as decades-old rivalries prevented it from agreeing on a single candidate.

It was time for Berlusconi to step in. Putting on his humble, beseeching face, he attempted to show that he cared principally about the nation's interests, and led calls for Napolitano to stand again. Technically, this wasn't allowed. A president of the republic can hold office for only one seven-year term. But this being Italy, and as no other names were suggested, the rules flew out the window. Napolitano protested, but not enough. And after several more cries of "twist my arm," King Giorgio, as the press began to refer to him, told his aides at the Quirinale Palace to stop packing.

But Italy still needed a government. So, incredibly, Napolitano chose the prime minister for this advanced Western democracy for the second time in 18 months. Enrico Letta, the new head of government, was a young, urbane and EU-friendly moderate from the center-left Democratic Party. He concocted a left-center-right Frankenstein's monster of a coalition, which tried to keep all of the parliament's factions happy, and which hardly achieved anything. By December, the economy had fallen by another 2 percent and public debt rose to 133 percent of GDP.[8]

The crumbling economy and dwindling market confidence weren't helped in the summer of 2013 when Berlusconi loyalists threatened to withdraw support from the Letta government unless he agreed to help Berlusconi out of his legal difficulties. To his credit, Letta refused outright.[9] At this point, any government was better than no government: pundits across the political spectrum agreed the collapse of Letta's stopgap coalition, feeble though the government was, would prove disastrous with the economy on a knife-edge. The attempt at political blackmail showed once again how Berlusconi and his cronies were happy to put their interests before those of the economically hamstrung nation.

It wouldn't be fair to say that the Letta government achieved nothing at all; it certainly gained some notoriety when Berlusconi's top ally in the cross-party Letta coalition government was accused of ordering an "extraordinary rendition" to help Kazakhstan's dictator, and Berlusconi's friend, President Nursultan Nazarbayev.

On May 29, 2013, the wife and six-year-old daughter of leading Kazakh dissident Mukhtar Ablyazov were arrested and deported on the orders of Rome's interior ministry, headed by Angelino Alfano. Alfano was also a senior member of Berlusconi's PDL party, and widely seen as the former premier's proxy in the cross-party coalition. This was the same Alfano who had, as justice minister in previous Berlusconi administrations, twice attempted to introduce immunity laws to shield the media mogul from prosecution—laws that were subsequently struck down as unconstitutional by the courts.

It was apparently under Alfano's direction that, incredibly, about 40 heavily armed police stormed a house in Rome to snatch Alma Shalabayeva and her young daughter. She was erroneously accused of possessing false documents and then whisked out of the country in a private jet, accompanied by a Kazakh official, before her lawyers had a chance to intervene.[10]

Within days, a court in Rome ruled her documents were in order and questioned the validity and speed of the deportation. Opposition politicians and newspapers accused Alfano of delivering the wife and child of Ablyazov to Kazakhstan at the behest of Berlusconi, who had described the Kazakh president as "a dear friend." Alfano denied this, and a senior civil servant soon fell on his sword. But within hours of quitting, the official, Giuseppe Procaccini, appeared to undermine Alfano's claims of innocence, saying, "Alfano told me to receive the Kazakh ambassador at the Interior Ministry and that it was a delicate issue."[11] Astonishingly, it later emerged that the Kazakh ambassador to Rome supervised the capture and arrest of Shalabayeva and her daughter from a command center in the Italian Interior Ministry. When events came to light, Letta ordered an internal inquiry. The embattled makeshift prime minister, who was trying to keep the wheels on a lumbering coalition and drag Italy from the abyss of endless recession, said the scandal had "embarrassed and discredited" the country. Parliamentarians demanded to know how and why this happened.

But Italy's parliament should have been equally concerned with what was happening closer to home. It appears that even that most august of parliamentary bodies, the cross-party Anti-mafia commission, the legislature's key watchdog on organized crime, which ought to be whiter than white, isn't beyond suspicion. At the end of 2013, Anti-mafia commission member Laura Garavini, a respected campaigner against organized crime, told me she was concerned about the backgrounds of at least two fellow commission members from Berlusconi's PDL party.

One member, Senator Claudio Fazzone, had been embroiled in controversy in 2008 when, as the PDL chief for the province of Latina, he battled to prevent the town council of Fondi from being dissolved, although investigators had found clear evidence the council had been infiltrated by the 'ndrangheta mafia group. Fazzone received support in his campaign to spare the Fondi town council from the Berlusconi government.

Garavini was not the only person to have reservations about a second commission member. In October 2013 jaws dropped in some quarters when Berlusconi's PDL party renominated the lawyer Carlo Sarro for a place on the commission. Sarro had acquired a dubious parliamentary record, having supported an amnesty on abusive building construction, typically favored by the Campania and Naples-based mob, the Camorra.[12] Another MP, Arturo Scotto, regional secretary for the environmentally orientated SEL party in Campania, issued a press release saying: "We read with incredulity the nomination of Carlo Sarro for the Anti-mafia Commission."[13] Suspicions over Sarro had been further raised because he was seen as close to Nicola Cosentino, Berlusconi's former junior finance minister, who was arrested in April 2014 on suspicion of extortion and mafia-related offenses. Back in 2009, during a previous stint on the commission, Sarro had wasted no time in weighing in to defend the suspected camorrista Cosentino and attacking the "manipulations and inventions" of the magistrates seeking to prosecute him.[14]

The story of Cosentino is itself a stain on the Italian parliament. Two years before his eventual arrest, magistrates had sought to take Cosentino into custody on suspicion of collusion with the Naples mafia. Proceedings against the MP and former Berlusconi minister were put on hold, however, when a majority of MPs—principally the center-right, but not only—voted to prevent magistrates from making the arrest. Prosecutors claimed Cosentino was the "national reference point" for the Casalesi clan of the Camorra, which has extensive interests in northern Italy, and even northern Europe, Australia and Canada. And, last year, the Supreme Court judges concurred.[15]

Leading mafia writer Roberto Saviano, who penned the book *Gomorra* and contributed to the hit film that it spawned, spoke for many when he condemned the *omertà*, or code of silence, invoked by the Italian parliament. In his open letter in *La Repubblica* he accused Cosentino, who was at that stage a PDL co-coordinator for Campania (the region of which Naples is the capital), of having been at the heart of a corrupt system that bought votes with favors and "destroyed a whole territory."[16] He was referring to the Camorra's lucrative trade in the illegal disposal of trash and toxic waste that has poisoned huge swathes of land north of Naples and seen dioxins taint the region's prized mozzarella cheese.

In December 2012, Saviano had warned that Berlusconi's decision to run for premier again was "disastrous news" for the fight against the mafia. He claimed that the ability of political parties to purchase votes "for €20 each" was a factor in the mogul's decision.[17]

When Berlusconi crows that his administrations have been tough on organized crime—by confiscating the wealth of jailed bosses and sending the troops into northern Naples every so often in attention-grabbing stunts—it's worth looking behind the headlines. Then you see not only dubious cronyism, but also an ambiguous attitude toward the mob, one made worse by the collateral damage from Berlusconi's self-serving law changes. Mobsters the length and breadth of Italy must have thought Christmas had come early back in September 2001, for example, when the Berlusconi government abolished the crime of false accounting, thereby closing one of the main avenues used by magistrates to attack mafia bosses.

Berlusconi himself denies any connections to the mob. And as we've seen, the statute of limitations precludes prosecutions against him for mafia association. But, by the start of 2013, his troubles were nonetheless escalating rapidly. The unlikely trio of Napolitano, Monti and Grillo had already toppled Berlusconi and kept him from power. Now two other enemies were preparing to attack. Milan's magistrates were homing in on a criminal conviction. But, before that, there was his estranged—and formidable—wife, Veronica Lario, to deal with. And in negotiations with someone who knew where the bodies were buried, the mogul had to be very careful indeed—no matter how demanding she was, or how much money she asked for.

CHAPTER 15

THE DEVIL'S ADVOCATES

By 2013, Berlusconi's reputation as the shadiest leader in the Western world was aided and abetted by his status as the Patron Saint of Italian Defense Attorneys: his career legal bill had topped the $250 million mark.[1] No doubt his lawyers say they're worth it. In February 2012, Berlusconi had finally cast away one of the millstones around his neck by escaping the David Mills bribery case, in which he was accused of paying the British lawyer $600,000 to lie under oath about his overseas slush funds. Thanks to all the legal maneuvers and holdups, the case expired under the statute of limitations, which Berlusconi had reduced from 15 to 10 years in 2005, with help from lawyer friends he'd shoved into politics.

One of the lawyers making hay was Piero Longo. After a judge announced that the Mills bribery charges had timed out, Longo solemnly told TV crews outside the court that Berlusconi and his defense were disappointed that the case had not continued, in order to allow a complete acquittal. Marco Travaglio, Berlusconi's journalistic *bête noire*, made the opposing argument—that the Teflon Don had slipped away again. "This is the sixth time the statute of limitations has stopped a trial involving Berlusconi. Anywhere else in the world the clock is stopped on the statute of limitations when the trial starts, but here it keeps on going," he said.[2] As he left the courtroom, peeved prosecutor Fabio De Pasquale said it was "useless to comment." But De Pasquale, the tortoise to Berlusconi's hare, wasn't done yet.

And the tycoon was fighting another very costly legal battle, but one that wasn't going so well: Berlusconi's alimony contest with his estranged wife, Veronica Lario. In the autumn of 2013, a court in Milan ordered a stunned Berlusconi to pay Lario €3 million ($4 million) a month. She also got to keep the $100 million Villa di Macherio, in which she had grown accustomed to a rather rarefied existence. According to one of my colleagues, the occasional photo obtained by the media shows Lario and her three children "living the sort of gracious life that Marie Antoinette must have enjoyed before everything went pear-shaped: frolicking in long skirts with goats and horses, listening solemnly while daughter Barbara tinkles on the white Steinway."[3]

Of all the key players in Berlusconi's life, Lario is probably the least typical, and the least understood. The former actress, from a middle-class family in the well-to-do left-wing stronghold of Bologna, has remained largely silent about her relationship with Berlusconi over the years, although some intriguing details have slipped out: for example, this media magnate's wife has not allowed their three children to watch television. She once noted: "From the 1980s onwards [the period in which her husband's broadcasts had sent Italian TV slithering downmarket], the television produced programs continually less appropriate for children."[4] She even quoted liberal philosopher Karl Popper on the subject: "He who makes television should be well aware of things to avoid in order to ensure the activity does not have anti-educative consequences." These comments seem to beg the question, once again, what did Veronica Lario see in Silvio Berlusconi (apart from, possibly, his generosity)?

Only when the worst of Berlusconi's sexual excesses hit the headlines in 2009 did she finally deliver her broadside in the press. But just five years earlier, back in 2004, she described herself as the "perfect wife" for the mogul, because she wasn't perturbed by his constant absences due to business or politics. She added that it was "pointless" trying to see their relationship in traditional terms.[5]

These days, there's no doubt, though, that the gloves are truly off. In May 2014, Berlusconi's trashy gossip sheet *Chi* ran a series of deliberately unflattering photos of the then 57-year-old former actress looking, well, 57 years old—a cardinal sin for the fairer sex in the land of fake lips and face-lifts. The article went on to note that she had put on weight, and the rag helpfully consulted "experts" on what kind of plastic surgery might help her combat the ageing process.

A week later, Lario hit back in a newspaper interview and once again highlighted her peculiar status as both one of the most important intimates in the life of Silvio Berlusconi and one of the most searching and articulate critics of much of what he stood for:

> There are three reasons for why I am speaking to a newspaper again. The first is that I consider the article an unacceptable attack on women like me who want to grow old without buying into the stereotype of "stay young at any cost." I'm nearly 60. Probably, according to current obsessive standards, I'm not ageing well. I'm not bothered about my waistline or the wrinkles on my neck. Is this sufficient reason to suggest I, and I deduce my peers, should visit a plastic surgeon? What kind of example are we giving to 16-year-olds who these days want liposuction as birthday presents?[6]

And in a dig at her ex-husband she added:

> It's an old story, best told by Oscar Wilde in [*The Picture of*] *Dorian Gray*. In a desperate attempt to maintain the appearance of your twenties, you remove yourself ever further from reality. Everything changes but you. I have a normal life. I'm a grandmother. Do I have to be insulted for this?

Of course nobody should be insulted for ageing gracefully. "A normal life," though? Even Lario's strongest supporters must have coughed at that remark. The hostile photo story in *Chi* appeared just a week or so after media reports suggesting that in order to retain her "normal" existence, Lario was now demanding an eye-popping €540 million ($720 million) one-off divorce payment (instead of the monthly €3 million payments). A cash-strapped Berlusconi insisted that €200 million ($260 million) was the most he could afford.[7] The latest *Forbes* estimate suggested he was worth $9 billion. But with a weak stock exchange and a TV empire struck by high overheads and tumbling advertising revenues, his liquidity wasn't what it had been. A court in Monza granted the divorce in February 2014. But in Milan, a separate alimony battle was still in full swing. That city's appeals court threw Berlusconi a bone in September 2014 by reducing his payments in the separation period from €3 million to €2 million a month, although the ruling could be appealed at the

Supreme Court. And, if the mogul's companies rose in the stock exchange, Lario would be entitled to go back to court, in the process currently under way in Monza, to demand a bigger handout. For this reason a definitive, one-off divorce payment to get Lario off his back for good appealed to Berlusconi. Most pundits thought a compromise somewhere between the €540 million and €200 million would emerge. Either way, Lario won't have to worry about paying the bills as she gets old.

Neither will his children. While Lario will enjoy her golden years with the hundreds of millions of dollars she'll get in the eventual settlement, Berlusconi's five children—Marina and Pier Silvio by his first marriage, and Barbara, Eleonora and Luigi by his second marriage—can also count on being multi-multimillionaires, if they aren't already.

Not that we know much about Berlusconi's family. From the information available, he seems an affectionate father. But, given how long Berlusconi has been in the public eye, surprisingly little is known about how the tycoon regards his sons or daughters, or his general likes and dislikes, or his thoughts on art, culture and life: he rarely if ever expresses an opinion on such things. His press interviews are invariably opportunities to justify himself, ward off accusations of wrongdoing, or promote his business or political strategies. Veronica Lario and some former Berlusconi associates, such as Vittorio Dotti, have another explanation, however, for the mogul's reticence on subjects other than business or legal travails—it might be that he simply doesn't have much to say. As Lario once noted, Berlusconi is a man without hobbies, one for whom success, recognition and even adulation are everything. In other words, perhaps we've already learned what there is to know.

Giuliano Urbani, the political pundit who worked closely with Berlusconi in setting up his Forza Italia powerbase, told me that in private the mogul had an "adorable" personality: vulgar but generous, charming and amusing. He noted, too, that it wasn't terribly different from the public face of the man. He added: "you never hear Berlusconi's thoughts on abstract things, or philosophy or things outside the immediate remit of his business or legal preoccupations, because he doesn't have any."

Berlusconi's children keep a low profile. The eldest, Marina and Pier Silvio, are dependable senior lieutenants in his business empire. His youngest children—Eleonora, born in 1986, and Luigi, born in 1988—have the lowest profiles of all, although Luigi, who has something of the young Silvio Berlusconi's boy-next-door good looks, has immersed himself successfully in his father's business after declaring an interest in finance and studying at Milan's Bocconi business school.

Barbara, the middle child, and the eldest of Lario's children, is probably the most interesting of the five. She broke the code of silence on family affairs, particularly those of her father, by criticizing his creepy relationship with Noemi Letizia, whose eighteenth birthday party he attended, to the outrage of her mother. "I was amazed," she told the Italian *Vanity Fair* in August 2009, adding that public officials should not make "a distinction between [their] public life and private life" and should promote moral values. "My story is that of a girl who lived her youth in a normal and tranquil fashion. I never frequented old men," she remarked tersely. "These are psychological links of which I have no experience."

Apparently, Berlusconi wasn't expecting such an attack from his nearest and dearest. The angry mogul was said to have told friends: "She reminds me of her mother," adding that no one had warned him the media ambush was coming. "It was like a cold shower." But, like her mother, she wasn't shy about criticizing the tycoon. In 2008 she said the conflicts of interest between Berlusconi's business empire and his political role were damaging to public life: "I am convinced that the question needs to be regulated." Although—again following her mother's example—political or ethical reservations haven't prevented her from taking financial advantage of her position. She's an adviser to the board of Fininvest and has even muscled in on the director's board of AC Milan, claiming the position of joint vice president of the club, to the chagrin of Adriano Galliani, Berlusconi's right-hand man there for 28 years.

Since the *Vanity Fair* comments, father and daughter have publicly patched things up. But Barbara Berlusconi's ambitiousness has seen her clash with the mogul's eldest child, her half sister, Marina. The hostility between these two women was no secret, as speculation mounted on who would inherit what when their father died, given Lario's perceived jockeying to put her children in the best possible position. But Berlusconi's worsening legal predicament would see the rivalry put on the back burner as the two "lionesses" started to worry, instead, about the future prospects of the business empire, as its founder's political power drained away.[8]

In December 2012, the mogul announced he was going steady, again. With his reputation as a dirty old man bolstered by a year of sleazy headlines, Berlusconi made a bid to silence the critics who said that he was a serial philanderer who preyed on very young women. The mogul, 76, let it be known he had become close to a former member of his fan club, 27-year-old Francesca Pascale, who was 20 years younger than his eldest children. But at least it was legal. Berlusconi's cheerleader-in-chief, Daniela Santanchè, told the press that Pascale was Italy's new "first lady" (even though Berlusconi was no longer prime minister). "Berlusconi introduces her as his girlfriend, and for me it is a beautiful thing. I know her as his girlfriend," she gushed.[9]

Pascale had worked as a shop assistant in Naples, and she'd served as a provincial councilor in his center-right PDL party, until she stepped down in July 2014. She was one of the founding members of a support group called "Silvio, we miss you." It was hard to imagine a partner more different from the left-leaning, independent-minded Veronica Lario.

A year later, with legal developments ensuring that the Rubygate affair was still very much in the public eye, his relationship with Pascale was again dished out to the press, this time as evidence that Berlusconi really was a family man. A saccharine cover feature in Italian *Vanity Fair*, showing Berlusconi with Francesca and Dudu, their pet dog, had much of the public guffawing—and some *Vanity Fair* readers ripping up their subscriptions. With the camera lens seemingly dipped in lard and the pair wearing enough makeup to re-plaster the inside of a school gymnasium, the shoot had a predictably staged feel.

The comment from reader "Rossana F." on the Italian *Vanity Fair* site was typical: "an old man, the girlfriend and a puppy—of course we want some lighter news but this is really squalid in its banality. What kind of message is it trying to put out?" The answer was that the mogul's PR had decided to use Pascale as evidence that the billionaire magnate was just a normal kind of guy—but perhaps one who'd been too generous and fallen victim to financial sharks and predatory women.

Pascale, who had first met Berlusconi six years earlier, said she hadn't attended the mogul's bunga bunga parties because she couldn't have tolerated the behavior of the other guests. She knew that the floozies and starlets whom Berlusconi had invited to discuss culture, current affairs and politics at his elegant Arcore dinners were determined to exploit the opportunity and threw "themselves at him" at every opportunity.

In another interview, with *Oggi* magazine, she said she discovered an "unacceptable" mess when she moved into his mansion with her poodle Dudu earlier in 2014. "Many people were taking advantage of him."

Pascale was making all the right noises, including an attack on the financial demands of Berlusconi's estranged wife, Lario. "In what kind of country is there no outcry from the public when a man is condemned to pay three million euros a month to his ex-wife?" said Pascale. Presumably, the same country that let the old crook make so much money in the first place.

But continuing the theme of how the host's generosity had been abused, she announced a "spending review" in her sybarite boyfriend's household. "I had to intervene. They were paying €80 ($110) a kilo for green beans, can you believe it? Huge crates of fish were being delivered to the house when everyone knows he doesn't eat fish, he even hates the smell." Veronica Lario had voiced her opposition to the allied invasion of Iraq. But she's never commented, publicly at least, on the price of vegetables.

With Berlusconi's racy personal history, it wouldn't have been surprising if someone had stepped up and claimed to have had a recent sexual relationship with the mogul. But instead such a claim was made of Pascale, not the ex–prime minister. In October 2013, a young woman declared that Berlusconi's girlfriend was a lesbian and that the high-profile relationship with Berlusconi was a PR sham. Michelle Bonev, a starlet turned film producer, said that she and Pascale had been lovers—or in her words "more than just friends."

"Francesca had never been with a man, because she likes women," Bonev said on the program *Servizio Pubblico*, hosted by Berlusconi's old TV foe, Michele Santoro. Pascale, said Bonev, was highly ambitious and jealous of the other women—whom she regarded as "tarts and sluts"—in the ex–prime minister's inner circle. "She's a woman without scruples, she does everything out of ambition, to gain power," said the Bulgarian actress. Berlusconi was not left out of the actress's sexual revelations. Bonev also claimed that she'd slept with the mogul himself after being promised TV work with his Mediaset empire. Perhaps, though, Berlusconi *was* changing his ways: Bonev added that "the contract never arrived."

Pascale dismissed the claims as lies and announced she was suing Bonev for €10 million ($13 million). She also demanded damages from Santoro, the host of the television talk show, and from Urbano Cairo, the owner of La7, the channel on which it was broadcast.

But the carefully constructed post–bunga bunga image of Berlusconi, the family man, appeared to have been dealt a serious blow once again by one of the young women who'd frequented those elegant dinners.

While much of the press dwelt on the sentimental aspects of Francesca Pascale's relationship with Berlusconi, a few observers pondered Bonev's comments about Pascale's ambitiousness. Shrewdly, she appears to have made good friends with Berlusconi's eldest child, Marina. The pair have even taken pouting selfies of themselves together, and Pascale has touted Marina Berlusconi's political potential. Berlusconi's daughter shows little desire—or indeed little aptitude—for a career in politics. But some have wondered if Francesca Pascale might harbor political ambitions of her own.

Despite his legal battles and scandal-packed private life—or perhaps because of them—Berlusconi still had an interest in lawmaking. But a seat in the Senate wasn't enough: no longer in government, he was unable to cook up save-Berlusconi legislation. He couldn't shake off the ominous feeling that the law was catching up with him.

On October 20, 2012, the mogul gave his first official testimony in the Rubygate sex and abuse of office trial, declaring that there had "never been scenes of a sexual nature" at his Arcore orgies. Berlusconi even called Hollywood A-lister George Clooney—who'd been invited to dinner once—to testify that the mogul's soirees were perfectly respectable. A bemused Clooney, who spends his summers loafing around Lake Como, declined, tersely declaring: "I've only met Berlusconi once and that was in an attempt to get aid into Darfur."

Six days later, on October 26, 2012, Berlusconi was convicted in the first degree (that is, with right of two subsequent appeals) in the separate tax fraud trial relating to slush funds from his media empire. B-movie producer Frank Agrama was also convicted for his part in the tax scam as Berlusconi's US go-between. The prosecution said Mediaset executives inflated the price for the TV rights of some 3,000 films as they re-licensed them internally to Berlusconi's networks, pocketing the difference. Three other defendants, including Berlusconi's best friend and Mediaset president Fedele Confalonieri, were acquitted. Four other defendants were cleared because the statute of limitations had kicked in. The former prime minister was not so lucky.

When the verdict was read out Berlusconi was holidaying at the Kenyan ranch of his friend and fellow billionaire Flavio Briatore, the mogul who had been wiretapped in April 2011 saying he thought the three-time premier was "not well." Berlusconi phoned his Mediaset Italia 1 network that evening to tell viewers that he'd been victimized once again by leftist magistrates. "It is a political conviction that I can justly define as incredible and intolerable. My lawyers and I never thought that such a conviction would be possible," Berlusconi said during his on-air rant.[10] Sure enough, his lawyers announced they'd appeal.

Fabio De Pasquale, a short, dogged prosecutor with a handlebar mustache, won the first-round conviction. He had previously lost out to the statute of limitations in his ten-year battle to nail Berlusconi on the Mills bribery charge. In theory, the tax fraud case should have been dead in the water, too, by now, despite De Pasquale insisting that Berlusconi was at "the top of the chain of command in the sector of television rights" when Mediaset inflated film costs by around $368 million from 1994 to 1998. Under the ten-year statute of limitations for tax crimes, Berlusconi could no longer be prosecuted in 2012. Cleverly, though, De Pasquale found a way to beat the statute: he argued that the tax benefits brought by diverting such huge amounts of cash overseas would be felt for five successive years. The dodged tax payments over this period diminished each year, but crucially, in 2003, there appeared to remain a sum of €7.3 million ($9.4 million) that Berlusconi had hidden from the taxman.[11] This was small change for the billionaire. But it was a saving that might prove very costly indeed.

Thanks to the magistrate's legal maneuver there was still a year left in which to have the conviction set in stone by the Supreme Court. De Pasquale told me before the two appeals that, despite the mogul's lawyers' desperate attempts to impede the process, he was confident that the statute of limitations would not save his prey this time. And he was right.

CHAPTER 16

THE FALL

In 2013 Berlusconi's luck ran out. Despite dozens of indictments and convictions in the previous two decades, his riposte to each and every attack on his integrity had been to remind us that prosecutors had never once been able to make a charge stick through both appeal hearings—a prerequisite for a definitive conviction in the Italian legal system. That was about to change, however.

We knew that provided he didn't bite the head off a baby and stick the video on YouTube, he was unlikely to do jail time—amnesties and the legislative scam he performed to keep septuagenarians out of prison would guarantee that. But justice—or what was left of it after two decades of politics by and for Italy's most powerful billionaire—was about to catch up with Silvio Berlusconi. This would also signal the beginning of the end of his grip on Italian politics.

His first legal defeat came in the second week of January when judges blocked his attempt to stall the Rubygate sex and corruption hearings that were scheduled before February's general election.[1] Berlusconi feared that salacious court reports or, God forbid, a guilty verdict ahead of the vote would spell curtains for his center-right's chances.

"A trial cannot be suspended for a general election campaign," snapped Berlusconi's red-haired nemesis, the female prosecutor Ilda Boccassini. The judge concurred. The impression that Berlusconi's legal team had been doing everything in its power to draw out the Rubygate trial was strengthened when it emerged that Ruby herself, El Mahroug, would not be called to testify by the defense: up to this point, Berlusconi's lawyers had demanded umpteen delays in order to organize her appearance in the witness box.

The fate of the Ruby case was out of Berlusconi's hands, at least for the time being. But in addition to the constant political machinations, there was plenty on the social calendar to keep him occupied—and plenty of incidents to ensure that the mogul remained in the headlines.

One such event was January's Holocaust Memorial ceremony in Milan, which marked the opening of the commemorative site at the city's Central Station. It was from this forbidding fascist-era structure that thousands of Italian Jews were sent in trains to the death camps. Generously deciding to come, even though organizers had overlooked his invitation, Berlusconi helped himself to a seat in the front row and could soon be seen dozing through the ceremony.

Afterward, however, he headed for the press microphones and opined that Benito Mussolini, the fascist dictator and Hitler ally, hadn't been that bad—apart from those slightly draconian race laws—and had done some "good things."[2] Perhaps he meant the trains ran on time back then, and not just the services carting people off to Auschwitz. At the Foreign Press Association in Milan, one Italian journalist, Michele Novaga, articulated the outrage of many. "I'm lost for words," he said. "He wasn't invited. He sat himself in the front row and then he slept through the event dedicated to the memory of those who were herded away in cattle cars and never seen again. And then he even said, that apart from the race laws, Mussolini governed well. What else could he have done? Snore? Fart noisily during the minutes of silence? Piss in the corner?"

With a lull in the Ruby trial process, Berlusconi also had the chance to throw himself into the election campaign. In any normal Western democracy, the pro-Mussolini remarks, and the crass and insensitive context in which they were uttered, would have proved election poison. But on Planet Italia, Berlusconi brushed it off. And as events described in Chapter 14 suggest, you don't win a general election three times and come very close in a fourth without a touch of political genius. This, plus the center-left's ability to pull defeat from the jaws of victory and the theatrics of Beppe Grillo, had left Italy with a hung parliament.

To a large extent, though, the general election was overshadowed by historic events at the Vatican. On February 13, 2013, the increasingly frail

Benedict XVI announced his decision to abdicate, thereby causing further turmoil in a Catholic Church already riven by scandal. Thus, by February 25, Italy found itself strangely rudderless: without a government and only a lame-duck pontiff to look to for spiritual sustenance. In retrospect, Benedict's decision can be viewed as a brave and radical move by a highly conservative and little-loved Pope—one that would rejuvenate the 2,000-year-old institution. If only Italy's disgraced politicians, from Berlusconi downward, had demonstrated such grace and integrity.

On March 13, the papal conclave elected a relatively unknown Argentine cardinal, Jorge Mario Bergoglio, as the 266th leader of the world's Catholics. It would prove an inspired choice. There was huge excitement at the prospect of a Pope with people skills, who spurned all the pomp and ceremony, who took selfies with young people and appeared a little less medieval in his attitude to women, gays, divorcees and non-Christians. Very soon, Bergoglio would also begin disengaging the Vatican from national politics, thus denying the center-right even more of the Catholic votes it had been able to count on for decades. Within a few weeks, the immediate fuss surrounding Pope Francis's election calmed down a little. Unfortunately for Berlusconi, the gradual diminution in interest in events at the Vatican and a period of relative political calm, thanks to the installation of a stopgap left-right coalition government, coincided with the buildup to the verdict in the Rubygate trial.

The mogul who had been able to brush off relatively innocuous-sounding charges, such as false accounting and tax evasion, feared he was on the verge of becoming a convicted sex criminal. That wouldn't sit well with his delusion of being Europe's Elder Statesman. In a final attempt to delay the inevitable, Berlusconi's lawyers appealed to the Supreme Court, asking that the proceedings be moved to another northern city, Brescia, where, out of reach of Milan's "communist magistrates," the mogul would be more likely to receive a fair trial. Italy's most senior judges gave this plea short shrift, too.[3] Berlusconi's team, who'd footed the bill for El Mahroug's lawyers, had decided months earlier it was too risky to allow the unpredictable 20-year-old to take the stand. Thus denied her five minutes in the sun, the "victim" in the Rubygate affair turned up outside Milan's Palace of Justice on April 4, 2013, to give the press and the prosecutors a piece of her mind.[4]

The paw prints of Berlusconi and his lawyer Niccolò Ghedini were all over El Mahroug's prepared statement, however, which was peppered with claims as spurious and repetitive as those in advertising spots that interrupt Mediaset quiz shows. This was demure Ruby: very little makeup, hair pulled back, shivering with anger and pride in a sober black coat. Ostensibly fighting back the tears, but skillfully failing to do so, El Mahroug protested her innocence in a quavering voice. She had suffered "real psychological torture" at the hands of magistrates and the press, who had sought to attack Berlusconi by muddying her name.

As a result of this campaign, she said, five minutes into the declaration, "many people regard me as a prostitute even if this trial has shown exactly the opposite is true." It wasn't clear what the exact opposite of a prostitute was. Perhaps a Red Cross missionary worker? No such person was ever seen at the bunga bunga nights. Although Nicole Minetti and another guest did that Sapphic-tinged striptease in a nun's costume.

El Mahroug was prepared to apologize, however, for having lied in claiming she was the granddaughter of former Egyptian president Hosni Mubarak, in an apparent attempt to absolve Berlusconi of the most serious charge he faced—that of abusing his powers. She then flashed to the circling media pack what she said was a fake passport that gave her the surname Mubarak. It's not clear why the media didn't insist on getting a closer look. Some people might have wondered, why, if she had used a forged identity, prosecutors weren't more interested in pursuing her for possession and use of false documents. Cynics responded that the magistrates had a bigger fish to fry on the charge of abuse of office.

On June 3, 2013, Berlusconi was running out of time and options in the Rubygate trial. With the verdict just three weeks away, the mogul's lawyer Ghedini in desperation—or perhaps simply out of exasperation—tried to shame the judges into absolving the ex-premier of sex and corruption charges by accusing them of bias. "Rightly or wrongly, we consider the court prejudiced," said Berlusconi's legal stooge. "In the course of this trial, I've had the feeling that I've created irritation among the judges. The state prosecutor has not appeared to cause the same annoyance." File under: that's a surprise.

Tall and thin, with something of the undertaker about him, Ghedini earns millions from Berlusconi; for many years he simultaneously collected a handy €140,000 salary as a member of parliament, although the records show he was hardly ever there.[5] He dismisses concerns about conflicts of interest with the same disdain as his master. Ghedini told the court in his nasal monotone that the prosecutors and judges shared a "cultural closeness," thereby echoing Berlusconi's constant refrain that all of Milan's magistrature was out to get him. The chief presiding judge, Giulia Turri, pulled the sort of expression that anyone might upon hearing their train had been delayed an additional five minutes.

On May 6, Giulio Andreotti, one of Berlusconi's most controversial predecessors as Italian prime minister, passed away at the age of 94. The reactions in some quarters to the news may have given Il Cavaliere a fillip, emphasizing as they did that in Italy legality is a matter of degree and that successfully bending the rules or even breaking the law can generate respect as long as you get away with it.

Seven-time premier Andreotti, the small, hunched figure who came to personify Italian politics' shady links with organized crime, probably took many of the country's darkest secrets with him to the grave. Known as "Beelzebub" on account of his (until that point) apparent immortality—as well as his presumed ties with Cosa Nostra and the Vatican—he engendered loathing in some quarters, but a grudging or even unabashed respect in others. Berlusconi was certainly in the latter group, having benefitted from Beelzebub's political patronage in the 1980s.

Antonio Ingroia, the former Sicilian anti-mafia magistrate, told me he believed that unlike Silvio Berlusconi—whom he said was targeted by the mob on account of his emerging wealth and power—Andreotti actively cultivated links with organized crime, the details of which are never likely to be revealed. In 2002, Andreotti was sentenced to 24 years in prison for ordering the murder in 1979 of an investigative journalist.[6] A year later, however, on his second appeal, he was cleared and served no time in prison. Andreotti was also accused of exchanging a "kiss of honor" with Cosa Nostra's then boss of bosses Salvatore "The Beast" Riina. "I'm being blamed for everything, except the Punic Wars," was his typically sardonic comment.

Despite the widespread assumption that Andreotti (the protagonist of Paolo Sorrentino's much-lauded film *Il Divo*) and the mafia were as thick as thieves, tributes came thick and fast. "He was as cunning as a fox," Bobo Craxi, a junior foreign minister and the son of late Andreotti ally and convicted criminal Bettino Craxi, told news channel Sky TG 24. Giulia Bongiorno, the center-right politician and high-powered defense lawyer, hired by Andreotti for many of his trials, paid her own tribute: "They'll say all sorts of things about him. But those who knew him will feel a great sense of loss." Gossips noted that given all the money she'd made from the old mafioso, her sense of loss was understandable.

And Berlusconi probably thought that if Beelzebub, one of his Christian Democrat benefactors, could get away with it, then why couldn't he?

The verdict in the most talked about sex-and-politics scandal since Bill Clinton's abuse of a cigar fell on June 24, 2013. Outside Milan's huge fascist-era court complex, under a powder-blue sky, there was the usual media scrum, aided and abetted by pro- and anti-Berlusconi protesters.

Fearing the worst, Berlusconi wasn't in court to hear the verdicts. He and his legal team—and not a few neutral observers—said the evidence showing he had sex with El Mahroug was circumstantial rather than damning. Both Berlusconi and El Mahroug denied sexual relations, and the prosecution had produced no witnesses to say they had seen the tycoon abuse the then 17-year-old. But the three female judges were in no doubt that El Mahroug's paid participation in the bunga bunga parties was legally sufficient. They not only convicted him on the sex charge and of abuse of office, but also rubbed his nose in it by dealing him heavier sentences than those called for by the prosecution. They upped the six-year requested jail term to seven years and agreed to prosecutors' demands for a lifetime ban on the mogul holding public office.

Berlusconi would have two chances to appeal the verdict before the sentences kicked in. And keen legal observers might have noted that changes to the penal code introduced by the Monti government could make it rather more difficult to prove that *concussione* (abuse of office) had occurred at the inevitable appeal.

But in another worrying development for the mogul, Judge Giulia Turri said that many of the witnesses—including Arcore partygoers, who gave testimony on Berlusconi's behalf—should be investigated for perjury. This demand was in part prompted by news in April 2012 that bank records showed Berlusconi had paid a total of €127,000 ($165,000) to three key witnesses shortly after the Rubygate trial began.[7]

A month later, in the parallel Rubygate 2 trial, the three associates who did the mogul's pimping were found guilty of procuring or helping to procure the underage El Mahroug. The motley trio of Nicole Minetti, the voluptuous dental hygienist–cum–politician; Emilio Fede, the former newsreader; and the bankrupt impresario Lele Mora, were also handed long jail terms.

Mora, who was filmed rounding up young women and driving them into the grounds of Berlusconi's Arcore mansion, and Emilio Fede, who was notorious for his verbal diarrhea and pro-Berlusconi bias while reading the news, both received seven-year sentences, which sounded a bit harsh. The beautiful Minetti (think supermodel on a normal 2,000-calorie-a-day diet), who rose rapidly to become a highly paid regional councilor for the mogul's PDL party, was sentenced to five years in jail for the lesser crime of aiding and abetting prostitution.[8] The court had heard she'd also "performed sexual acts for money," including that strip show in a nun's outfit.

During her trial she declared that she organized the bunga bunga parties out of a "real feeling of love" for the perma-tanned ex-premier. Minetti, who had added some glamor, if not much political discourse, to boring Lombardy council meetings by sashaying into the chamber in skinny jeans, designer shades and seven-inch heels, was perhaps the most exquisite example of the perverse patrimonialism in Berlusconi's Italy, where high cheekbones and shamelessness are more important than a decent résumé. Minetti was sunning herself in Spain when the verdicts were read out. She issued a statement through her lawyer saying she was "stunned by the excessive punishment." At least she would have a couple more years to go shopping and take luxury holidays, before her appeals ran out.

The judges also asked prosecutors to investigate suspicions that Berlusconi, his lawyers Niccolò Ghedini and Piero Longo, and El Mahroug had lied under oath while testifying in Mora's, Fede's and Minetti's defense.

Another greedy Arcore "dinner guest," Moroccan model Imane Fadil, announced she was suing all three Berlusconi cronies for forcing her "to take part in Berlusconi's parties and have sex with him by taking advantage of her dire financial circumstances." Being a bunga bunga girl had ruined Fadil's ambitions to work in television, harrumphed her lawyer, Danila De Domenico. Sympathy glands were resolutely unresponsive. Everyone knew that, in Italy, partying with Berlusconi was probably the quickest way for young women to get a job on TV.

The vultures were circling. The impression that Berlusconi and his cronies were no longer getting away with it was growing all the time.

Despite the humiliation he felt at being labeled a sex criminal, Berlusconi knew the Ruby case still had a long way to go, with the right to two more appeals. It was the tax fraud charge relating to his media empire that represented the clear and present danger. Ghedini (no doubt rightly) accused prosecutors—and the judges—of doing everything to ensure that the mogul's first and second appeals were done and dusted by the fall, before the statute of limitations kicked in and killed the case. On May 8, Milan's appeals court confirmed the guilty verdict and the sentence of four years in prison and a five-year ban on holding public office.[9] There now appeared sufficient time to complete the second appeal and reach a definitive verdict. If the Supreme Court of Cassation confirmed the first appeal ruling, then—after two decades of dodging justice—Berlusconi would have a criminal record and answer to the law.

By the end of July 2013, a strange torpor had settled on one Rome location: the Supreme Court of Cassation. In the baking midsummer heat Romans would traditionally head for the hills or to the beach at Ostia. But the inexorable recession and changing work patterns meant the mass monthlong exodus was becoming a thing of the past and the usual bustle in the capital now continued through the summer months. This made the lack of commotion at the epicenter of Italy's most eagerly anticipated legal verdict of recent times all the more surprising. On the west bank of the Tiber, Italy's Supreme Court, a neobaroque mess known by Romans as "Il Palazzaccio" ("The Ugly Palace"), was due to rule on Friday, August 1, whether or not Silvio Berlusconi would be forever labeled a criminal. But outside there were none of the usual pro-Berlusconi "supporters"—some of whom are paid €10 to stand around and holler their appreciation for the Dear Leader.[10]

Even the perma-tanned tycoon kept his mouth closed for several days, apart from some low-key remarks to the effect that he would stand and take any punishment like a man. Of course, no one believed him. The billionaire mogul had been told by his lawyers to put a sock in it so as not to irritate the judges. But hints about the protests that would follow were he found guilty were quick in coming. On the eve of the verdict, Berlusconi ultra-loyalist Daniela Santanchè tweeted—without a hint of irony—that "tomorrow could be the last day of democracy."

———

That's not how most people saw it when, shortly after 7 p.m. the next day, Supreme Court Judge Antonio Esposito uttered the world "guilty," ruling that the billionaire had hidden millions of euros from his media empire in overseas slush funds in order to avoid tax payments.[11] The verdict was the media mogul's first definitive conviction in over 50 court cases.

The silence among the crowd of reporters who'd gathered in Rome in anticipation of the verdict was broken by a single "Yes!" Significantly, this was uttered by an Italian journalist. Finally, after two decades of indictments, convictions and overturned sentences; of close shaves and lucky escapes; after millions of man hours by lawyers and investigators, impeded by self-serving law changes and moving goalposts, Berlusconi, the most powerful man in Italy, the most loved in some quarters and easily the most reviled in many others, had been brought to justice.

Despite the celebrations that the verdict produced in most quarters, the reaction from the political opposition, locked with Berlusconi supporters in an uneasy left-right coalition government, was, by necessity, muted. Center-left prime minister Enrico Letta merely called for "respect for the magistrature and the sentence."

So it was left to Berlusconi's fellow demagogue, and most brutal critic, Beppe Grillo, to express what most of Italy felt on this historic day. "The Wall divided Germany for 28 years. The tax evader, the friend of mafiosi, the card-carrying mason, has polluted, corrupted, and paralyzed Italian politics for 21 years, since entering the field in 1993 in order to avoid prison. It is a wall that has separated Italy from democracy. Today this wall, an image, an optical illusion, kept alive by the special effects of newspapers and television, has fallen."

The Supreme Court cut Berlusconi's original four-year prison sentence to just a year under measures to reduce overcrowding in Italy's crumbling prisons. His US partner in crime, Frank Agrama, the film producer who'd brought the world *Dawn of the Mummy* and *Queen Kong* in addition to helping Berlusconi cook the books, was sentenced by the Supreme Court to three years in jail for tax fraud. He, too, denies all charges. His sentence was cut under the same amnesty.[12] Thanks to the law introduced to free his crooked lawyer Previti from prison, Berlusconi's jail time was commuted to house arrest or community service. Nonetheless,

Italian reporters were rubbing their hands at the thought of Berlusconi swapping his tailored navy suit for orange overalls.

Soon after the conviction senior parliamentary supporters arrived at Palazzo Grazioli, Berlusconi's Rome residence, where the tycoon had awaited the verdict with his lawyers, family members and closest associates. The prosecutor's office in Milan didn't waste any time dispatching *carabinieri* to officially notify Berlusconi of his sentence. And the next day, officers from Rome's police headquarters arrived at Palazzo Grazioli to confiscate the former prime minister's passports (ordinary and diplomatic) and to take his fingerprints.

There's no doubt that a definitive criminal conviction hit Berlusconi—and his loved ones—very hard indeed. Perhaps, after so much time—it was 36 years since Berlusconi had persuaded the young finance police officer Massimo Maria Berruti to work for him rather than press ahead with the Milano 2 exchange-control violation probe—a part of the mogul had come to regard himself as invincible. One of Berlusconi's loyal secret service bodyguards recalled the scene at Palazzo Grazioli. "It was terrible: for him, for his children, for all of us. Marina and Pier Silvio were there with him and they were both crying. Berlusconi, seeing them in this state, tried cracking a joke: 'Will you bring me some oranges in prison?' But you could see it was forced."[13]

On Sunday, August 4, a tearful Berlusconi appeared on a podium outside his Palazzo Grazioli, just across from the Palazzo Venezia, where Mussolini had addressed the Italian people. "I'm here, I'm staying here and I will not give in," Berlusconi blubbered to hundreds of elderly supporters, brought up from Calabria by the busload. But, if the event was staged, the mogul's emotions were real: he was really crying, weeping, even. "He wasn't faking . . . He closed his eyes. His face was purple," noted one reporter from *Corriere della Sera*.[14]

Political observers waited to see if, in the rage that would inevitably follow, Berlusconi would order his parliamentary troops to bring down the fragile left-right coalition government. But his PDL lieutenants played down the possibility of pulling the rug from under Enrico Letta's administration. They were obviously too weak themselves to benefit from a quick return to the polls.

But, true to form, Berlusconi began working on one of his video rants. Some critics say it is improper for major TV networks to provide the mogul with a free platform for his ten-minute propaganda spots. But other pundits say that the homemade monologues are so obviously deluded and self-serving that they probably backfire. Mediaset insiders say that the red mist really descended on the former prime minister while shooting the video. His old pal Fedele Confalonieri had to convince him to discard the first apoplectic take.

In any case, the nine-minute message that appeared that evening was bad enough. Berlusconi claimed he had been the victim of a "real judicial frenzy without equal in the civilized world." Halfway through the video, he pursed his lips and put his hand to his heart. He began to tremble lightly, with rage. "In the course of the work done in nearly 20 years for my country, and now nearly at the end of my active life, I receive as a reward, accusations and a sentence based on absolutely nothing, which even takes away my personal freedom and political rights. Is that how Italy recognizes the sacrifices and work of its best citizens?"

Shamelessly, the convicted tax fraud had stuck a big EU flag—an institution he had spent the best part of two years berating—as well as Italy's Tricolore flag by his desk to appear more statesman-like. And like all great performers he believed every word he said.

The Supreme Court judges decided that the other part of the tax fraud sentence, which banned Berlusconi from holding public office—and thereby a seat in the Senate—for five years, should be sent back to Milan's appeals court, with orders that it be reduced for technical reasons to a period of between three and five years.[15]

But the court's ruling was academic: everyone knew the tax fraud conviction itself should trigger the former prime minister's expulsion from the Senate under the Severino law. If he was kicked out of the Senate and denied parliamentary privileges, Berlusconi would not only be humiliated—he would also be more vulnerable to further arrests, since prosecutors would not require parliamentary approval to detain him. He'd had to hand in his passports, so fleeing to his villa in Antigua was off the table—at least for now. Could the year get any worse? In a word, yes.

Fearful of the legal dangers to which he would be exposed, Berlusconi fought tooth and nail against the implementation of the Severino law for the next three months. This legislation, named after the technocrat minister and eminent criminal lawyer Paola Severino, who'd introduced it in 2011, rules that people with definitive convictions resulting in jail sentences of more than two years are banned from holding public office (including Senate seats) for six years. Berlusconi's supporters declared that the law could not be applied to events that occurred before the legislation was created—a claim denied by several law experts, and by Severino herself.[16]

As ever, the mogul put his own concerns ahead of the national interest and attempted to extort a get-out-of-jail card from the fragile left-right coalition, which was busy trying to keep speculators at bay and dragging Italy from its longest recession since World War II. Veteran political pundit Professor James Walston noted that with the markets continuing to look for signs of instability in Italy, "a collapse of the government now would be disastrous."

But that didn't stop Berlusconi supporters, including PDL ministers in the coalition, from telling Prime Minister Letta that they would pull the plug on the government unless he told his center-left parliamentarians to stop the expulsion. Letta called the criminals' bluff. "I don't accept blackmail or inadmissible ultimatums," he said.[17] Six weeks later, on October 2, Berlusconi once again asked his center-right parliamentarians to bring down the government, setting up a confidence vote with the aim of pulling the rug away. Ostensibly, his reason for this was opposition to fiscal policy. But everyone knew he was furious about the approaching parliamentary ban.

This time, however, a large section of his own supporters rebelled before the vote. In the most humiliating U-turn in his two-decade parliamentary career, Berlusconi was forced to vote with the rebels and back the government at the last moment. From his seat on the floor of the house Prime Minister Letta could be seen laughing at Berlusconi. With key PDL defectors, including former doormat Angelino Alfano, forming a new breakaway party, Berlusconi decided on November 16 to dissolve the PDL—or at least change its name back to Forza Italia. Not that this changed much.

The mogul's minions reacted to his humiliations as they'd always done, by slating the turncoats and singing The Boss's praises. Berlusconi's family newspaper *Il Giornale* set out to put the record straight on November 22, the fiftieth anniversary of JFK's assassination, by noting that the mogul and the late-lamented US president had much in common, including wealth, political success and "an overwhelming passion for beautiful women."[18] To everyone else, it appeared the rot had truly set in and Berlusconi was becoming a sad caricature of himself.

Three days later the press crowded into the new HQ of Berlusconi's reformed Forza Italia in the center of Rome to hear the beleaguered mogul reveal details of a new US "super witness" who would prove that the billionaire wasn't a tax dodger. The witness had mysteriously come forward now—a decade after the tax fraud indictment and two days before Berlusconi was due to be kicked out of parliament—with evidence that his Mediaset empire had not *knowingly* inflated the costs of buying film rights in order to channel money into overseas slush funds. Berlusconi was vehement that the new development proved his innocence. But his explanation of the evidence was so convoluted and incomprehensible that even Italian correspondents who prided themselves on knowing the ins and outs of the case exchanged blank stares. In essence, an assistant to the B-movie producer Agrama, said to be at the center of the TV rights tax scam, claimed Agrama had told her that Berlusconi was in the dark about the whole business.[19] But the journalists in the room recalled Berlusconi claiming for years he'd never even met Agrama—until an unhelpful photo of them posing together turned up.

The next day, Berlusconi's faithful servant Ghedini arrived at the Foreign Press Association, just on the other side of Via del Corso, to explain developments to the world's press. I asked him an (im)pertinent question: whether the emergence of the super witness had involved an exchange of money. The legal stooge, with his dead eyes and piranha mouth, looked at me as if I'd just made an improper suggestion regarding the good character of his mother. It didn't matter; everyone knew Berlusconi was on the ropes. The next day, on November 27, 2013, Berlusconi officially became *persona non grata* at Palazzo Madama, Italy's upper chamber of parliament.[20] He made sure he wasn't there to witness the expulsion vote. He declared from Palazzo Grazioli: "Democracy is in mourning." To most observers, though, it felt like democracy had finally woken up.

In the run-up to Christmas 2013, Team Berlusconi changed tack and launched a Facebook page "written" by Dudu the dog, who was proving more popular than its owners, Francesca Pascale and her ageing boyfriend. Lovey-dovey pics of Berlusconi and Pascale in women's mags produced jibes from all but the most hard-core Berlusconi supporters. Pascale, who'd upped the ante for her new role in Italian society with full face paint, brutally retouched eyebrows and Chanel suits, didn't endear herself to recession-mired Italy by spending most of her waking hours on luxury shopping trips. Others referred disparagingly to her nocturnal obligations and wondered if she hadn't earned her money.

Dudu, the pair's dog, was seen as positive PR. In a social-networking gimmick, which, in the words of one correspondent, "went beyond farce," Dudu dispensed trite, Paulo Coelho–level aphorisms and acted as a cheerleader for the mogul. Berlusconi supporters who were bored of the shopping channel probably liked it, and Il Cavaliere hadn't got where he was worrying about insulting people's intelligence. Inevitably, pranksters left sarcastic comments. "Does Dudu the dog eat money like his master?" asked one cynic.

Dudu responded with Confucian poise: "Friends, I ask you not to rise to the provocations. We're here only to love each other." Heartless suppositions on what had first attracted 27-year-old Francesca to her billionaire fiancé were batted away by indignant friends and supporters.

The ex–prime minister's PR team made the most of things when Berlusconi's old pal Vladimir Putin rocked up in Rome to sign some Russian-Italian trade deals. The Russian bully called round for dinner with his politically wounded friend and Berlusconi's gossip rag *Chi* ran photos of Putin playing fetch with the mogul's fluffy white dog in the corridors of Palazzo Grazioli.[21]

But at the national level, even Berlusconi was starting to doubt if the love was still there for him anymore. On New Year's Eve it emerged he'd given his Forza Italia troops in the northern city of Turin a typically self-centered pep talk, insisting he'd battle on. "I am an old man; I cannot permit myself to end my human adventure, my history as a businessman, as a sportsman, as a statesman, as a loser." But it also sounded like a valedictory speech. Proudly unapologetic regarding all the fun he'd had along the way, Italian politics' Don Giovanni was finally being dragged under by the state's own Commendatore, the magistrature. Berlusconi was looking ahead to a bleak 2014, with no seat in parliament, community service punishment, fresh indictments and a criminal record that no amount of money could scrub away.

CHAPTER 17

FADING AWAY

Berlusconi the criminal had been kicked out of parliament. The Severino law meant the 77-year-old couldn't stand for public office for the next six years. But still he declared he'd fight on. It's tempting to ask what—apart from Italy's law enforcement agencies—he was fighting. He had nothing left to prove, apart from his innocence, and that would be monumentally difficult.

Rumors resurfaced that he might flee abroad to Antigua and party in his Caribbean villa till he dropped. But the purveyors of that notion had forgotten that, as a confirmed criminal, the ex–prime minister's passports—both ordinary and diplomatic—had been confiscated by the authorities. So, why couldn't he simply stay put in one of his Italian pleasure palaces and be fed peeled grapes by scantily clad women, and die with a smile on his face? The answer was that Berlusconi was used to getting his own way. He felt humiliated and longed to rearrange the justice system, for his own ends, again. But the chances of that, despite attempts to revitalize his Forza Italia party, seemed slimmer all the time.

More immediately he had to brace himself for the period of community service. Judges accepted Berlusconi's request to serve his punishment at a hospice for Alzheimer's patients. At 9:45 a.m. on May 9, 2014, the mogul began his first-ever sentence after a cat-and-mouse game with Italian law enforcement that had lasted the best part of four decades. It's true that not many convicts turn up for their punishment in a bulletproof limousine with a raft of personal security men. Heavily made up, with his preferred semi-casual attire of dark suit and black sweater, the three-time premier made an unusually low-key entrance. The usual saccharine grin was absent; instead the mogul's expression was a mix of resignation and condescension.

A protestor in a clown's hat shouted: "Go to prison!" as the tycoon stepped out of his car at the Sacra Famiglia Hospice near Milan. But not everyone was as hostile to the disgraced former prime minister. Two middle-aged female relatives of elderly Alzheimer's patients at the Church-run institution surprised a reporter from left-wing Rai 3 television in the days before Berlusconi's arrival by declaring their support for the miscreant. "It's terrible. Poor man, those judges were out to get him," said one of them.

Still, it was safe to say that the majority of Italians thought he'd finally got what he deserved—or perhaps less than he deserved, with a four-year prison sentence for tax evasion commuted to 12 months community service, entailing just one four-hour session per week.

Being Berlusconi, he sought to put a positive spin on this humiliation, which he'd fought tooth and nail to avoid. "I'm actually pleased because in my life I have always helped people," he said. He even talked up his aptitude as a health worker during a prior radio interview. "It took me just 10 days to learn the different treatment methods that can be used." Massimo Restelli, head of the hospice's care services, swiftly asserted that the media magnate would be accompanied at all times by a professional healthcare worker specialized in Alzheimer's care. Restelli even appeared concerned that the convict might suffer stage fright. "We ask everyone, including Berlusconi, to observe, to listen and not to get performance anxiety," he said.[1]

"Performance anxiety"? That wasn't very likely. Mr. Vaudeville had a captive audience that wasn't even able to heckle. Perhaps they should have let in the man in the clown outfit.

Stefano Apuzzo, a reporter from *La Repubblica*, managed to sneak into the hospice while Berlusconi was there and took a video on his smartphone. He saw the mogul in a white coat, sitting or strolling around in the center's recreation room, chatting and cracking jokes with staff and a few elderly patients in wheelchairs.[2] Apuzzo noted that Berlusconi, healthcare worker, "appeared at ease." But as the old fraudster loafed around in front of the helpless elderly citizens he was supposed to be assisting, it looked like a scene by Harold Pinter. Ever the gentleman, though, he presented a female member of staff with a necklace.

Berlusconi had opted for community service rather than house arrest because his movements and political activity would be slightly less encumbered; he was, after all, still the head of a major political party. But despite some attempts to spur on the troops, his Forza Italia party was still facing humiliation in the approaching EU elections. Aware of his voters' demographic, he sought to resuscitate the campaign by enticing ageing voters with promises of free false teeth.[3] This gimmick to revive the fortunes of his ailing political movement followed a similar proposal a month earlier to sponsor homeless cats and dogs.

It all seemed so desperate. Giuliano Urbani, the former Bocconi University academic, and the nearest thing that Berlusconi's party had to a political guru, saw a Forza Italia/PDL movement that was withering away. The risible free dentures gambit was, he said, "the clearest proof the dream was gone."[4] It was Urbani's electoral analysis back in 1994 that proved pivotal in Berlusconi's decision to stand for office. But now the political scientist saw a party, which had originally appealed to young as well as older voters, incapable of attracting the same broad demographic.

Berlusconi's key spokesman and confidante Paolo Bonaiuti had just jumped ship, too. The defection of a supporter as important, and hitherto loyal, as Bonaiuti showed that Forza Italia was "falling like a house of cards," said Urbani. Most pundits concurred. Berlusconi's party would inevitably linger on, but only as a nostalgic shell; instead of figures like Bonaiuti and Urbani, who at least gave Berlusconi's movement some sound behind-the-scenes counsel and clever PR, the mogul now turned for advice to the lightweights and hangers-on he had picked up after he'd gone off the rails.

In a November 2013 newspaper interview, Vittorio Sgarbi, Berlusconi's former TV attack dog and fellow sybarite, had described the ex–prime minister's plight in typically pithy terms. The mogul's inner circle now consisted of "the incapable, traitors, people on the make, idiots," plus "lawyers who swindle him," he barked. "Silvio Berlusconi's is a human tragedy, but also a political catastrophe due to his worst enemy: Silvio Berlusconi. He doesn't understand the daily tragedy of having to spend his days with Pascale and Dudu the dog."

Berlusconi tried to get around the ban on holding office by running for a position in the European Parliament. In March 2014, Giovanni Toti, one of the new breed of political lightweights now "advising" him, stated that it was "certain" that Berlusconi would be a candidate when Europeans headed for the polls on May 22 to 25. But European Justice Commissioner Viviane Reding gave this statement short shrift: the mogul's crafty election bid "won't be happening," she said. EU law was, she said, "very clear" regarding his ineligibility.

Later in the year, in September, his lawyers claimed that judges in the European Court of Human Rights in Strasbourg had agreed to review the fairness of his tax fraud conviction. The court immediately let it be known that it had made no such decision. But in any case, one source very close to the prosecution that had nailed him in August 2013 told me that such applications to the Strasbourg court, provided they're not handwritten in red crayon, tend to be considered out of courtesy. The source added that in the unlikely event the court eventually found in favor of Berlusconi, it wouldn't have the power to quash the conviction. Experts, such as Giorgio Sacerdoti, a professor of international and European law at the Bocconi University, concurred.

But Berlusconi soldiered on. On May 16, with just a week to go to the European elections and his poll ratings riding lower than his trousers at the business end of an Arcore dinner party, Berlusconi tried to distance himself from some of the black sheep of his Forza Italia party. One was convicted mafioso Dell'Utri, who had just started his seven-year prison term in Palermo. Another was suspected Camorra collaborator Nicola Cosentino. And then there was ex-minister Claudio Scajola, who had been arrested the week before, accused of helping Amedeo Matacena, another PDL figure convicted of mafia association, to evade capture.[5]

But the bigger news concerned who was deserting Berlusconi, not the other way around. The very same day that the mogul was on TV claiming that neither Dell'Utri, nor Cosentino nor Scajola had been much involved in Forza Italia parliamentary politics for a long time, Cesare Previti—Darth Vader to Berlusconi's Emperor—joined the growing list of defectors announcing their support for the mogul's center-right rival Angelino Alfano.[6]

On Friday May 23, 2014, just 24 hours before the European poll, Berlusconi took the unusual step of agreeing to answer questions posed by a row of mostly unsympathetic journalists. This was far removed from his preferred setup of a friendly chat with a sympathetic presenter on a Mediaset channel. Facing a panel of interrogators makes it difficult for him to hold court and manipulate the debate. But he was desperate for votes.

A journalist from *Corriere della Sera* asked him why his European election campaign had flopped so spectacularly. In his response, the ex-premier appeared irritable, even angry. His voice was cracked and croaky. He fidgeted awkwardly on his seat. Plastered in orange pancake, he looked waxen and tired. It was a sign of the changing times when Maurizio Belpietro, formerly one of Berlusconi's most supine supporters in the media, dealt brusquely with the mogul, at one point telling him curtly, "Let me finish the question." But even stranger was the impression that some of his media foes in the studio felt a little sorry for him. Perhaps I felt sorry for him, just watching the performance. Despite everything he's done—and got away with—Berlusconi doesn't have the sort of face it's easy to hate. Even when he's angry, you know he's never more than a few seconds away from doing something amusing/appalling. His face is not confused and dyspeptic like George W. Bush, there's no saturnine glare like Nixon. Perhaps, over the decades, opponents have underestimated the effect of his ability to keep laughing, or at least keep the voters laughing.

Still, the X factor was wearing thin. On election day, support for his party in the European poll (in which the national political groupings compete for seats at the European level as they would at home) collapsed to 16.8 percent compared to the 35.3 percent he'd won in the previous European election.[7] Before the poll, with no chance of undoing his criminal record he'd even surrendered his "knighthood" for services to business. He was now the "ex-Cavaliere."

By the spring of 2014 something else had changed. Or rather something had vanished, and it was this that really marked the fall of Silvio Berlusconi. It was an absence, not a rude arrival, so people weren't really aware of it as it happened. For the first time in two decades Italians were no longer talking about him.

For twenty years, at every dinner party, on every trip to the local bar or train journey, his name was mentioned; his exploits prompted discussion, vilification, sniggers—but mostly sighs—from Italians who'd come to view him like death or taxes. As the days lengthened, though, Italians got on with their lives; people began to forget him. The newspapers continued to print stories about his attempts to influence the latest coalition government to his own ends. But ordinary Italians didn't read the papers, which were fuller than ever of reports on political reform and economic doom and gloom. And, crucially, there was less Berlusconi on the television. I even sensed a reluctance among some Italians to discuss him; Berlusconi hadn't been obliterated, but he was fading away, and they were happy to adopt the pragmatic approach to twenty years of national humiliation by turning the other cheek.

Berlusconi still continued to exert political influence. He had the biggest center-right grouping in parliament, after all. So Matteo Renzi, the latest stopgap (and unelected) prime minister, needed to cooperate with the mogul to pass important reforms.

Renzi, just 39 years old, was the third politician in a row to sneak into the prime minister's seat via the back door. This ambitious and ruthless politician was the mayor of Florence when he unseated his colleague Enrico Letta as head of the Democratic Party in December 2013, just weeks after declaring he had absolutely no such plans. This ambush was a clear signal that he also intended to snatch the prime ministership from Letta. He achieved this three months later, in February 2014, by calling a party confidence vote on Letta, which everyone knew the incumbent premier couldn't win. Letta quit, and, with the Democratic Party the biggest component of the coalition government, President Napolitano was obliged to name Renzi the new head of the government.

Renzi was known as the "new Tony Blair," on account of his modernizing tendencies and PR skills. In truth, Renzi owed as much to Berlusconi as to the former British prime minister. From the mogul he learned the importance of presentation and the media and, in particular, the power of personalizing politics. A bit cocky, but down-to-earth and quick witted, Italy's youngest-ever premier promised big changes in 100 days. But six months later, not much had changed, except that Renzi was now talking about a make-or-break period of 1,000 days to reform the country.[8]

The Italian economy was in the same position it had been for the past five years, or maybe 25 years, struggling to keep its head above water, with a precarious coalition battling to introduce changes needed to overhaul parliament and the electoral and justice systems. Berlusconi might now have a lower public profile, but signs of his contribution over the past two decades to the sclerotic state of Italy were everywhere for Italians who cared to look.

On July 18, 2014, after a year of fading prestige and power, the old crook enjoyed a major reprieve. An appeals court cleared the former prime minister of all charges in the Rubygate case, in which he was accused of paying for sex with an underage prostitute and abusing his office to conceal the crime. Although Berlusconi was already banned from holding public office and had a permanent criminal record, it was the Ruby case that had threatened to utterly destroy him. The mogul had appeared so terrified of the Rubygate charges that a few days before the verdict in the first appeal he wrote a huge article, covering two full pages in the Berlusconi family paper *Il Giornale*, declaring his innocence. In the piece, Berlusconi recalled the night Ruby had first come to Arcore—as if it were the most natural thing in the world for a married 73-year-old premier to host unknown teenage girls for dinner.[9] Ruby had told everyone about her family ties to Hosni Mubarak, he wrote. He believed she was 24 years old. And he could exclude "with absolute peace of mind that there had ever been embarrassing scenes of a sexual nature." Perhaps it all hinged on your definition of "embarrassing."

A jail sentence—the thing that he probably dreads the most—had actually been in the cards, thanks to the underage prostitution charge. In order to appease the law-and-order lobby, part of the legal package that the prime minister had introduced in 2005—so that he and Cesare Previti could avoid jail—stipulated that sex criminals cannot avoid custodial sentences. Not long after a panel of three judges had cleared the mogul, one of their number, Enrico Tranfa, president of the second section of Milan's courts of appeals, dramatically quit—apparently in protest at the majority verdict.

The appeals judges published their detailed reasoning in October. It showed that while they (or at least the two who'd considered him innocent) thought there was sufficient evidence to show Berlusconi had indulged in sexual acts with the young Moroccan, the prosecution had failed to prove the mogul *knew* Ruby was underage at the time.[10] On the abuse of office charge, no one believed that the mogul had seriously considered Karima "Ruby" El Mahroug to be the granddaughter of President Hosni Mubarak. The judge's ruling was likely based on a new law drafted by the Monti government, which came into effect after Berlusconi's original conviction, that changed the rules regarding such prosecutions: from 2014 onward "abuse of office" occurs only when the person doing the favor has been offered a tangible financial or professional reward.

The change to the penal code was made by former premier Mario Monti's justice minister, Paola Severino. It was this minister's legislation that ensured convicted tax fraud Berlusconi was banned from parliament. Once again, Italian law gave with one hand and took away with the other. As this book went to press, the Supreme Court was preparing to consider the Milan prosecutors' appeal for a retrial, setting out in 61 pages the evidence showing that Berlusconi had known El Mahroug was underage when he invited her to his orgies, and that he had abused his powers in pressing for her release from the police cell.

The three stooges, Fede, Mora and Minetti, who'd done the mogul's pimping, were not so lucky when the verdicts on their first appeal were announced in November 2014. Their sentences were cut, on the basis they hadn't known El Mahroug was underage. But they were still left with significant jail terms for prostitution-related offenses. In March 2015 the Supreme Court upheld Berlusconi's acquittals, with judges deciding that the abuse-of-office charge was invalid and that there was insufficient evidence that the mogul knew El Mahroug had been underage. Berlusconi now had more time to focus on his disintegrating Forza Italia party and the ongoing trial in the southern city of Bari in which he was charged with bribing the pimp and coke dealer Gianpaolo Tarantini to lie to prosecutors who were investigating the tycoon's sex parties.

It's worth noting that three weeks after the controversial decision to clear him at first appeal, one of El Mahroug's former lawyers popped up to say how sordid the whole Rubygate affair had been.

The attorney Egidio Verzini intimated that the young Moroccan had received a sum of over €6 million ($7.9 million) after the scandal broke. "Ruby understood from the start that this was the opportunity of a lifetime and was determined to get a large amount of money out of it," Verzini said.[11] As this book went to press, El Mahroug was one of a number of young women being investigated on suspicion of giving false statements to investigators about their experiences at the bunga bunga parties.

Verzini said he decided to stop defending El Mahroug after three months, when she eschewed the "legal route" he'd advocated. This entailed suing Emilio Fede for having brought her to the bunga bunga parties in the first place. Verzini claimed that deliberate outside interference had railroaded his strategy: "They suggested a different approach to Ruby and not the legal path that I'd advised. At that point I decided to end my relationship with the client, given that what was being proposed appeared to contradict the norms of our legal system."[12]

But he admitted, too, that he had been unhappy about the squalor surrounding him. Apparently, his conscience was jolted when his own legal assistant remarked with disgust on "the dozens of extremely young women ready for anything in the villa at Arcore," and "the incredible amounts of money paid to all those girls by a prime minister over 70." Feeling uncomfortable that continuing to defend El Mahroug would amount to doing Berlusconi's bidding, the lawyer quit. "I'm not a moralist. I like women, money and a good life, too. But there is a limit," he said. Before the mogul's cronies could accuse Verzini of being a leftist agitator, he remarked: "I've always been on the right, politically. But I stopped believing in *this right* a long time ago."[13] Shortly after he quit as El Mahroug's lawyer, he said he was visited by two men he'd never seen before, who warned him in no uncertain terms not to talk about the affair.

Some people, though, can be counted on to never to keep their mouths closed. A few days later, Berlusconi's old crony Emilio Fede showed why journalists and satirists consider him the gift that keeps on giving. In conversations secretly recorded by the former newsreader's personal trainer, Fede described Berlusconi's early business model, at a time when the mogul "didn't have a lira," as "mafia, mafia, mafia, money, mafia, money." The by now ex–TV news anchor also blurted out that Berlusconi had set up 60 overseas slush funds to pay for Dell'Utri's silence regarding the pair's links to the mob. The oddly upstanding fitness consultant, Gaetano Ferri, went straight to the authorities after hearing the conversation, which was soon plastered over the newspapers.[14]

It's too late for the mogul to be convicted for mafia association, like his pal Dell'Utri. But at the time this book went to press, Berlusconi still had the Senator De Gregorio bribery charges to fight. He was hopeful the statutes of limitation would kill this case. But by February 2015 prosecutors had the bit between their teeth in the Ruby 3 perjury case, maintaining the mogul had continued to make large payments to witnesses in the original Rubygate trial. And another indictment, for inducing his pimp Tarantini to perjure himself (to conceal the mogul's shady private life), appeared imminent. Deep down, Berlusconi knew his final years would pass with his nemeses the magistrates snapping ever closer at his heels. They have already drawn blood with the tax fraud conviction, and further legal defeats are likely.

So what does the future have in store for the 78-year-old mogul? He might take pride in handing over his fabulous wealth to the Berlusconi dynasty. But the frosty relationship between his most ambitious children, his daughters Marina, 47, and Barbara, 29, born of his first and second wives, respectively, suggests this might not go smoothly either. Following their father's tax fraud conviction and eviction from parliament, all five siblings are thought to have put their differences aside, at least for now, as they consider the fate that might await Fininvest without their father and three-time prime minister to nurture it. Berlusconi's declining political fortunes have prompted speculation about the future of not just his Forza Italia party but also the business empire with which the party has enjoyed a symbiotic relationship over the years.

There is certainly evidence of the business benefits Berlusconi has enjoyed thanks to his dominant political role. Analysts talked about the "Berlusconi premium" enjoyed by Mediaset shares when he was in office. Research published in February 2014 found a significant pro-Mediaset bias in the allocation of advertising spending during Berlusconi's political tenure. The authors said companies tried to court political advantage by directing advertising to the mogul-premier's TV channels.[15] And now without the support of a prime minister—or at least a powerful center-right political party—will the Berlusconi empire fall victim to the center-left, or even magistrates, determined to dismantle it, as some people (even those on the center-left) have suggested to me? The suggested scenario has led to speculation that Marina Berlusconi will stand for office in order to ensure the survival of the Berlusconi dynasty. But the mogul's oldest daughter shows very little enthusiasm for the idea.

The brutal recession also hit Mediaset's TV advertising revenues very hard. The company, which had been able to bear its high overheads during the boom years, had to look for cuts across the board during the long, hard downturn. In the last 12 months the outlook has picked up somewhat with predictions of a stronger TV advertising market by 2014–2015. But without Berlusconi pulling the strings in government and even Rai boardrooms, can it be sure of keeping hold of its 62 percent of the TV ad market?

Meanwhile, rumors continue to swirl over the future of Berlusconi's AC Milan football club. In late 2014, ticket sales were falling, and there were suggestions he might be forced to sell it.

By the end of 2014, the mogul's ultimate ambition, to be president of the republic, was a prospect no longer touted even by his most optimistic supporters. Berlusconi, like his operatic equivalent Don Giovanni, had had a lot of fun along the way, but his fall from power was now almost complete. True, his big companies Mediaset, Mondadori and Mediolanum are not about to fold. But with their larger-than-life owner no longer on the scene, how much will the Italian public, or the rest of the world, even care? For the spectators, the participants and the man himself, it was always about Berlusconi.

In northern Italy, the summer of 2014 was a washout. Berlusconi was marooned for the most part at his Arcore villa HQ. Gray skies and rain meant even the beautiful gardens and swimming pool were off-limits most of the time. For the past twenty years, he'd spent August in his paradise seaside home of Villa Certosa by the turquoise waters of Sardinia's Costa Smeralda (emerald coast). But the judges had ruled this pleasure palace was out-of-bounds for the convict, as were his homes in idyllic spots on lakes Como and Maggiore.

So he stayed in and watched films with fiancée Francesca Pascale. It was tempting to imagine the old playboy was finally preparing to settle down. Pascale seemed up for it. She talked about the ring he'd given her. But Berlusconi himself appeared to be getting cold feet, saying he was too old. And the presence of a Mrs. Pascale-Berlusconi on the inheritance list might complicate things a bit. Toward the end of the year, some reports suggested the strain was beginning to show. And the mogul's straight-talking middle child, Barbara Berlusconi, said in another Italian *Vanity Fair* article that it was "unlikely" that her father would ever marry again.

Berlusconi used the period of virtual house arrest to go on one of his periodic fitness regimes. This meant high-protein meals and a ban on carbs and his favorite pizza. The long dining table at Arcore that had once seen hookers and starlets push overcooked pasta around their plates before stripping off for bunga bunga sessions now played host to just Berlusconi, his family and his young companion, as they solemnly ate chicken and vegetables.

Over the summer, Berlusconi saw a few of his oldest friends, including his bosom pal Confalonieri. These solitary visitors, his closest associates—the ones who hadn't been jailed or deserted Forza Italia—were told to eat before they came, to ensure the mogul wasn't tempted to lay on more crowd-pleasing—and calorific—fare. One of the guests was Denis Verdini, a key Forza Italia figure in charge of the mogul's negotiations with Prime Minister Matteo Renzi over justice and parliamentary reforms. Berlusconi wanted to ensure changes that were favorable to the center-right in the next general election—an election in which his participation was banned.

By Christmas 2014 it was reported that even his chief political go-between Verdini was about to jump ship. Forza Italia was sinking. Membership had collapsed from 400,000 to 60,000. Accounts were in the red and it had just sacked 50 workers. During a forlorn 2014 Forza Italia Christmas dinner on the outskirts of Rome, Berlusconi took the microphone, as he'd always done, and regaled the bored diners with self-aggrandizing jokes. But even the lackeys were no longer laughing at the cabaret act that didn't know when to quit.[16]

Berlusconi's sense of both entitlement and frustration manifested itself in growing exasperation with events unfolding in the wider world. According to the few who had access to him in the later part of the year, he insisted that the mounting chaos in Libya was proof that his pragmatic approach to dealings with Gaddafi had been the right one. Events in Ukraine showed how the West had mishandled relations with his old friend Vladimir Putin. He even offered Prime Minister Matteo Renzi the benefit of his diplomatic experience to help smooth things over with Russia, to help make up for the actions of the United States, NATO and Europe that had "incredibly and irresponsibly" wiped out the progress made in the relationship with Russia since the end of the Cold War. Renzi didn't take him up on his offer.

"I was right on everything, and not just on foreign policy, but they stopped me governing," he fumed. For "they," read: Mario Monti, Giorgio Napolitano and the European powers, who appear to have acted in a Machiavellian manner to dispose of Berlusconi before he dragged Italy off the cliff. In Emperor Berlusca's mind, the fact that the worst of the sovereign debt crisis was averted paled in comparison to his perceived humiliation. It never occurred to him to blame himself for what had happened. For a man who'd achieved so much, and one who'd got away with even more, his punishment was now his inability to appreciate how incredibly lucky he'd been—thus far, at least—in four astonishing and shameless decades.

Back in that Catholic boarding school in the 1940s, when he was already doing his classmates' homework for money, or in the 1950s when he crooned on cruise ships, or even in the 1960s when he sold his first modest property development in Via Alciati, if you'd told Berlusconi then what he would go on to do and how he'd do it, perhaps even he would have been amazed, too.

EPILOGUE

When the mogul left parliament for the last time, two-thirds of Italy may have popped open the Prosecco. But how much is there to cheer about? In a nutshell, very little. Their country—*il bel paese*—still feels, for all its natural and artistic splendor, its endless sunshine and peerless cuisine, like a beautiful but badly run museum or a fantasy retirement location for rich Americans and northern Europe's middle classes. Even so, it remains the most alluring country in Europe, if not the world. Its sensual delights and wonderful people explain why all the German, Swedish, Danish, Dutch and Finnish journalists I've met in Italy are in no hurry to return to their efficient, clean, orderly and dull home countries. They know that it would be like going from color TV back to black-and-white. But with the wheels finally coming off the Berlusconi show and so much less news to file, it might soon be time for them to dust off the suitcases and head for Fiumicino airport.

For bright young Italians without the right family connections, however, a one-way flight to London, Paris or Berlin might be their *only* hope of getting a job. And this costly brain drain hasn't stopped because Berlusconi is on the way out; neither has the pervasive self-interest nor the fractured party political system that allowed him to win three elections.

Matteo Renzi, the current prime minister—at least when this book went to press (though given the speed with which Italy gets through governments, it's not worth betting your life's savings he'll be there till 2018)—wants to address the political instability by moving toward a two-party system like that in America or the UK. He has his work cut out. Still, the young, brash Renzi might represent Berlusconi's most lasting achievement: the creation of a center-left that's a bit savvier. It certainly took them long enough. Renzi is far from perfect, of course. Berlusconi in his final government promoted ministers and councilors whom he wanted to sleep with. Renzi, on the other hand, appears to choose colleagues—very often attractive and female—because they don't pose a threat or won't overshadow him politically. Neither selection strategy bodes particularly well.

Renzi needs all the help he can muster to drag Italy out of its economic hole. Youth unemployment is approaching 50 percent, and investment as a proportion of economic output in 2013 was at the lowest level since World War II.[1] By the summer of 2014, Italy was heading for deflation. This, combined with its no-growth economy, meant the mountainous national debt would be even harder to pay off. Some economists were predicting another sovereign debt crisis within 12 months.

Berlusconi could argue that Italy's problems are not all his fault. Of course, he'd probably argue they're not his fault at all. But what else did he achieve, apart from helping to create Renzi—or "Renzusconi"—and presiding over the country's continued economic decline? To the dismay of most of his countrymen, he seems to have joined the exclusive list of quintessentially Italian things alongside the Colosseum, Fiat 500s, Leonardo da Vinci, pizza Margherita and, of course, the mafia. In terms of his contribution to Western culture, Berlusconi will be able to claim the credit when the term "bunga bunga" enters the English dictionary; with over three-quarters of a million Google references, it appears that status isn't far away.[2] And of course, he has also appalled, astonished and entertained the rest of us for the best part of 20 years.

He's in no doubt about his status. "I am, far and away, the best prime minister that Italy has ever had in its 150-year-history," he said in 2009, when his third attempt at government was already unraveling.[3] But the things that any reasonably ambitious Italian prime minister might have hoped to achieve given three terms in office—improving living standards, reducing corruption, making inroads against tax evasion and organized crime, protecting the cultural patrimony, reforming justice and politics—seem as far away as ever. This shouldn't come as a surprise: it has always been clear that the anticommunist who made a quick buck in Soviet Russia, the libertine who faked piety to get Catholic votes, the economic liberal who presided over a media monopoly, was only ever in it for one thing. "His only value is money and his only objective to save himself," former employee Vittorio Dotti noted last year.[4]

Some opponents are still calling for the morass of his help-himself legislation to be dismantled in order to bring the Berlusconi age to an end. That will take some doing. But more difficult will be countering his tacit message that greed, self-interest and a lax attitude to the law can pay dividends—something that many Italians already suspected. Some of the strongest adherents to this creed helped Berlusconi and profited handsomely themselves. That's why Il Cavaliere has been able to ride roughshod over the country for so long. Perhaps Italians should start looking in the mirror rather than blaming everything on one brilliant but unscrupulous entrepreneur. As one of his critics, the singer Giorgio Gaber, remarked, "I don't fear Berlusconi himself, I fear the Berlusconi in me."

NOTES

CHAPTER 1: STARTING AS HE MEANT TO CONTINUE

1. Maria Latella, *Tendenza Veronica* (Milan: BurRizzoli, 2009), 107.
2. Vittorio Dotti and Andrea Sceresini, *L'Avvocato del Diavolo* (Milan: Chiarelettere, 2014), 35.
3. Paul Ginsborg, *Silvio Berlusconi: Television, Power and Patrimony* (London: Verso, 2005), 14.
4. "Your Early Business Career," *The Economist*, July 31, 2003, http://www.economist.com/node/1921934 (accessed: May 2, 2014).
5. "Your Early Business Career," *The Economist.*
6. Carlo Cosmelli, "Mafia, politica e affari: sette domande al Cavaliere," *Micromega*, July 3, 2009, http://temi.repubblica.it/micromega-online/mafia-politica-e-affari-sette-domande-al-cavaliere (accessed: May 3, 2014).
7. "Diritti Mediaset, chiesti 3 anniper il parlamentare Pdl Berruti," *La Stampa*, January 23, 2011, http://www.lastampa.it/2011/02/23/italia/politica/diritti-mediaset-chiesti-anniper-il-parlamentare-pdl-berruti-nHG6iIHhN6zEJE55cBQ6CK/pagina.html (accessed: July 15, 2014).
8. Pino Corrias, Massimo Gramellini and Curzio Maltese, *Colpo Grosso* (Milano: Dalai Editore, 1994), 47.
9. Mario Portanova, "Tangenti, truffe, abusi edilizi: l'incredibile storia del prete-manager Luigi Verzé," *Il Fatto Quotidiano*, January 2, 2012, www.ilfattoquotidiano.it/2012/01/02/tangenti-truffe-abusi-edilizi-lincredibile-storia-prete-manager-luigi-verze/181051/ (accessed: May 6, 2014); Michael Day, "Mario Cal: The Mysterious Suicide That Has Rocked the Vatican," *The Independent*, October 3, 2011, http://www.independent.co.uk/news/world/europe/mario-cal-the-mysterious-suicide-that-has-rocked-the-vatican-2364712.html (accessed: May 6, 2014).
10. Alexander Stille, *The Sack of Rome* (New York: Penguin, 2007), 30.
11. Dotti and Sceresini, *L'Avvocato del Diavolo*, 36.
12. "Your Early Business Career," *The Economist.*
13. Stille, *The Sack of Rome*, 34.
14. Claudia Fusani, "La Contessa Rangoni Michiavelli: 'Cosi Berlusconi ha truffato mia congnata,'" *L'Unita*, August 13, 2010, www.unita.it/italia/la-contessa-rangoni-machiavelli-laquo-cos-igrave-berlusconi-ha-truffato-mia-cognata-raquo-1.159160 (accessed: May 6, 2014).
15. Giuseppe D'Avanzo, "Lodo Mondadori, Previti condannato; La Cassazione conferma la sentenza d'appello," *La Repubblica*, July 14, 2007, http://www.repubblica.it/2007/07/sezioni/cronaca/cassazione-previti/lodo-condanna/lodo-condanna.html (accessed: May 6, 2014).

CHAPTER 2: DIRTY CASH

1. Claudia Fusani, "La Contessa Rangoni Michiavelli: 'Cosi Berlusconi ha truffato mia congnata,'" *L'Unita*, August 13, 2010, www.unita.it/italia/la-contessa-rangoni-machiavelli-laquo-cos-igrave-berlusconi-ha-truffato-mia-cognata-raquo-1.159160 (accessed: May 6, 2014).
2. Marco Travaglio, *Montanelli e il Cavaliere: Storia di un Grande e di un Piccolo Uomo* (Milan: Garzanti, 2004), 16.
3. "Paolo Borsellino, la sua ultima intervista censurata dale tv," *Controinformazione Indipendente*, August 11, 2013, https://www.youtube.com/watch?v=NDyfC3Z_d5A (accessed: May 15, 2014).
4. Alexander Stille, *The Sack of Rome* (New York: Penguin, 2007), 45.
5. "Paolo Borsellino, la sua ultima intervista censurata dale tv," *Controinformazione Indipendente*, May 21, 1992.
6. "Mangano e il cavallo: dopo la condanna Dee'Utri continua a mentire," *Il fatto Quotidiano*, June 29, 2010, www.ilfattoquotidiano.it/2010/06/29/mangano-e-il-cavallo-dopo-la-condanna-dellutri-continua-a-mentire/33657/ (accessed: July 12, 2014).
7. "Dell'Utri garante tra Berlusconi e boss," *La Repubblica*, June 6, 2013, http://ricerca.repubblica.it/repubblica/archivio/repubblica/2013/09/06/dellutri-garante-tra-berlusconi-boss.html (accessed: May 9, 2014).
8. Giovanni Bianconi, "Dell'Utri in viaggio con 50 chili di bagali, fuga evidente," *Corriere Della Sera*, April 29, 2004, http://www.corriere.it/cronache/14_aprile_29/dell-utri-viaggio-50-chili-bagagli-fuga-evidente-f5cc4238-cf59-11e3-bf7e-201ea72c5359.shtml (accessed: May 16, 2014).
9. Nick Pisa, "Berlusconi 'Paid £300,000 Protection Money to Mafia,'" *The Daily Telegraph*, May 22, 2011, http://www.telegraph.co.uk/news/worldnews/silvio-berlusconi/8529314/Berlusconi-paid-300000-protection-money-to-Mafia.html (accessed: May 11, 2014).
10. Stille, *The Sack of Rome*, 58.
11. Stille, *The Sack of Rome*, 52.
12. John Carlin, "All Hail Berlusconi," *The Observer*, January 18, 2004, http://www.theguardian.com/world/2004/jan/18/italy.features (accessed: May 12, 2014).
13. Vittorio Dotti and Andrew Sceresini, *L'Avvocato del Diavolo* (Milan: Chiarelettere, 2014), 51.
14. Paul Ginsborg, *Silvio Berlusconi: Television, Power and Patrimony* (London: Verso, 2005), 38.
15. Dotti and Sceresini, *L'Avvocato del Diavolo*, 52.

CHAPTER 3: REALPOLITIK

1. "Vent'anni fa il lancio di monetine contro Craxi all'Hotel Raphael," *Corriere Della Sera*, April 30, 2013, http://roma.corriere.it/roma/notizie/politica/13_aprile_30/craxi-raphael-ventanni-dopo-212905795963.shtml (accessed: May 18, 2014).
2. "Berlusconi Appears in Court," *BBC News*, May 5, 2003, http://news.bbc.co.uk/2/hi/europe/2995497.stm (accessed: May 18, 2014).
3. Laura Colby, "Benedetti on Bribes: Would Do It Again if Needed," *New York Times*, May 19, 1993, http://www.nytimes.com/1993/05/19/news/19iht-ital_10.htm (accessed: May 20, 2014).
4. Vittorio Dotti and Andrew Sceresini, *L'Avvocato del Diavolo* (Milan: Chiarelettere, 2014), 90.
5. Dotti and Sceresini, *L'Avvocato del Diavolo*, 93.
6. Alexander Stille, *The Sack of Rome* (New York: Penguin, 2007), 103.
7. Stille, *The Sack of Rome*, 100.
8. Dotti and Sceresini, *L'Avvocato del Diavolo*, 44.

9. Paul Ginsborg, *Silvio Berlusconi: Television, Power and Patrimony* (London: Verso, 2005), 31.
10. Philip Willan, in email to author, May 13, 2014.
11. Andrew Gumbel, "Obituary: Franco Di Bella," *The Independent*, December 23, 1997, http://www.independent.co.uk/news/obituaries/obituary-franco-di-bella-1290357.html (accessed: May 15, 2014).
12. Gumbel, "Obituary: Franco Di Bella."
13. "Belzebu e Belfagor nel complotto della P2," *La Repubblica*, May 23, 1984, http://ricerca.repubblica.it/repubblica/archivio/repubblica/1984/05/23/belzebu-belfagor-nel-complotto-della-p2.html (accessed: May 15, 2014).
14. "Your Early Business Career," *The Economist*, July 31, 2003, http://www.economist.com/node/1921934 (accessed: May 20, 2014).
15. Philip Willan, *The Vatican at War: From Blackfriars Bridge to Buenos Aires* (Bloomington: iUniverse, 2013), 102.
16. Dotti and Sceresini, *L'Avvocato del Diavolo*, 29.
17. Marco Travaglio, *Montanelli e il Cavaliere: Storia di un Grande e di un Piccolo Uomo*, (Milan: Garzanti, 2004), 28.
18. Stille, *The Sack of Rome*, 145.
19. Vittorio Dotti and Andrea Sceresini, *L'Avvocato del Diavolo* (Milan: Chiarelettere, 2014), 69.
20. Dotti and Sceresini, *L'Avvocato del Diavolo*, 72.
21. Dotti and Sceresini, *L'Avvocato del Diavolo*, 78.
22. Lizzy Davies, "Berlusconi Brother Sparks Fury over Balotelli Remark," *The Guardian*, February 6, 2013, http://www.theguardian.com/world/2013/feb/06/berlusconi-brother-fury-balotelli-remark (accessed: May 25, 2014).
23. Ginsborg, *Silvio Berlusconi: Television, Power and Patrimony*, 55.
24. "In Quotes: Berlusconi in His Own Words," *BBC News*, August 2, 2013, http://news.bbc.co.uk/2/hi/europe/3041288.stm (accessed: May 20, 2014).
25. Stille, *The Sack of Rome*, 118.
26. Stille, *The Sack of Rome*, 118.
27. Barbacetto, Gomez and Travaglio, *Mani Pulite*, 403.

CHAPTER 4: ESCAPE ROUTE

1. Stephen P. Koff, *Italy: From the 1st to the 2nd Republic* (London: Routledge, 2002), 21.
2. Fiona Leney, "The Sleaze Factor: Clean Hands Team Fails to Wash Away Tangentopoli Dirt," *The Independent*, October 25, 1994, http://www.independent.co.uk/news/world/the-sleaze-factor-cleanhands-team-fails-to-wash-away-tangentopoli-dirt-fiona-leney-looks-at-italys-cathedral-of-corruption-where-each-day-a-new-sector-of-society-is-investigated-1444839.html (accessed: May 20, 2014).
3. Gianni Barbacetto, "Mani pulite, anno zero," *Societacivile 2004*, http://www.societacivile.it/focus/articoli_focus/mani_pulite.html (accessed: August 18, 2014).
4. Gianni Barbacetto, Peter Gomez and Marco Travaglio, *Mani Pulite: La Vera Storia* (Roma: Editori Riuniti, 2002), 97.
5. "Craxi: tutti I processi e le condanne," *La Repubblica*, January 19, 2000, http://www.repubblica.it/online/politica/craxi1/processi/processi.html (accessed: August 18, 2014).
6. Paul Ginsborg, *Silvio Berlusconi: Television, Power and Patrimony* (London: Verso 2005), 84.
7. Alexander Stille, *The Sack of Rome* (New York: Penguin, 2007), 135.
8. Marco Travaglio, *Ad Personam: 1994–2010. Così Destra e Sinistra Banno Privatizzato la Democrazia* (Milan: Chiarelettere, 2010), 35.
9. Travaglio, *Ad Personam*, 35.
10. Stille, *The Sack of Rome*, 152.

11. Paul Ginsborg, *Silvio Berlusconi: Television, Power and Patrimony* (London: Verso, 2005), 65.
12. Maria Latella, *Tendenza Veronica* (Milan: BurRizzoli, 2009), 51.
13. Stille, *The Sack of Rome*, 144.
14. Latella, *Tendenza Veronica*, 73.
15. "1994—Dicesa in campo," www.youtube.com/watch?v=B8-uIYqnk5A (accessed: June 10, 2014).
16. Michael Day, "Senior Italian Politician Charged with Defamation Aggravated by Racial Discrimination," *The Independent*, November 7, 2013, http://www.independent.co.uk/news/world/europe/senior-italian-politician-charged-with-defamation-aggravated-by-racial-discrimination-8927534.html (accessed: May 25, 2014).
17. Stille, *The Sack of Rome*, 159.
18. Martin Bull and Martin Rhodes, *Italy—A Contested Polity* (New York: Routledge, 2009), 233.
19. Stille, *The Sack of Rome*, 183.
20. Marco Travaglio, *Montanelli e il Cavaliere: Storia di un Grande e di un Piccolo Uomo* (Milan: Garzanti, 2004), 86.
21. Travaglio, *Montanelli e il Cavaliere*, 88.
22. Travaglio, *Montanelli e il Cavaliere*, 99.
23. Travaglio, *Ad Personam*, 45.
24. Travaglio, *Ad Personam*, 35.
25. Alberto Vannucci, "The Controversial Legacy of 'Mani Pulite': A Critical Analysis of Italian Corruption and Anti-Corruption Policies," *Bulletin of Italian Politics*, vol. 1 (2009), 233–264.

CHAPTER 5: GETTING HIS HANDS DIRTY

1. Marco Travaglio, *Ad Personam: 1994–2010. Così Destra e Sinistra Hanno Privatizzato la Democrazia* (Milan: Chiarelettere, 2010), 69.
2. Vittorio Dotti and Andrea Sceresini, *L'Avvocato del Diavolo* (Milan: Chiarelettere, 2014), 15.
3. Dotti and Sceresini, *L'Avvocato del Diavolo*, 96.
4. Dotti and Sceresini, *L'Avvocato del Diavolo*, 117.
5. Travaglio, *Ad Personam*, 50.
6. Travaglio, *Ad Personam*, 193.
7. Travaglio, *Ad Personam*, 57.
8. Travaglio, *Ad Personam*, 127.
9. Travaglio, *Ad Personam*, 59.
10. Travaglio, *Ad Personam*, 64.
11. Alexander Stille, *The Sack of Rome* (New York: Penguin, 2007), 199.
12. Stille, *The Sack of Rome*, 186.
13. Conti Paolo, "Rai: finisce 3 a 2 la partita delle nomine," *Corriere della Sera*, September 18, 1994, http://archiviostorico.corriere.it/1994/settembre/18/RAI_finisce_partita_delle_nomine_co_0_94091813818.shtml (accessed: May 25, 2014).
14. Stille, *The Sack of Rome*, 195.
15. Paolo Posteraro, *Povera Italia. Da Craxi a Renzi: I Peggiori Anni della Nostra Vita* (Rome: Newton Compton Editori, 2014), 129.
16. Paul Ginsborg, *Silvio Berlusconi: Television, Power and Patrimony* (London: Verso, 2005), 75.
17. Ginsborg, *Silvio Berlusconi*, 77.
18. Ginsborg, *Silvio Berlusconi*, 80.
19. Gianni Barbacetto, Peter Gomez and Marco Travaglio, *Mani Pulite: La Vera Storia*, (Roma: Editori Riuniti, 2002), 218.
20. Stille, *The Sack of Rome*, 214.
21. Barbacetto, Gomez and Travaglio, *Mani Pulite*, 48.

22. Travaglio, *Ad Personam*, 73.
23. Travaglio, *Ad Personam*, 69.
24. Stille, *The Sack of Rome*, 190.

CHAPTER 6: JUSTICE FOR SALE

1. Vittorio Dotti and Andrea Sceresini, *L'Avvocato del Diavolo* (Milan: Chiarelettere, 2014), 70.
2. Paul Ginsborg, *Silvio Berlusconi: Television, Power and Patrimony* (London: Verso 2005), 84.
3. "Italy, former Italian Prime Minister Silvio Berlusconi wins referendum that could have forced him to break up his TV empire," *ITN News*, June 12, 1995, http://www.itnsource.com/shotlist//RTV/1995/06/12/605201568/?s=elects (accessed: August 20, 2014).
4. Gianni Barbacetto, Peter Gomez and Marco Travaglio, *Mani Pulite: La Vera Storia* (Roma: Editori Riuniti, 2002), 526.
5. Barbacetto, Gomez and Travaglio, *Mani Pulite*, 524.
6. Alexander Stille, *The Sack of Rome* (New York: Penguin, 2007), 218.
7. Barbacetto, Gomez and Travaglio, *Mani Pulite*, 528.
8. Marco Travaglio, "Berlusconi, storia dell'evasore-corruttore da Craxi a Mills," *Il Fatto Quotidiano*, August 8, 2013, http://www.ilfattoquotidiano.it/2013/08/08/berlusconi-storia-dellevasore-corruttore-da-craxi-a-mills/679749/ (accessed: June 2, 2014).
9. Travaglio, "Berlusconi, storia dell'evasore-corruttore da Craxi a Mills."
10. Peter Gomez and Antonella Mascal, *Il Regalo di Berlusconi* (Milan: Chiarelettere, 2009), 188.
11. Gomez and Mascal, *Il Regalo di Berlusconi*, 201.
12. Nick Pisa, "Tessa Jowell's husband David Mills 'very relieved' after Italian court quashes bribery conviction," *Daily Mail*, February 26, 2010, http://www.dailymail.co.uk/news/article-1253672/Tessa-Jowells-estranged-husband-David-Mills-faces-jail-corruption-charges-Italian-supreme-court-ruling.html (accessed: June 2, 2014).
13. Travaglio, "Berlusconi, storia dell'evasore-corruttore da Craxi a Mills."
14. Barbacetto, Gomez and Travaglio, *Mani Pulite*, 423.
15. Barbacetto, Gomez and Travaglio, *Mani Pulite*, 422.
16. Barbacetto, Gomez and Travaglio, *Mani Pulite*, 424.
17. Barbacetto, Gomez and Travaglio, *Mani Pulite*, 430.
18. Dotti and Sceresini, *L'Avvocato del Diavolo*, 13.
19. Barbacetto, Gomez and Travaglio, *Mani Pulite*, 447.
20. Stille, *The Sack of Rome*, 237.
21. Paolo Biondani and Carlo Porcedda, *Il Cavaliere Nero: Il Tesoro Nascosto di Silvio Berlusconi* (Milan: Chiarelettere, 2013), 145.
22. Ron Dicker, "Mother Teresa Humanitarian Image 'a Myth,' New Study Says," *Huffington Post*, March 4, 2013, www.huffingtonpost.com/2013/03/04/mother-teresa-myth_n_2805697.html (accessed: June 5, 2014).
23. Stille, *The Sack of Rome*, 230.
24. Ginsborg, *Silvio Berlusconi: Television, Power and Patrimony*, 88.
25. Barbacetto, Gomez and Travaglio, *Mani Pulite*, 699.
26. Mario Calabresi, "Berlusconi: 'Ho avuto un cancro alla prostata," *La Repubblica*, July 23, 2000, www.repubblica.it/online/politica/malattia/parla/parla.html (accessed: June 6, 2014).

CHAPTER 7: THE GORY YEARS

1. Giancarlo Mola, "Berlusconi: 'La mia biografia in tutte le famiglie italiane,'" *La Repubblica*, April 11, 2001, www.repubblica.it/online/politica/campagnacinque/libro/libro.html (accessed: June 10, 2013).

2. Alexander Stille, *The Sack of Rome* (New York: Penguin, 2007), 255.
3. Vittorio Dotti and Andrea Sceresini, *L'Avvocato del Diavolo* (Milan: Chiarelettere, 2014), 39.
4. Luca Rifcolfi, *Tempo Scaduto. Il 'Contratto con gli Italian' alla Prova dei Fatti* (Bologna: Il Mulino, 2006).
5. Marco Travaglio, *Ad Personam: 1994–2010. Cosi Destra e Sinistra Hanno Privatizzato la Democrazia* (Milan: Chiarelettere, 2010), 195.
6. Travaglio, *Ad Personam*, 206.
7. Rizzo Sergio, "Le doppie dimissioni del ministro di sangue dc," *Corriere della Sera*, May 5, 2010, http://archiviostorico.corriere.it/2010/maggio/05/doppie_dimissioni_del_ministro_sangue_co_9_100505011.shtml (accessed: August 20, 2014); Gianni Barbacetto, Peter Gomez and Marco Travaglio, *Mani Pulite: La Vera Storia* (Roma: Editori Riuniti, 2002), 594.
8. Carlo Macrì, "Ex-Minister Scajola and Ex-FI Deputy Matacena Arrested," *Corriere della Sera*, May 8, 2014, http://www.corriere.it/english/14_maggio_08/ex-minister-scajola-and-ex-fi-deputy-matacena-arrested-22c7f4e6-d6a1-11e3-b1c6-d3130b63f531.shtml (accessed: July 10, 2014).
9. Travaglio, *Ad Personam*, 199.
10. Travaglio, *Ad Personam*, 214.
11. Travaglio, *Ad Personam*, 219.
12. "Italy's Worst Case of Corruption," *The Guardian*, August 7, 2003, www.theguardian.com/world/2003/aug/07/italy (accessed: June 25, 2014).
13. Paolo Biondani and Carlo Porcedda, *Il Cavaliere Nero: Il Tesoro Nascosto di Silvio Berlusconi* (Milan: Chiarelettere, 2013), 146.
14. Bruce Johnston and Julian Coman, "Brussels Horror as Berlusconi Fills in as Foreign Minister," *The Daily Telegraph*, January 13, 2002, http://www.telegraph.co.uk/news/worldnews/europe/italy/1381309/Brussels-horror-as-Berlusconi-fills-in-as-foreign-minister.html (accessed: June 26, 2014).
15. Steven Erlanger, "Italy's Premier Calls Western Civilization Superior to Islamic World," *New York Times*, September 26, 2001, www.nytimes.com/2001/09/27/world/italy-s-premier-calls-western-civilization-superior-to-islamic-world.html (accessed: June 26, 2014).
16. "Berlusconi Vaunts Italy's Secretaries," *BBC News*, September 24, 2003, http://news.bbc.co.uk/2/hi/europe/3137406.stm (accessed: June 26, 2014).
17. "Berlusconi e l'inglese," *Mister Media*, October 30, 2012, www.youtube.com/watch?v=_9c-ji9L2lI (accessed: June 26, 2014).
18. "Silvio Berlusconi vs MRP Schulz; Relive the Moment," *EurActiv*, April 16, 2008, www.youtube.com/watch?v=0bPqaqGJ5Js (accessed: June 26, 2014).
19. "Berlusconi's Doctor Confirms Facelift," *ABC News*, January 18, 2004, http://www.abc.net.au/news/2004-01-18/berlusconis-doctor-confirms-facelift/121352 (accessed: June 26, 2014).
20. Malcolm Moore, "Cherie Blair Had Best Night of Her Life with Silvio Berlusconi," *The Daily Telegraph*, June 5, 2008, www.telegraph.co.uk/news/worldnews/europe/italy/2080817/Cherie-Blair-had-best-night-of-her-life-with-Silvio-Berlusconi.html (accessed: June 27, 2014).
21. Nick Pisa, "Tony Blair Begged Wife Cherie to Protect Him from Berlusconi's Bandanna," *The Daily Telegraph*, May 24, 2009, http://www.telegraph.co.uk/news/worldnews/europe/italy/5377843/Tony-Blair-begged-wife-Cherie-to-protect-him-from-Berlusconis-bandanna.html (accessed: June 27, 2014).
22. "Visit to Italy: The Gasparri Law—Observations and Recommendations by the OSCE Representative on the Freedom of the Media," June 7, 2005, www.osce.org/fom/15827 (accessed: June 27, 2014).
23. "Visit to Italy: The Gasparri Law."
24. David Blaine Walker, *Institutional Reform in Contemporary Italian Politics: Electoral Systems* (Ann Arbor, MI: ProQuest, 2011), 61.

25. "OSCE Media Watchdog Says New Italian Legislation Insufficient to Curb Media Concentration," June 7, 2005, www.osce.org/fom/46498 (accessed: January 11, 2015).
26. Stille, *The Sack of Rome*, 280.
27. Michael Day, "Berlusconi Payback," *Variety*, April 24, 2008, http://variety.com/2008/scene/news/berlusconi-payback-1117984575/ (accessed: June 28, 2014).
28. Day, "Berlusconi Payback."
29. "Basta Berlusconi," *The Economist*, April 6, 2006, www.economist.com/node/6772333 (accessed: June 29, 2014).
30. Marco Travaglio, in interview with author on Italian politics, June 2, 2014.
31. Peter Popham, "Berlusconi Throws Legal System into Chaos to Save Ally," *The Independent*, October 8, 2005, http://www.independent.co.uk/news/world/europe/berlusconi-throws-legal-system-into-chaos-to-save-ally-318026.html (accessed: June 29, 2014).
32. Biondani and Porcedda, *Il Cavaliere Nero*, 121.

CHAPTER 8: GETTING AWAY WITH IT

1. John Hooper, "Berlusconi Collapses at Political Rally," *The Guardian*, November 27, 2006, http://www.theguardian.com/world/2006/nov/27/italy.johnhooper (accessed: July 3, 2014).
2. "Berlusconi a Cleveland. Cossiga: 'Operato al cuore, intervento riuscito,'" *Il Sole 24 Ore*, December 18, 2006, http://www.ilsole24ore.com/art/SoleOnLine4/Attualita ed Esteri/Attualita/2006/12/sbio161206berlusconiusa.shtml?uuid=d6580fe0-8cea-11db-8307-00000e25108c&DocRulesView=Libero (accessed: December 11, 2014).
3. Beppe Severgnini, "Il Cavaliere spiegto ai posteri: Dieci motivi per 20 anni di 'regno,'" *Corriere della Sera*, October 27, 2010, www.corriere.it/politica/10_ottobre_27/severgnini-berlusconi-spiegato-ai-posteri-dieici-motivi-per-venti-anni_4f712cd0-e18e-11df-9076-00144f02aabc.shtml (accessed: July 5, 2014).
4. Marco Travaglio, *È Stato la Mafia* (Milan: Chiarelettere, 2014), 94.
5. Gianni Barbacetto, Peter Gomez and Marco Travaglio, *Mani Pulite: La Vera Storia* (Roma: Editori Riuniti, 2002), 223.
6. Alexander Stille, *The Sack of Rome* (New York: Penguin, 2007), 241.
7. Travaglio, *È Stato la Mafia*, 89.
8. Marco Travaglio, *Ad Personam: 1994–2010. Così Destra e Sinistra Hanno Privatizzato la Democrazia* (Milan: Chiarelettere, 2010), 276.
9. Travaglio, *Ad Personam*, 279.
10. Travaglio, *Ad Personam*, 281.
11. Travaglio, *Ad Personam*, 282.
12. "Berlusconi perde la causa con Travaglio," *Corriere della Sera*, March 7, 2006, www.corriere.it/Primo_Piano/Politica/2006/03_Marzo/07/travaglio.shtml (accessed: July 7, 2014).
13. Stefano Corradino, "Berlusconi e il disturbo vincente. Intervista allo psichiatra Luigi Cancrini," *Articolo 21*, July 3, 2009, http://archivi.articolo21.org/317/notizia/berlusconi-e-il-disturbo-vincente-intervista-allo.html (accessed: January 11, 2015).
14. Beppe Grillo, "Ruby Forever," *Beppe Grillo's Blog*, January 2011, www.beppegrillo.it/en/2011/01/ruby_forever_1.html (accessed: July 6, 2014).
15. Paul Ginsborg, *Silvio Berlusconi: Television, Power and Patrimony* (London: Verso, 2005), 109.
16. "I pm: 3 anni e 8 mes du carcere a Berlusconi," *Corriere della Sera*, June 19, 2012, archiviostorico.corriere.it/2012/giugno/19/anni_mesi_carcere_Berlusconi_co_8_120619045.shtml (accessed: July 7, 2014).
17. "Italy ex-PM Silvio Berlusconi to Face Bribery Charge," *BBC News*, October 23, 2013, http://www.bbc.com/news/world-europe-24641233 (accessed: July 8, 2014).
18. "Italy ex-PM Silvio Berlusconi to Face Bribery Charge," *BBC News*, October 23, 2013.

CHAPTER 9: FIDDLING WHILE ROME BURNS

1. Curzio Maltese, *La Bolla: La Pericolosa Fine del Sogno Berlusconiani* (Milan: Feltrinelli, 2009), 79.
2. Phil Stewart, "Italy's Berlusconi Wins Immunity from Prosecution," Reuters, July 22, 2008, www.reuters.com/article /2008/07/22/us-italy-immunity-idUSL 222100720080722 (accessed: July 8, 2014).
3. Barbie Latza Nadeau, "Basta! Berlusconi's Wife Bails," *The Daily Beast*, May 4, 2009, http://www.thedailybeast.com/articles/2009/05/04/berlusconis-9-billion-divorce.html (accessed: July 10, 2014).
4. "Berlusconi: Left Has Uglier Women," *BBC News*, April 9, 2008, news.bbc.co.uk/1 /hi/world/europe/7338415.stm (accessed: July 10, 2014).
5. Maria Latella, *Tendenza Veronica* (Milan: BurRizzoli, 2009), 127.
6. John Follain, "'Lesbian' Clinch More Embarrassment for Berlusconi," *The Sunday Times*, July 5, 2009, http://www.thesundaytimes.co.uk/sto/news/world_news /article176363.ece (accessed: July 10, 2014).
7. Gabriella De Matteis and Giuliano Foschini, "D'Addario in lacrime sesso e politica ecco le mie notti con Berlusconi," *La Repubblica*, November 28, 2014, http://ricerca .repubblica.it/repubblica/archivio/repubblica/2014/11/28/daddario-in-lacrime -sesso-e-politica-ecco-le-mie-notti-con-berlusconi12.html (accessed: December 18, 2014).
8. Tom Kington, "Could Barbara Montereale's Revelations Break Silvio Berlusconi's Grip on Power?" *The Observer*, June 21, 2009, http://www.theguardian.com/world /2009/jun/21/berlusconi-italy-barbara-montereale (accessed: July 11, 2014).
9. Michael Day and Peter Popham, "Italian Stallions: The Sex Lives of Mussolini and Berlusconi," *The Independent*, November 24, 2009, http://www.independent.co.uk /news/world/europe/italian-stallions-the-sex-lives-of-mussolini-and-berlusconi -1826454.html (accessed: July 11, 2014).
10. Nick Squires, "Sleaze Threatens to Topple Silvio Berlusconi as Friends Warn over Scandals," *Daily Telegraph*, June 21, 2009, www.telegraph.co.uk/news/worldnews /europe/italy/5588183/Sleaze-threatens-to-topple-Silvio-Berlusconi-as-friends -warn-over-scandals.html (accessed: July 12, 2014).
11. "Feste e ragazze, fini preoccupato 'A rischio la fiducia dei cittadini,'" *La Repubblica*, June 19, 2009, www.repubblica.it/2009/06/sezioni/politica/berlusconi-divorzio-8 /avvenire-al-premier/avvenire-al-premier.html (accessed: January 2015).
12. Michael Day, "Vatican Blamed for Bogus Dirt That Ousted Catholic Editor," *The Independent*, February 4, 2010, http://www.independent.co.uk/news/world/europe /vatican-blamed-for-bogus-dirt-that-ousted-catholic-editor-1889071.html (accessed: July 12, 2014).
13. John Hooper, "'Don't Embarrass Italy before G8 summit,' President Urges Media," *The Guardian*, June 29, 2009, www.theguardian.com/world/2009/jun/29/silvio -berlusconi-g8-summit-allegations (accessed: July 12, 2014).
14. "Berlusconi Says Obama Is 'Tanned,'" *BBC News*, November 8, 2008, http://news .bbc.co.uk/1/hi/world/europe/7715016.stm (accessed: July 12, 2014).
15. Anita Singh, "Queen Is 'Not Amused' by Berlusconi Gaffe," *Daily Telegraph*, April 3, 2009, www.telegraph.co.uk/finance/g20-summit/5099649/Queen-is-not-amused-by -Berlusconi-gaffe.html (accessed: July 14, 2014).
16. Michael Day, "Berlusconi Turns to Gaddafi and G8 for Comfort," *The Independent*, June 29, 2009, http://www.independent.co.uk/news/world/europe/berlusconi-turns -to-g8-and-gaddafi-for-comfort-1722950.html (accessed: July 14, 2014).
17. Stefan Faris, "Bye Bye Gaddafi: How Italy Will Profit from the New Libyan Regime," *Time*, August 4, 2011, http://content.time.com/time/world/article/0,8599,2090116,00 .html (accessed: July 8, 2014).
18. Committee to Protect Journalists, http://cpj.org/killed/europe/russia/ (accessed: July 10, 2014).

19. Michael Day, "Putin Accused of Giving Berlusconi Cut from Energy Deals," *The Independent*, December 3, 2010, http://www.independent.co.uk/news/world/europe/putin-accused-of-giving-berlusconi-cut-from-energy-deals-2149802.html (accessed: July 12, 2014).
20. Day, "Putin Accused of Giving Berlusconi Cut from Energy Deals."
21. "Franceschini in calzini turchesi: 'Tutti come il giudice Mesiano,'" *La Repubblica*, October 18, 2009, www.repubblica.it/2009/10/sezioni/politica/giustizia-14/giustizia-14/giustizia-14.html (accessed: July 15, 2014).
22. Michael Day, "Top News Reader Quits in Protest at Berlusconi," *The Independent*, May 25, 2010, http://www.independent.co.uk/news/world/europe/tv-news-reader-quits-in-protest-at-berlusconi-1981964.html (accessed: July 15, 2014).
23. John Hooper, "Berlusconi: Italy Earthquake Victims Should View Experience as Camping Weekend," *The Guardian*, April 8, 2009, http://www.theguardian.com/world/2009/apr/08/italy-earthquake-berlusconi (accessed: July 15, 2014).
24. Michael Day, "'Apocalypse' on Railway in Tuscany," *The Independent*, July 1, 2009, www.independent.co.uk/news/world/europe/apocalypse-on-railway-in-tuscany-1726203.html (accessed: July 20, 2014).
25. Alessandra Rizzo, "Berlusconi Attacker Apologizes for 'Superficial, Cowardly and Impetuous' Act," *The Huffington Post*, December 14, 2009, http://www.huffingtonpost.com/2009/12/14/berlusconi-attacker-apolo_n_392033.html (accessed: July 18, 2014).
26. Sara Nicoli, "Cucu, la Merkel e 'inchiavabile,'" *Il Fatto Quotidiano*, September 10, 2011, http://www.ilfattoquotidiano.it/2011/09/10/cucu-la-merkel-e-%E2%80%9Cinchiavabile%E2%80%9D/156545/ (accessed: July 18, 2014).

CHAPTER 10: BERLUSCONI'S NOT WELL

1. Nick Squires, "Silvio Berlusconi Picks Starlets for European Elections," *Daily Telegraph*, April 22, 2009, http://www.telegraph.co.uk/news/worldnews/europe/italy/5200992/Silvio-Berlusconi-picks-starlets-for-European-elections.html (accessed: July 20, 2014).
2. Squires, "Silvio Berlusconi Picks Starlets for European Elections."
3. Peter Gomez, Marco Lillo and Marco Travaglio, *Papi: Uno Scandalo Politico* (Milan: Chiarelettere, 2009), 148.
4. Giuseppe D'Avanzo and Conchita Sannino, "Cosi papi Berlusconi entro nella vita di Noemi," *La Repubblica*, May 24, 2009, http://www.repubblica.it/2009/05/sezioni/politica/berlusconi-divorzio-2/parla-gino/parla-gino.html (accessed: July 22, 2014).
5. "Roberto Maroni (Lega Nord)—Ministro dell'Interno," *MicroMega*, http://temi.repubblica.it/micromega-online/maroni-roberto-lega-nord-ministro-dellinterno (accessed: July 20, 2014).
6. Gomez, Lillo and Travaglio, *Papi*, 17.
7. Gomez, Lillo and Travaglio, *Papi*, 18.
8. Michael Day, "Drama Topper Is at Center of Wire-Tap Storm," *Variety*, July 17, 2008, http://variety.com/2008/scene/news/rai-chiefs-move-to-sack-sacca-1117989087/ (accessed: July 19, 2014).
9. Gomez, Lillo and Travaglio, *Papi*, 45.
10. Nick Vivarelli, "Berlusconi Fuels Rai-Mediaset Rivalry," *Variety*, June 27, 2008, https://variety.com/2008/scene/markets-festivals/berlusconi-fuels-rai-mediaset-rivalry-1117988229/ (accessed: July 20, 2014).
11. Gomez, Lillo, and Travaglio, *Papi*, 69.
12. Carlo Bonini and Piero Colaprico, "Silenzi, prestiti e favore: cosi Berlusconi ha pagato le Olgettine e i fedelissimi," *La Repubblica*, October 27, 2011, http://inchieste.repubblica.it/it/repubblica/rep-it/2011/10/27/news/silenzi_prestiti_e_favori_cos_berlusconi_ha_pagato_le_olgettine_e_i_fedelissimi-23945879/ (accessed: July 21, 2014).

13. Nick Vivarelli, "Murdoch, Berlusconi Tension Builds," *Variety*, December 3, 2008, http://variety.com/2008/tv/news/murdoch-berlusconi-tension-builds-1117996735/ (accessed: July 8, 2014).
14. Michael Day, "Sky TV Broadcast Angers Berlusconi," *Variety*, April 17, 2009, http://variety.com/2009/scene/markets-festivals/skytv-broadcast-angers-berlusconi-1118002560/ (accessed: July 10, 2014).
15. Michael Day and Peter Popham, "Murdoch Is Waging a Vendetta against Me, Says Berlusconi," *The Independent*, June 5, 2009, http://www.independent.co.uk/news/world/europe/murdoch-is-waging-a-vendetta-against-me-says-berlusconi-1697328.html (accessed: July 8, 2014).
16. http://silvioperilnobel.blogspot.co.uk/ (accessed: July 20, 2014).
17. Anushay Hossain, "Femicide in Italy: Domestic Violence Persists Despite New Laws," *Forbes*, August 26, 2013, http://www.forbes.com/sites/worldviews/2013/08/26/femicide-in-italy-domestic-violence-persists-despite-new-laws/ (accessed: August 12, 2014).
18. Michael Day, "Murder in Calabria: Fabiana's Fate Shames Italy," *The Independent*, June 2, 2013, www.independent.co.uk/news/world/europe/murder-in-calabria-fabianas-fate-shames-italy-8640816.html (accessed: July 15, 2013).
19. James Walston, "Berlusconi's Real Woman Problem," *Foreign Policy*, February 14, 2014, http://www.foreignpolicy.com/articles/2011/02/14/berlusconis_real_Woman_Problem?wp_login_redirect=0 (accessed: July 15, 2014).

CHAPTER 11: RUBYGATE AND BUNGA BUNGA

1. "Ruby, chiesto rinvio a giudizio per Fede, Minetti e Mora," *Il Fatto Quotidiano*, May 6, 2011, http://www.ilfattoquotidiano.it/2011/05/06/ruby-chiesto-rinvio-a-giudizio-per-fede-minetti-e-mora/109438/ (accessed: September 3, 2014).
2. "Il caso Ruby," *La Repubblica*, http://inchieste.repubblica.it/it/repubblica/rep-it/2011/04/12/news/il_caso_ruby-14836804/ (accessed: July 17, 2014).
3. Piero Colaprico, *Le Cene Eleganti* (Milan: Feltrinelli, 2011), 20.
4. "Il caso Ruby," *La Repubblica*.
5. "Il caso Ruby," *La Repubblica*.
6. Colaprico, *Le Cene Eleganti*, 95.
7. Philip Willan, "Meet Ilda Boccassini, the Lady Who Scares the Italian Mob," *Daily Telegraph*, July 18, 2010, http://www.telegraph.co.uk/news/worldnews/europe/italy/7896506/Meet-Ilda-Boccassini-the-lady-who-scares-the-Italian-Mob.html (accessed: July 18, 2014).
8. Michael Day, "Anti-Mafia Judge Sets Sight on Italy's Corrupt Official," *The Independent*, December 2, 2011, http://www.independent.co.uk/news/world/europe/antimafia-judge-sets-sights-on-italys-corrupt-officials-6270762.html (accessed: July 18, 2014).
9. Marianne Aprile, "Le donne del Cavaliere?" *Oggi*, September 21, 2011, www.oggi.it/attualita/notizie/2011/09/21/le-donne-del-cavaliere-sono-ben-131 (accessed: July 18, 2014).
10. Colaprico, *Le Cene Eleganti*, 112.
11. Barbie Latza Nadeau, "Will Berlusconi Get the Boot?" *The Daily Beast*, November 7, 2011, http://www.thedailybeast.com/articles/2010/11/07/silvio-berlusconis-bunga-bunga-parties.html (accessed: July 17, 2014).
12. Tom Kington, "Italy in Suspense As 'Bunga Bunga' Trial Poised to Lift Lid on Berlusconi's Antics," *The Observer*, April 3, 2011, http://www.theguardian.com/world/2011/apr/03/italy-silvio-berlusconi-trial (accessed: July 18, 2014).
13. "Il caso Ruby," *La Repubblica*.
14. Peter Gomez, Marco Lillo, and Marco Travaglio, *Papi; Uno Scandalo Politico* (Milan: Chiarelettere, 2009), 265.

15. Colaprico, *Le Cene Eleganti*, 236.
16. Colaprico, *Le Cene Eleganti*, 190.
17. Colaprico, *Le Cene Eleganti*, 238.

CHAPTER 12: FINAL FLING

1. "Constitutional Court Curbs Berlusconi Immunity Law," *France 24*, January 14, 2011, www.france24.com/en/20110113-italy-top-court-curbs-silvio-berlusconi-immunity-law-trials (accessed: July 19, 2014).
2. Roberto Mancini, "Berlusconi's Gift to the Media," *The Guardian*, June 29, 2009, http://www.theguardian.com/commentisfree/libertycentral/2009/jun/29/berlusconi-mafia-wiretapping (accessed: July 17, 2014).
3. "Constitutional Court Curbs Berlusconi Immunity Law."
4. Doug Longhini, "Amanda Knox Prosecutor Giuliano Mignini Back in Court as a Defendant," *CBS News*, November 2, 2011, http://www.cbsnews.com/news/amanda-knox-prosecutor-giuliano-mignini-back-in-court-as-a-defendant/ (accessed: July 9, 2014).
5. "Mostro Firenze: Annullate condanne a pm Mignini e Giuttari," *Ansa*, November 22, 2011, http://www.ansa.it/web/notizie/rubriche/cronaca/2011/11/22/visualizza_new.html_15027818.html (accessed: September 20, 2014).
6. Barbie Latza Nadeau, *Angel Face* (New York: Beast Books, 2010), 94.
7. "L'Anm: 'Processo breve amnistia permanente che uccide almeno 15 mila processi," *Il Messaggero*, April 14, 2011, http://www.ilmessaggero.it/articolo_app.php?id=37837&sez=HOME_INITALIA&npl=&desc_sez (accessed: July 19, 2014).
8. Paolo Biondani and Carlo Porcedda, *Il Cavaliere Nero: Il Tesoro Nascosto di Silvio Berlusconi* (Milan: Chiarelettere, 2013), 146.
9. Michael Day, "Leave Libya or We Will Bring You Down, Allies Tell Berlusconi," *The Independent*, May 3, 2012, http://www.independent.co.uk/news/world/europe/leave-libya-or-we-will-bring-you-down-allies-tell-berlusconi-2278065.html (accessed: July 20, 2014).
10. "Milan Train Segregation Idea Row," *BBC News*, May 9, 2009, http://news.bbc.co.uk/2/hi/world/europe/8041974.stm (accessed: July 21, 2014).
11. John Hooper, "Silvio Berlusconi Faces Humiliation as Milan Voters Support Left-wing Mayor," *The Guardian*, May 20, 2011, http://www.theguardian.com/world/2011/may/30/silvio-berlusconi-defeat-in-milan (accessed: July 21, 2014).
12. "Top 10 World Economy Ranking," *Econpost*, February 21, 2011, http://econpost.com/worldeconomy/world-economy-ranking (accessed: July 22, 2014).
13. "Italy Scandal: Silvio Berlusconi in 'Sex Boast,'" *BBC News*, September 17, 2011, http://www.bbc.co.uk/news/world-europe-14960214 (accessed: January 12, 2015).
14. "Italy Scandal: Silvio Berlusconi in 'Sex Boast.'"
15. "ECB Told Italy to Make Budget Cuts," *BBC News*, September 29, 2011, http://www.bbc.co.uk/news/business-15104967 (accessed: July 22, 2014).
16. "Tremonti e Berlusconi, rapporto finito: 'Silvio dimettiti, il problema sei tu,'" *Il Fatto Quotidiano*, November 3, 2011, http://www.ilfattoquotidiano.it/2011/11/03/tremonti-e-berlusconi-volano-gli-stracci-silvio-dimettiti-il-problema-sei-tu/168160/ (accessed: July 22, 2014).
17. Michael Day, "Berlusconi Humiliated by IMF Scrutiny," *The Independent*, November 5, 2011, http://www.independent.co.uk/news/world/europe/berlusconi-humiliated-by-imf-scrutiny-6257549.html (accessed: July 22, 2014).
18. Michael Day, "Italy Wakes Up to Life after Berlusconi," *The Independent*, November 9, 2011, http://www.independent.co.uk/news/world/europe/italy-wakes-up-to-life-after-berlusconi-6259186.html (accessed: January 12, 2015).
19. Day, "Italy Wakes Up to Life after Berlusconi."
20. Daniela Manca, "Piersilvio Berlusconi: 'Il nuovo governo? Per Mediaset puo essere boaccata d'ossigeno,'" *Corriere della Sera*, November 19, 2011, http://www

.corriere.it/economia/11_novembre_19/manca_buon_senso_6db08818-1283-11e1-b297-12e8887ffed4.shtml (accessed: July 10, 2014).

CHAPTER 13: BLAME THE GERMANS

1. Perry Anderson, "The Italian Disaster," *London Review of Books*, vol. 36 (May 22, 2014), http://www.lrb.co.uk/v36/n10/perry-anderson/the-italian-disaster (accessed: June 28, 2014).
2. Michael Day, "Ten Years On, Italy Still Split over Craxi," *The Independent*, January 20, 2010, http://www.independent.co.uk/news/world/europe/ten-years-on-italy-still-split-over-craxi-1873172.html (accessed: July 11, 2014).
3. Marco Travaglio, *Viva il Re* (Milan: Chiarelettere, 2013), 118.
4. Anderson, "The Italian Disaster."
5. Marcus Walker, Stacy Meichtry and Charles Forelle, "Deepening Crisis over Euro Pits Leader against Leader," *Wall Street Journal*, December 30, 2011, http://online.wsj.com/news/articles/ SB10001424052970203391104577124480046463576 (accessed: July 25, 2014).
6. "How Goldman Sachs Helped Mask Greece's Debt," *BBC News*, February 20, 2012, http://www.bbc.co.uk/news/world-europe-17108367 (accessed: August 22, 2014).
7. "La 'bomba' di Grillo contro Equitalia," *Tempo*, January 3, 2012, http://www.iltempo.it/politica/2012/01/03/la-bomba-di-grillo-contro-equitalia-1.19450 (accessed: July 15, 2014).
8. Michael Day, "Caving In to Pressure: Why Mario Monti's Technocrats Couldn't Repair Italy after Silvio Berlusconi's Government Collapsed," *The Independent*, February 22, 2013, http://www.independent.co.uk/news/world/europe/caving-in-to-pressure-why-mario-montis-technocrats-couldnt-repair-italy-after-silvio-berlusconis-government-collapsed-8507736.html (accessed: July 15, 2014).
9. Day, "Caving In to Pressure."
10. Steven Scherer, "Berlusconi Says Idea That Italy Should Dump Euro Was a 'Joke,'" *Reuters*, June 2, 2012, http://www.reuters.com/article/2012/06/02/us-berlusconi-euro-idUSBRE8510AW20120602 (accessed: July 15, 2014).
11. Sara Nicoli, "Cucu, la Merkel e 'inchiavabile,'" *Il Fatto Quotidiano*, September 10, 2011, www.ilfattoquotidiano.it/2011/09/10/cucu-la-merkel-e-%E2%80%9Cinchiavabile%E2%80%9D/156545 (accessed: July 15, 2014).
12. "Berlusconi's Phone Call Leaves Merkel Waiting," *BBC News*, April 4, 2009, news.bbc.co.uk/2/hi/europe/7983006.stm (accessed: July 25, 2014).
13. Michael Day, "Mario Monti: 'I Convinced Thatcher That the Maastricht Treaty Was a Good Idea,'" *The Independent*, October 15, 2012, www.independent.co.uk/news/people/profiles/mario-monti-i-convinced-thatcher-that-the-maastricht-treaty-was-a-good-idea-8210955.html (accessed: July 25, 2014).
14. Eric J. Lyman, "Newspaper Berlusconi Controls Says Germany's Merkel Is Heading a 'Fourth Reich,'" *The Hollywood Reporter*, August 7, 2012, http://www.hollywoodreporter.com/news/silvio-berlusconi-newspaper-germany-merkel-fourth-reich-359090 (accessed: July 16, 2014).
15. Marco Travaglio, *Ad Personam: 1994–2010. Così Destra e Sinistra Hanno Privatizzato la Democrazia* (Milan: Chiarelettere, 2010), 467.
16. Pablo Onate, "Italian Members of Parliament Are Paid Substantially Higher Salaries Than Those in Other Western European Countries," *LSEblogs*, http://blogs.lse.ac.uk/europpblog/2013/09/02/italian-members-of-parliament-are-paid-substantially-higher-salaries-than-those-in-other-west-european-countries/ (accessed: September 7, 2014).
17. "Notes on a Scandal," *Nature*, vol. 471 (March 9, 2011), 135-136, http://www.nature.com/nature/journal/v471/n7337/full/471135b.html?WT.ec_id=NATURE-20110310 (accessed: August 10, 2014).

18. "Falso il master della Santanche: e lei si infuria: campagna ridicola," *Corriere della Sera*, March 24, 2011, http://www.corriere.it/politica/11_marzo_22/santanche-bocconi-oggi_3ea66fe2-54a1-11e0-a5ef-46c31ce287ee.shtml (accessed: August 8, 2014).
19. Michael Day, "Family Fiefdoms Blamed for Tainting Italian Universities," *The Independent*, September 25, 2010, http://www.independent.co.uk/news/world/europe/family-fiefdoms-blamed-for-tainting-italian-universities-2089120.html (accessed: August 9, 2014).
20. Madeleine Johnson, "The Deeper Woe," *The American*, July 4, 2011, www.theamericanmag.com/article_print.php?article=2877&show_images=1 (accessed: August 9, 2014).
21. "Sequestro lampo e ricatto per Spinelli, il 'cassiere' di Berlusconi: sei arresti," *Corriere della Sera*, November 19, 2012, http://milano.corriere.it/milano/notizie/cronaca/12_novembre_19/arresti-sequestro-collaboratore-berlusconi-2112765091596.shtml (accessed: July 24, 2014).
22. Michael Day, "Raphael's Deposition: Renaissance Masterpiece Warped by Rome Museum's Faulty Airconditioning," *The Independent*, September 1, 2014, http://www.independent.co.uk/arts-entertainment/art/news/raphaels-deposition-renaissance-masterpiece-warped-by-rome-museums-faulty-air-conditioning-9704807.html (accessed: September 8, 2014).
23. Gabriele Cereda, "C'è Berlusconi in sala, standing ovation sulla sequenza finale di '2012' a Vimercate," *La Repubblica*, December 8, 2009, http://milano.repubblica.it/dettaglio/ce-berlusconi-in-sala-standing-ovation-sulla-sequenza-finale-di-2012-a-vimercate/1799151 (accessed: August 10, 2014).
24. Cereda, "C'è Berlusconi in sala."

CHAPTER 14: DEMAGOGUES

1. Marco Politi, Vatican expert, personal interview with the author, September 10, 2014.
2. Michael Day, "Italy Faces Constitutional Crisis over Coma Woman," *The Observer*, February 8, 2008, www.theguardian.com/world/2009/feb/08/englaro-italy-vatican (accessed: August 10, 2014).
3. Michael Day, "A Father's Plea: Let My Daughter Die in Peace," *The Observer*, February 8, 2008, http://www.theguardian.com/world/2009/feb/08/eluana-englaro-assisted-suicide (accessed: August 8, 2014).
4. Day, "A Father's Plea: Let My Daughter Die in Peace."
5. "Via dalla Rai Santoro, Biagi e Luttazzi," *La Repubblica*, April 18, 2002, http://www.repubblica.it/online/politica/rainominedue/berlu/berlu.html (accessed: July 30, 2014).
6. Edward Cody, "French Ex-President Chirac Convicted of Corruption," *The Washington Post*, December 15, 2011, http://www.washingtonpost.com/world/french-ex-president-chirac-convicted-of-corruption/2011/12/15/gIQAfp97vO_story.html (accessed: September 22, 2014).
7. John Hooper, "Italy's Web Guru Tastes Power as New Political Movement Goes Viral," *The Guardian*, January 3, 2013, www.theguardian.com/world/2013/jan/03/italy-five-star-movement-internet (accessed: August 10, 2014).
8. Perry Anderson, "The Italian Disaster," *London Review of Books*, vol. 36 (May 22, 2014), http://www.lrb.co.uk/v36/n10/perry-anderson/the-italian-disaster (accessed: August 11, 2014).
9. Michael Day, "We Won't Be Blackmailed," *The Independent*, July 30, 2013, www.independent.co.uk/news/world/europe/we-wont-be-blackmailed-italys-fragile-coalition-government-close-to-collapse-as-centerleft-prime-minister-enrico-letta-warns-people-of-freedom-party-that-he-wont-buckle-over-silvio-berlusconi-8780580.html (accessed: August 11, 2014).

10. "Caso Kazakistan, ombre su Alfano. Gli uomini del ministro sapevano del blitz," *Il Fatto Quotidiano*, July 14, 2013, http://www.ilfattoquotidiano.it/2013/07/14/caso-kazakistan-ombre-su-alfano-uomini-del-ministro-sapevano-del-blitz/655452/ (accessed: August 12, 2014).
11. "Caso Shalabayeva, si dimette Procaccini. Il legale: 'Polizia sapeva chi è Alm,'" *La Repubblica*, July 16, 2013, http://www.repubblica.it/politica/2013/07/16/news/caso_ablyazov_il_pdl_in_trincea_per_alfano_oggi_la_relazione_di_pansa_incognite_sfiducie-63064280/ (accessed: August 12, 2014).
12. Vincenzo Iurillo, "Antimafia: In commissione Sarro, parlamentare Pdl fan del condono edilizio," *Il Fatto Quotidano*, October 13, 2013, http://www.ilfattoquotidiano.it/2013/10/13/antimafia-in-commissione-sarro-pdl-senatore-fan-del-condono-edilizio/741784/ (accessed: September 23, 2014).
13. "Antimafia: Inopportuna nomina Sarro, legato a Cosentino," October 14, 2013, http://selmade.it/antimafia-inopportuna-nomina-sarro-legato-a-cosentino/ (accessed: January 12, 2015).
14. "Pdl, Papa e Sarro su caso Cosentino: "Mistificazione della realtà," *Napoli Today*, October 23, 2009, http://www.napolitoday.it/politica/elezioni/elezioni-regionali-2010/cosentino-indagato-risposta-pdl-commissione-antimafia.html (accessed: January 12, 2015).
15. "La Cassazione: 'Cosentino è ancora referente dei casalesi,'" *La Repubblica*, September 16, 2014, http://napoli.repubblica.it/cronaca/2014/09/16/news/la_cassazione_cosentino_ancora_referente_dei_casalesi-95930169/ (accessed: September 23, 2014).
16. Roberto Saviano, "Il patto scellerato," *La Repubblica*, January 13, 2012, www.repubblica.it/politica/2012/01/13/news/saviano_cosentino-28017990/ (accessed: August 8, 2014).
17. Michael Day, "Anti-mafia Campaigner Roberto Saviano Sues Gangsters Who Ordered His Death," *The Independent*, December 11, 2012, http://www.independent.co.uk/news/world/europe/antimafia-campaigner-roberto-saviano-sues-gangsters-who-ordered-his-death-8406282.html (accessed: December 19, 2014).

CHAPTER 15: THE DEVIL'S ADVOCATES

1. "Profile: Silvio Berlusconi, Italian Ex-Prime Minister," *BBC News*, May 9, 2014, www.bbc.co.uk/news/world-europe-11981754 (accessed: August 12, 2014).
2. Tom Kington, "Silvio Berlusconi Bribery Case Thrown Out of Court," *The Guardian*, February 25, 2012, http://www.theguardian.com/world/2012/feb/25/silvio-berlusconi-bribery-case-court (accessed: September 3, 2014).
3. Peter Popham, "Hit and Run: Viva Veronica!" *The Independent*, May 6, 2009, http://www.independent.co.uk/news/people/hit-and-run/hit—run-viva-veronica-1679796.html (accessed: August 12, 2014).
4. Maria Latella, *Tendenza Veronica* (Milan: BurRizzoli, 2009), 99.
5. Latella, *Tendenza Veronica*, 77.
6. Maria Latella, "Esclusiva con Veronica Lario: 'Vittima di agguati fotografici: mi attaccano perche non temo di invecchiare,'" *Il Messaggero*, May 18, 2014, www.ilmessaggero.it/societa/persone/veronica_lario_intervista_invecchiare/notizie/695650.shtml (accessed: August 12, 2014).
7. "Berlusconi, Veronica Lario vuole €540 milioni per divorzio. È Battaglia," *Il Fatto Quotidiano*, May 8, 2014, www.ilfattoquotidiano.it/2014/05/08/berlusconi-lespresso-veronica-lario-vuole-da-silvio-540-milioni-per-divorzio-e-guerra/978393/ (accessed: August 12, 2014).
8. Ettore Livini, "E nel nome del padre è pace tra le due sorelle," *La Repubblica*, October 20, 2013, http://ricerca.repubblica.it/repubblica/archivio/repubblica/2013/10/29/nel-nome-del-padre-pace-tra.html (accessed: September 22, 2014).
9. Nick Squires, "Meet Silvio Berlusconi's New Girlfriend Francesca Pascale—50 Years His Junior," *Daily Telegraph*, December 12, 2012, http://www.telegraph.co.uk/news

/worldnews/silvio-berlusconi/9740323/Meet-Silvio-Berlusconis-new-girlfriend-Francesca-Pascale-50-years-his-junior.html (accessed: August 19, 2014).

10. Michael Day, "Former Italian Prime Minister Silvio Berlusconi Sentenced to a Year in Jail for Tax Fraud," *The Independent*, October 26, 2012, http://www.independent.co.uk/news/world/europe/former-italian-prime-minister-silvio-berlusconi-sentenced-to-a-year-in-jail-for-tax-fraud-8228441.html (accessed: September 6, 2014).
11. Paolo Biondani and Carlo Porcedda, *Il Cavaliere Nero: Il Tesoro Nascosto di Silvio Berlusconi* (Milan: Chiarelettere, 2013), 123.

CHAPTER 16: THE FALL

1. "Processo Ruby, i giudici: 'No alla sospensione lle elezioni,'" *Il Fatto Quotidiano*, January 14, 2014, http://www.ilfattoquotidiano.it/2013/01/14/processo-ruby-difesa-berlusconi-chiede-legittimo-impedimento-per-elezioni/468937/ (accessed: September 4, 2014).
2. "Berlusconi: Mussolini fece anche cose buone," *Corriere della Sera*, January 27, 2013, www.corriere.it/politica/13_gennaio_27/berlusconi-leggi-razziali_c33e2904-6866-11e2-b978-d7c19854ae83.shtml (accessed: September 4, 2014).
3. "Cassazione: no a trasferimento, i processi di Berlusconi restano a Milano," *La Repubblica*, May 6, 2013, www.repubblica.it/politica/2013/05/06/news/berlusconi_cassazione_in_camera_consiglio_per_decidere_su_trasferimento_processi-58165375/ (accessed: September 4, 2014).
4. "Ruby si sfoga a Milano. Io utilizzata dai PM per attaccare Berlusconi," *Mnews.it*, April 4, 2013, www.youtube.com/watch?v=ZNo2nqZOW18 (accessed: September 4, 2014).
5. "On. Niccolò Ghedini," *Openparlamento*, http://parlamento16.openpolis.it/parlamentare/ghedini-niccol%C3%B2/1587 (accessed: September 4, 2014).
6. Mino Pecorelli, "Omicidio Pecorelli, Andreotti condannato," *La Repubblica*, November 17, 2002, www.repubblica.it/online/politica/propeco/andreotti/andreotti.html (accessed: September 5, 2014).
7. Tom Kington, "Silvio Berlusconi Paid €127,000 to Witnesses in Trial," *The Guardian*, April 12, 2012, http://www.theguardian.com/world/2012/apr/12/silvio-berlusconi-paid-witnesses-ruby-trial (accessed: September 3, 2014).
8. Angelo Mincuzzi, "Ruby bis, Mora e Fede condannati a 7 anni. Nicole Minetti a 5," *Il Sole 24 Ore*, July 19, 2013, www.ilsole24ore.com/art/notizie/2013-07-19/oggi-sentenza-processo-ruby-091708.shtml?uuid=AbnvQYFI (accessed: September 4, 2014).
9. Angelo Mincuzzi, "Diritti tv Mediaset, Berlusconi condannato a quattro anni in appello," *Il Sole 24 Ore*, May 8, 2013, www.ilsole24ore.com/art/notizie/2013-05-08/respinta-giudici-rinvio-udienza-095612.shtml?uuid=Abvuk1tH (accessed: September 5, 2014).
10. Alessandra Paolini, "Pdl, figuranti pagati per riempire la piazza: 'Ci danno 10 euro, arrotondiamo la pensione,'" *La Repubblica*, March 24, 2013, www.repubblica.it/politica/2013/03/24/news/figuranti_pagati_manifestazione_pdl-55243399/ (accessed: September 4, 2014).
11. "Conferma ta la condanna per Berlusconi il Cavaliere ottiene solo lo stop all'interdizione," *Corriere della Sera*, August 1, 2013, www.corriere.it/politica/13_agosto_01/berlusconi-cassazione-sentenza_fd399324-fa87-11e2-9aaf-71b689b7d489.shtml (accessed: September 3, 2014).
12. Deborah Ball and Charles Forelle, "Berlusconi Makes Last-Ditch Bid to Reopen Case," *Wall Street Journal*, November 25, 2013, http://online.wsj.com/news/articles/SB10001424052702304011304579220091260566298 (accessed: September 6, 2014).
13. Francesco Bei, *La Caduta* (Parma: Guanda, 2013), 34.
14. Bei, *La Caduta*, 42.

15. "Berlusconi. Dopo la condanna definitiva, cosa succederà al Cavaliere?" *Tempi*, August 2, 2013, www.tempi.it/silvio-berlusconi-mediaset-condanna-definitiva-cosa-succede-ora-al-cavaliere-interdizione-ineleggibilita-incompatibilita-senato-carcere-domiciliari#.UuKSxvY1giE (accessed: September 4, 2014).
16. "Giustizia, Severino: 'Mia legge buon compromesso tra giustizialismo e il nulla,'" *Il Fatto Quotidiano*, November 27, 2013, http://tv.ilfattoquotidiano.it/2013/11/27/giustizia-severino-mia-legge-giusto-compromesso-tra-giustizialismo-e-non-fare-nulla/255640/ (accessed: September 5, 2014).
17. "Caso Berlusconi, Letta al PDL: Non accetto ricatti," *SkyTG24*, August 28, 2013, http://video.sky.it/news/politica/caso_berlusconi_letta_al_pdl_non_accetto_ricatti/v168697.vid (accessed: September 3, 2014).
18. Alessandro Sallusti, "Un Kennedy ad Arcore," *Il Giornale*, November 22, 2013, www.ilgiornale.it/news/interni/969695.html (accessed: August 25, 2014).
19. "Diritti tv, Berlusconi: 12 nuove testimonianze," *Il Sole 24 Ore*, November 25, 2013, www.ilsole24ore.com/art/notizie/2013-11-25/processo-diritti-tv-mediaset-berlusconi-annuncia-nuove-carte-stati-uniti—150713.shtml?uuid=ABvBdZf (accessed: September 2, 2014).
20. "Berlusconi non e piu Senatore, Palazzo Madama dice si alla decadenza," *Il Sole 24 Ore*, November 27, 2013, www.ilsole24ore.com/art/notizie/2013-11-27/il-giorno-piu-di-berlusconi-senato-vota-decadenza-ex-premier-e-protesta-scende-piazza-075957.shtml?uuid=ABFUC4f (accessed: September 5, 2014).
21. Nick Squires, "Vladimir Plays Ball with Berlusconi Poodle," *Daily Telegraph*, December 4, 2013, http://www.telegraph.co.uk/news/worldnews/silvio-berlusconi/10494736/Vladimir-Putin-plays-ball-with-Berlusconi-poodle.html (accessed: September 8, 2014).

CHAPTER 17: FADING AWAY

1. "Restelli: 'Berlusconi aiutera i malati di Alzheimer a mangiare ma non gli fara il bagno, niente ansia di prestazione," *La Repubblica*, May 1, 2014, http://www.repubblica.it/politica/2014/05/01/news/restelli_berlusconi_aiuter_i_malati_di_alzheimer_a_mangiare_ma_non_gli_far_il_bagno_niente_ansia_da_prestazione-84948521/ (accessed: August 14, 2014).
2. "Come ho filmato Berlusconi nella casa di riposo," *La Repubblica*, June 30, 2014, http://video.repubblica.it/politica/cosi-ho-filmato-berlusconi-nella-casa-di-riposo/170864/169384 (accessed: August 20, 2014).
3. "'Daro la dentiera gratis a tutti' Il marketing odontoiatrico di Silvio," *La Repubblica*, May 12, 2014, http://ricerca.repubblica.it/repubblica/archivio/repubblica/2014/05/12/daro-la-dentiera-gratis-a-tutti-il-marketing-odontoiatrico-di-silvio10.html (accessed: August 14, 2014).
4. Andrea Montanari, "Urbani: 'Forza Italia crolla come un castello di carte," *La Repubblica*, April 15, 2014, www.repubblica.it/politica/2014/04/15/news/urbani_forza_italia_crolla_come_un_castello_di_carte-83648804/ (accessed: August 14, 2014).
5. "Scajola arrestato dalla Dia," *La Repubblica*, May 8, 2014, www.repubblica.it/cronaca/2014/05/08/news/arrestato_scajola-85533400/ (accessed: August 14, 2014).
6. "Berlusconi scarica Scajola e Dell'Utri," *L'Aria che Tira*, http://www.la7.it/laria-che-tira/video/berlusconi-scarica-scajola-e-dell%E2%80%99utri-16-05-2014-131882 (accessed: August 14, 2014); "Anche Previti lascia Silvio e sostiene Alfano," *La Stampa*, May 16, 2014, http://www.lastampa.it/2014/05/16/italia/politica/anche-previti-lascia-silvio-e-sostiene-alfano-VKS2tTNeJbAeCtSAtUUlVP/pagina.html (accessed: August 14, 2014).
7. "Results of the 2014 European Elections," *European Parliament*, http://www.results-elections2014.eu/en/country-results-it-2014.html (accessed: September 8, 2014).

8. Liam Moloney, "Italy's Renzi Presents New Reform Package," *Wall Street Journal*, August 29, 2014, http://online.wsj.com/articles/italys-renzi-presents-new-reform-package-1409340446 (accessed: September 25, 2014).
9. Silvio Berlusconi, "La verità di Berlusconi," *Il Giornale*, July 14, 2014, http://www.ilgiornale.it/news/politica/verit-berlusconi-1037374.html (accessed: September 10, 2014).
10. "Ruby, B. assolto perché legge è cambiata: 'Telefonate in Questura abuso, non reato,'" *Il Fatto Quotidiano*, http://www.ilfattoquotidiano.it/2014/10/16/processo-ruby-i-giudici-prostituzione-certa-ma-berlusconi-non-sapeva-eta/1157359/ (accessed: December 18, 2014).
11. Paolo Biondani, "Quanti milioni per Ruby," *L'Espresso*, August 7, 2014, 32–35.
12. Biondani, "Quanti milioni per Ruby."
13. Biondani, "Quanti milioni per Ruby."
14. Davide Milosa, "Fede: 'Ruby? Silvio scopava, scopava. Su Dell'Utri: Solo lui sa sulla mafia,'" *Il Fatto Quotidiano*, July 23, 2014, http://www.ilfattoquotidiano.it/2014/07/23/fede-ruby-silvio-scopava-scopava-su-dellutri-solo-lui-sa-sulla-mafia/1069456/ (accessed: August 28, 2014).
15. Rachel Sanderson, "Berlusconi's Empire Faces a Tricky Future without Him," *Financial Times*, May 28, 2014, http://www.ft.com/cms/s/0/f11b725c-e680-11e3-9a20-00144feabdc0.html#axzz3Bgpw3TLe (accessed: August 18, 2014).
16. Carmelo Lopapa, "L'Addio di Verdini a Forza Italia," *La Repubblica*, December 17, 2014, 11.

EPILOGUE

1. Gavin Jones and James Mackenzie, "How Italy Became a Submerging Economy," *Reuters*, July 14, 2014, http://www.reuters.com/article/2014/07/14/us-italy-economy-submerging-specialrepor-idUSKBN0FJ0QT20140714 (accessed: July 16, 2014).
2. Kathryn Westcott, "At Last an Explanation for 'Bunga Bunga,'" *BBC News*, February 5, 2011, http://www.bbc.co.uk/news/world-europe-12325796 (accessed: September 16, 2014).
3. Vittorio Dotti and Andrea Sceresini, *L'Avvocato del Diavolo* (Milan: Chiarelettere, 2014), 196.
4. Dotti and Sceresini, *L'Avvocato del Diavolo*, 196.

BIBLIOGRAPHY

"1994–Dicesa in campo," www.youtube.com/watch?v=B8-uIYqnk5A (accessed June 10, 2014).

"Anche Previti lascia Silvio e sostiene Alfano," *La Stampa*, May 16, 2014, http://www.lastampa.it/2014/05/16/italia/politica/anche-previti-lascia-silvio-e-sostiene-alfano-VKS2tTNeJbAeCtSAtUUlVP/pagina.html (accessed August 14, 2014).

Anderson, Perry. "The Italian Disaster," *London Review of Books*, vol. 36 (May 22, 2014), http://www.lrb.co.uk/v36/n10/perry-anderson/the-italian-disaster (accessed June 28, 2014).

Aprile, Marianne. "Le Donne del Cavaliere?" *Oggi*, September 21, 2011, www.oggi.it/attualita/notizie/2011/09/21/le-donne-del-cavaliere-sono-ben-131 (accessed July 18, 2014).

Ball, Deborah, and Charles Forelle. "Berlusconi Makes Last-Ditch Bid to Reopen Case," *Wall Street Journal*, November 25, 2013, http://online.wsj.com/news/articles/SB10001424052702304011304579220091260566298 (accessed September 6, 2014).

Barbacetto, Gianni. Societacivile 2004, http://www.societacivile.it/focus/articoli_focus/mani_pulite.html (accessed August 18, 2014).

Barbacetto, Gianni, Peter Gomez and Marco Travaglio. *Mani Pulite: La Vera Storia* (Roma: Editori Riuniti, 2002).

"Basta Berlusconi," *The Economist*, April 6, 2006, www.economist.com/node/6772333 (accessed June 29, 2014).

Bei, Francesco. *La Caduta* (Parma: Guanda, 2013).

"Belzebu e Belfagor nel complotto della P2," *La Repubblica*, May 23, 1984, http://ricerca.repubblica.it/repubblica/archivio/repubblica/1984/05/23/belzebu-belfagor-nel-complotto-della-p2.html (accessed May 15, 2014).

Berlusconi, Silvio. "La verità di Berlusconi," *Il Giornale*, July 14, 2014, http://www.ilgiornale.it/news/politica/verit-berlusconi-1037374.html (accessed September 10, 2014).

"Berlusconi Appears in Court," *BBC News*, May 5, 2003, http://news.bbc.co.uk/2/hi/europe/2995497.stm (accessed May 18, 2014).

"Berlusconi. Dopo la condanna definitiva, cosa succederà al Cavaliere?" *Tempi*, August 2, 2013, www.tempi.it/silvio-berlusconi-mediaset-condanna-definitiva-cosa-succede-ora-al-cavaliere-interdizione-ineleggibilita-incompatibilita-senato-carcere-domiciliari#.UuKSxvY1giE (accessed September 4, 2014).

"Berlusconi e l'inglese," *Mister Media*, October 30, 2012, www.youtube.com/watch?v=_9c-ji9L2lI (accessed June 26, 2014).

"Berlusconi: Left Has Uglier Women," *BBC News*, April 9, 2008, news.bbc.co.uk/1/hi/world/europe/7338415.stm (accessed July 10, 2014).

"Berlusconi: Mussolini fece anche cose buone," *Corriere della Sera*, January 27, 2013, www.corriere.it/politica/13_gennaio_27/berlusconi-leggi-razziali_c33e2904-6866-11e2-b978-d7c19854ae83.shtml (accessed September 4, 2014).

"Berlusconi non e piu Senatore, Palazzo Madama dice si alla decadenza," *Il Sole 24 Ore*, November 27, 2013, www.ilsole24ore.com/art/notizie/2013-11-27/il-giorno-piu-di-berlusconi-senato-vota-decadenza-ex-premier-e-protesta-scende-piazza-075957.shtml?uuid=ABFUC4f (accessed September 5, 2014).

"Berlusconi perde la causa con Travaglio," *Corriere della Sera*, March 7, 2006, www.corriere.it/Primo_Piano/Politica/2006/03_Marzo/07/travaglio.shtml (accessed July 7, 2014).

"Berlusconi Says Obama Is 'Tanned,'" *BBC News*, November 8, 2008, http://news.bbc.co.uk/1/hi/world/europe/7715016.stm (accessed July 12, 2014).

"Berlusconi scarica Scajola e Dell'Utri," *L'Aria che Tira*, http://www.la7.it/laria-che-tira/video/berlusconi-scarica-scajola-e-dell%E2%80%99utri-16-05-2014-131882 (accessed August 14, 2014).

"Berlusconi Vaunts Italy's Secretaries," *BBC News*, September 24, 2003, http://news.bbc.co.uk/2/hi/europe/3137406.stm (accessed June 26, 2014).

"Berlusconi, Veronica Lario vuole €540 milioni per divorzio. È Battaglia," *Il Fatto Quotidiano*, May 8, 2014, www.ilfattoquotidiano.it/2014/05/08/berlusconi-lespresso-veronica-lario-vuole-da-silvio-540-milioni-per-divorzio-e-guerra/978393/ (accessed August 12, 2014).

"Berlusconi's Doctor Confirms Facelift," *ABC News*, January 18, 2004, http://www.abc.net.au/news/2004-01-18/berlusconis-doctor-confirms-facelift/121352 (accessed June 26, 2014).

"Berlusconi's Phone Call Leaves Merkel Waiting," *BBC News*, April 4, 2009, news.bbc.co.uk/2/hi/europe/7983006.stm (accessed July 25, 2014).

Bianconi, Giovanni. "Dell'Utri in viaggio con 50 chili di bagali, fuga evidente," *Corriere della Sera*, April 29, 2004, http://www.corriere.it/cronache/14_aprile_29/dell-utri-viaggio-50-chili-bagagli-fuga-evidente-f5cc4238-cf59-11e3-bf7e-201ea72c5359.shtml (accessed May 16, 2014).

Biondani, Paolo, "Quanti milioni per Ruby," *L'Espresso*, August 7, 2014, 32–35.

Biondani, Paolo, and Carlo Porcedda. *Il Cavaliere Nero: Il Tesoro Nascosto di Silvio Berlusconi* (Milan: Chiarelettere, 2013).

Blaine Walker, David. *Institutional Reform in Contemporary Italian Politics: Electoral Systems*, (Ann Arbor, MI: ProQuest, 2011).

Bonini, Carlo, and Piero Colaprico. "Silenzi, prestiti e favore: cosi Berlusconi ha pagato le Olgettine e i fedelissimi," *La Repubblica*, October 27, 2011, http://inchieste.repubblica.it/it/repubblica/rep-it/2011/10/27/news/silenzi_prestiti_e_favori_cos_berlusconi_ha_pagato_le_olgettine_e_i_fedelissimi-23945879/ (accessed July 21, 2014).

Bull, Martin, and Martin Rhodes. *Italy—A Contested Polity* (New York: Routledge, 2009).

Calabresi, Mario. "Berlusconi: 'Ho avuto un cancro alla prostata," *La Repubblica*, July 23, 2000, www.repubblica.it/online/politica/malattia/parla/parla.html (accessed June 6, 2014).

Carlin, John. "All Hail Berlusconi," *The Observer*, January 18, 2004, http://www.theguardian.com/world/2004/jan/18/italy.features (accessed May 12, 2014).

"Caso Berlusconi, Letta al PDL: Non accetto ricatti" *SkyTG24*, August 28, 2013, http://video.sky.it/news/politica/caso_berlusconi_letta_al_pdl_non_accetto_ricatti/v168697.vid (accessed September 3, 2014).

"Caso Kazakistan, ombre su Alfano. Gli uomini del ministro sapevano del blitz," *Il Fatto Quotidiano*, July 14, 2013, http://www.ilfattoquotidiano.it/2013/07/14/caso-kazakistan-ombre-su-alfano-uomini-del-ministro-sapevano-del-blitz/655452/ (accessed August 12, 2014).

"Caso Shalabayeva, si dimette Procaccini. Il legale: 'Polizia sapeva chi è Alm,'" *La Repubblica*, July 16, 2013, http://www.repubblica.it/politica/2013/07/16/news/caso_ablyazov_il_pdl_in_trincea_per_alfano_oggi_la_relazione_di_pansa_incognite_sfiducie-63064280/ (accessed August 12, 2014).

"Cassazione: no a trasferimento, i processi di Berlusconi restano a Milano," *La Repubblica*, May 6, 2013, www.repubblica.it/politica/2013/05/06/news/berlusconi_cassazione

_in_camera_consiglio_per_decidere_su_trasferimento_processi-58165375/ (accessed September 4, 2014).

Cereda, Gabriele. "C'è Berlusconi in sala, standing ovation sulla sequenza finale di '2012' a Vimercate," *La Repubblica*, December 8, 2009, http://milano.repubblica.it/dettaglio/ce-berlusconi-in-sala-standing-ovation-sulla-sequenza-finale-di-2012-a-vimercate/1799151 (accessed August 10, 2014).

"Claudio Fazzone, plentipotenziario di Berlusconi," *Lettere 43*, January 2, 2014, http://www.lettera43.it/politica/claudio-fazzone-plenipotenziario-di-berlusconi_43675119023.htm (accessed July 30, 2014).

Cody, Edward. "French Ex-President Chirac Convicted of Corruption," *The Washington Post*, December 15, 2011, http://www.washingtonpost.com/world/french-ex-president-chirac-convicted-of-corruption/2011/12/15/gIQAfp97vO_story.html (accessed September 22, 2014).

Colaprico, Piero. *Le cene eleganti* (Milan: Fentrinelli, 2011).

Colby, Laura. "Benedetti on Bribes: Would Do It Again if Needed," *New York Times*, May 19, 1993, http://www.nytimes.com/1993/05/19/news/19iht-ital_10.htm (accessed May 20, 2014).

"Come ho filmato Berlusconi nella casa di riposo," *La Repubblica*, June 30, 2014, http://video.repubblica.it/politica/cosi-ho-filmato-berlusconi-nella-casa-di-riposo/170864/169384 (accessed August 20, 2014).

Committee to Protect Journalists, http://cpj.org/killed/europe/russia/ (accessed July 10, 2014).

"Conferma ta la condanna per Berlusconi il Cavaliere ottiene solo lo stop all'interdizione," *Corriere della Sera*, August 1, 2013, www.corriere.it/politica/13_agosto_01/berlusconi-cassazione-sentenza_fd399324-fa87-11e2-9aaf-71b689b7d489.shtml (accessed September 3, 2014).

Conti, Paolo. "Rai: Finisce 3 a 2 la partita delle nomine," *Corriere della Sera*, September 18, 1994, http://archiviostorico.corriere.it/1994/settembre/18/RAI_finisce_partita_delle_nomine_co_0_94091813818.shtml (accessed May 25, 2014).

Corrias, Pino, Massimo Gramellini and Curzio Maltese. *Colpo Grosso* (Milan: Dalai Editore, 1994).

Cosmelli, Carlo. "Mafia, politica e affari: Sette domande al Cavaliere," *Micromega*, July 3, 2009, http://temi.repubblica.it/micromega-online/mafia-politica-e-affari-sette-domande-al-cavaliere (accessed May 3, 2014).

"Craxi: Tutti i processi e le condanne," *La Repubblica*, January 19, 2000, http://www.repubblica.it/online/politica/craxi1/processi/processi.html (accessed August 18, 2014).

"'Darò la dentiera gratis a tutti' Il marketing odontoiatrico di Silvio," *La Repubblica*, May 12, 2014, http://ricerca.repubblica.it/repubblica/archivio/repubblica/2014/05/12/daro-la-dentiera-gratis-a-tutti-il-marketing-odontoiatrico-di-silvio10.html (accessed August 14, 2014).

D'Avanzo, Giuseppe, and Conchita Sannino. "Cosi papi Berlusconi entro nella vita di Noemi," *La Repubblica*, May 24, 2009, http://www.repubblica.it/2009/05/sezioni/politica/berlusconi-divorzio-2/parla-gino/parla-gino.html (accessed July 22, 2014).

Davies, Lizzy. "Berlusconi Brother Sparks Fury over Balotelli Remark," *The Guardian*, February 6, 2013, http://www.theguardian.com/world/2013/feb/06/berlusconi-brother-fury-balotelli-remark (accessed May 25, 2014).

Day, Michael. "A Father's Plea: Let My Daughter Die in Peace," *The Observer*, February 8, 2008, http://www.theguardian.com/world/2009/feb/08/eluana-englaro-assisted-suicide (accessed August 8, 2014).

Day, Michael. "Anti-Mafia Judge Sets Sight on Italy's Corrupt Official," *The Independent*, December 2, 2011, http://www.independent.co.uk/news/world/europe/antimafia-judge-sets-sights-on-italys-corrupt-officials-6270762.html (accessed July 18, 2014).

Day, Michael. "'Apocalypse' on Railway in Tuscany," *The Independent*, July 1, 2009, www.independent.co.uk/news/world/europe/apocalypse-on-railway-in-tuscany-1726203.html (accessed July 20, 2014).

Day, Michael. "Berlusconi Humiliated by IMF Scrutiny," *The Independent*, November 5, 2011, http://www.independent.co.uk/news/world/europe/berlusconi-humiliated-by-imf-scrutiny-6257549.html (accessed July 22, 2014).

Day, Michael. "Berlusconi Payback," *Variety*, April 24, 2008, http://variety.com/2008/scene/news/berlusconi-payback-1117984575/ (accessed June 28, 2014).

Day, Michael. "Berlusconi Turns to Gaddafi and G8 for Comfort," *The Independent*, June 29, 2009, http://www.independent.co.uk/news/world/europe/berlusconi-turns-to-g8-and-gaddafi-for-comfort-1722950.html (accessed July 14, 2014).

Day, Michael. "Caving In to Pressure: Why Mario Monti's Technocrats Couldn't Repair Italy after Silvio Berlusconi's Government Collapsed," *The Independent*, February 22, 2013, http://www.independent.co.uk/news/world/europe/caving-in-to-pressure-why-mario-montis-technocrats-couldnt-repair-italy-after-silvio-berlusconis-government-collapsed-8507736.html (accessed July 15, 2014).

Day, Michael. "Drama Topper Is at Centre of Wire-Tap Storm," *Variety*, July 17, 2008, http://variety.com/2008/scene/news/rai-chiefs-move-to-sack-sacca-1117989087/ (accessed July 19, 2014).

Day, Michael. "Family Fiefdoms Blamed for Tainting Italian Universities," *The Independent*, September 25, 2010, http://www.independent.co.uk/news/world/europe/family-fiefdoms-blamed-for-tainting-italian-universities-2089120.html (accessed August 9, 2014).

Day, Michael. "Former Italian Prime Minister Silvio Berlusconi Sentenced to a Year in Jail for Tax Fraud," *The Independent*, October 26, 2012, http://www.independent.co.uk/news/world/europe/former-italian-prime-minister-silvio-berlusconi-sentenced-to-a-year-in-jail-for-tax-fraud-8228441.html (accessed September 6, 2014).

Day, Michael. "Italy Faces Constitutional Crisis over Coma Woman," *The Observer*, February 8, 2008, www.theguardian.com/world/2009/feb/08/englaro-italy-vatican (accessed August 10, 2014).

Day, Michael. "Leave Libya or We Will Bring You Down, Allies Tell Berlusconi," *The Independent*, May 3, 2012, http://www.independent.co.uk/news/world/europe/leave-libya-or-we-will-bring-you-down-allies-tell-berlusconi-2278065.html (accessed July 20, 2014).

Day, Michael. "Mario Cal: The Mysterious Suicide That Has Rocked the Vatican," *The Independent*, October 3, 2011, http://www.independent.co.uk/news/world/europe/mario-cal-the-mysterious-suicide-that-has-rocked-the-vatican-2364712.html (accessed May 6, 2014).

Day, Michael. "Mario Monti: 'I Convinced Thatcher That the Maastricht Treaty Was a Good Idea,'" *The Independent*, October 15, 2012, www.independent.co.uk/news/people/profiles/mario-monti-i-convinced-thatcher-that-the-maastricht-treaty-was-a-good-idea-8210955.html (accessed July 25, 2014).

Day, Michael. "Murder in Calabria: Fabiana's Fate Shames Italy," *The Independent*, June 2, 2013, www.independent.co.uk/news/world/europe/murder-in-calabria-fabianas-fate-shames-italy-8640816.html (accessed July 15, 2013).

Day, Michael. "Putin Accused of Giving Berlusconi Cut from Energy Deals," *The Independent*, December 3, 2010, http://www.independent.co.uk/news/world/europe/putin-accused-of-giving-berlusconi-cut-from-energy-deals-2149802.html (accessed July 12, 2014).

Day, Michael. "Raphael's Deposition: Rennaisance Masterpiece Warped by Rome Museum's Faulty Airconditioning," *The Independent*, September 1, 2014, http://www.independent.co.uk/arts-entertainment/art/news/raphaels-deposition-renaissance-masterpiece-warped-by-rome-museums-faulty-air-conditioning-9704807.html (accessed September 8, 2014).

Day, Michael. "Senior Italian Politician Charged with Defamation Aggravated by Racial Discrimination," *The Independent*, November 7, 2013, http://www.independent.co.uk/news/world/europe/senior-italian-politician-charged-with-defamation-aggravated-by-racial-discrimination-8927534.html (accessed May 25, 2014).

Day, Michael. "Sky TV Broadcast Angers Berlusconi," *Variety*, April 17, 2009, http://variety.com/2009/scene/markets-festivals/skytv-broadcast-angers-berlusconi-1118002560/ (accessed July 10, 2014).

Day, Michael. "Ten Years On, Italy Still Split over Craxi," *The Independent*, January 20, 2010, http://www.independent.co.uk/news/world/europe/ten-years-on-italy-still-split-over-craxi-1873172.html (accessed July 11, 2014).

Day, Michael. "Top News Reader Quits in Protest at Berlusconi," *The Independent*, May 25, 2010, http://www.independent.co.uk/news/world/europe/tv-news-reader-quits-in-protest-at-berlusconi-1981964.html (accessed July 15, 2014).

Day, Michael, and Peter Popham. "Italian Stallions: The Sex Lives of Mussolini and Berlusconi," *The Independent*, November 24, 2009, http://www.independent.co.uk/news/world/europe/italian-stallions-the-sex-lives-of-mussolini-and-berlusconi-1826454.html (accessed July 11, 2014).

Day, Michael, and Peter Popham. "Murdoch Is Waging a Vendetta against Me, Says Berlusconi," *The Independent*, June 5, 2009, http://www.independent.co.uk/news/world/europe/murdoch-is-waging-a-vendetta-against-me-says-berlusconi-1697328.html (accessed July 8, 2014).

"Dell'Utri garante tra Berlusconi e boss," *La Repubblica*, June 6, 2013, http://ricerca.repubblica.it/repubblica/archivio/repubblica/2013/09/06/dellutri-garante-tra-berlusconi-boss.html (accessed May 9, 2014).

D'Emilio, Frances, and Juan Zamorano. "Robert Seldon Lady, Ex-CIA Station Chief Arrested in Panama," *Huffington Post*, July 18, 2013, http://www.huffingtonpost.com/2013/07/18/robert-seldon-lady-arrested-panama_n_3618062.html (accessed August 16, 2014).

Dicker, Ron. "Mother Teresa Humanitarian Image 'a Myth,' New Study Says," *Huffington Post*, March 4, 2013, www.huffingtonpost.com/2013/03/04/mother-teresa-myth_n_2805697.html (accessed June 5, 2014).

"Diritti tv, Berlusconi: 12 nuove testimonianze," *Il Sole 24 Ore*, November 25, 2013, www.ilsole24ore.com/art/notizie/2013-11-25/processo-diritti-tv-mediaset-berlusconi-annuncia-nuove-carte-stati-uniti—150713.shtml?uuid=ABvBdZf (accessed September 2, 2014).

Dotti, Vittorio, and Andrea Sceresini. *L'Avvocato del Diavolo* (Milan: Chiarelettere, 2014).

"ECB Told Italy to Make Budget Cuts," *BBC News*, September 29, 2011, http://www.bbc.co.uk/news/business-15104967 (accessed July 22, 2014).

Erlanger, Steven. "Italy's Premier Calls Western Civilization Superior to Islamic World," *New York Times*, September 26, 2001, www.nytimes.com/2001/09/27/world/italy-s-premier-calls-western-civilization-superior-to-islamic-world.html (accessed June 26, 2014).

"Falso il master della Santanche: E lei si infuria: Campagna ridicola," *Corriere della Sera*, March 22, 2011, http://www.corriere.it/politica/11_marzo_22/santanche-bocconi-oggi_3ea66fe2-54a1-11e0-a5ef-46c31ce287ee.shtml (accessed August 8, 2014).

Faris, Stefan. "Bye Bye Gaddafi: How Italy Will Profit from the New Libyan Regime," *Time*, August 4, 2011, http://content.time.com/time/world/article/0,8599,2090116,00.html (accessed July 8, 2014).

"Fazzone, Claudio. Plentipotenziario di Berlusconi," *Lettere 43*, January 2, 2014, http://www.lettera43.it/politica/claudio-fazzone-plenipotenziario-di-berlusconi_43675119023.htm (accessed July 30, 2014).

Ferrucci, Alessandro. "Quando il dittatore kazako disse a B.: 'Vieni nella mia dacia, portati il pigiama,'" *Il Fatto Quotidiano*, July 18, 2013, http://www.ilfattoquotidiano.it/2013/07/18/quando-dittatore-kazako-disse-a-berlusconi-vieni-nella-mia-dacia-portati-pigiama/659664/ (accessed August 15, 2014).

Follain, John. "'Lesbian' Clinch More Embarrassment for Berlusconi," *The Sunday Times*, July 5, 2009, http://www.thesundaytimes.co.uk/sto/news/world_news/article176363.ece (accessed July 10, 2014).

France 24, January 14, 2011, www.france24.com/en/20110113-italy-top-court-curbs-silvio-berlusconi-immunity-law-trials (accessed July 19, 2014).

"Franceschini in calzini turchesi: 'Tutti come il giudice Mesiano,'" *La Repubblica*, October 18, 2009, www.repubblica.it/2009/10/sezioni/politica/giustizia-14/giustizia-14/giustizia-14.html (accessed July 15, 2014).

Fusani, Claudia. "La Contessa Rangoni Michiavelli: 'Cosi Berlusconi ha truffato mia cognata,'" *L'Unita*, August 13, 2010, www.unita.it/italia/la-contessa-rangoni-machiavelli-laquo-cos-igrave-berlusconi-ha-truffato-mia-cognata-raquo-1.159160 (accessed May 6, 2014).

Ginsborg, Paul. *Silvio Berlusconi: Television, Power and Patrimony* (London: Verso, 2005).

"Giustizia, Severino: 'Mia legge buon compromesso tra giustizialismo e il nulla,'" *Il Fatto Quotidiano*, November 27, 2013, http://tv.ilfattoquotidiano.it/2013/11/27/giustizia-severino-mia-legge-giusto-compromesso-tra-giustizialismo-e-non-fare-nulla/255640/ (accessed September 5, 2014).

Gomez, Peter, and Antonella Mascal. *Il Regalo di Berlusconi* (Milan: Chiarelettere, 2009).

Gomez, Peter, Marco Lillo and Marco Travaglio. *Papi: Uno Scandalo Politico* (Milan: Chiarelettere, 2009).

Grillo, Beppe. "Ruby Forever," Beppe Grillo's Blog, January 2011, www.beppegrillo.it/en/2011/01/ruby_forever_1.html (accessed July 6, 2014).

Gumbel, Andrew. "Obituary: Franco Di Bella," *The Independent*, December 23, 1997, http://www.independent.co.uk/news/obituaries/obituary-franco-di-bella-1290357.html (accessed May 15, 2014).

Hooper, John. "Berlusconi Collapses at Political Rally," *The Guardian*, November 27, 2006, http://www.theguardian.com/world/2006/nov/27/italy.johnhooper (accessed July 3, 2014).

Hooper, John. "Berlusconi: Italy Earthquake Victims Should View Experience as Camping Weekend," *The Guardian*, April 8, 2009, http://www.theguardian.com/world/2009/apr/08/italy-earthquake-berlusconi (accessed July 15, 2014).

Hooper, John. "'Don't Embarrass Italy before G8 Summit, President Urges Media," *The Guardian*, June 29, 2009, www.theguardian.com/world/2009/jun/29/silvio-berlusconi-g8-summit-allegations (accessed July 12, 2014).

Hooper, John. "Italy's Web Guru Tastes Power as New Political Movement Goes Viral," *The Guardian*, January 3, 2013, www.theguardian.com/world/2013/jan/03/italy-five-star-movement-internet (accessed August 10, 2014).

Hooper, John. "Silvio Berlusconi Faces Humiliation as Milan Voters Support Leftwing Mayor," *The Guardian*, May 20, 2011, http://www.theguardian.com/world/2011/may/30/silvio-berlusconi-defeat-in-milan (accessed July 21, 2014).

Hossain, Anushay. "Femicide in Italy: Domestic Violence Persists Despite New Laws," *Forbes*, August 26, 2013, http://www.forbes.com/sites/worldviews/2013/08/26/femicide-in-italy-domestic-violence-persists-despite-new-laws/ (accessed August 12, 2014).

"How Goldman Sachs Helped Mask Greece's Debt," *BBC News*, February 20, 2012, http://www.bbc.co.uk/news/world-europe-17108367 (accessed August 22, 2014).

"I pm: 3 anni e 8 mes du carcere a Berlusconi," *Corriere della Sera*, June 19, 2012, archiviostorico.corriere.it/2012/giugno/19/anni_mesi_carcere_Berlusconi_co_8_120619045.shtml (accessed July 7, 2014).

"Il caso Ruby," *La Repubblica*, April 12, 2011, http://inchieste.repubblica.it/it/repubblica/rep-it/2011/04/12/news/il_caso_ruby-14836804/ (accessed July 17, 2014).

"Imi-Sir, il dispositivo della sentenza della sesta sezione della Cassazione," *La Repubblica*, May 4, 2006, http://www.repubblica.it/2006/04/sezioni/cronaca/imi-sir/dispositivo-sentenza/dispositivo (accessed May 6, 2014).

"In Quotes: Berlusconi in His Own Words," *BBC News*, http://news.bbc.co.uk/2/hi/europe/3041288.stm (accessed May 20, 2014).

"Italy ex-PM Silvio Berlusconi to Face Bribery Charge," *BBC News*, October 23, 2013, http://www.bbc.com/news/world-europe-24641233 (accessed July 8, 2014).

"Italy, Former Italian Prime Minister Silvio Berlusconi Wins Referendum That Could Have Forced Him to Break Up His TV Empire," *ITN News*, http://www.itnsource.com/shotlist//RTV/1995/06/12/605201568/?s=elects (accessed August 20, 2014).

"Italy's Worst Case of Corruption," *The Guardian*, August 7, 2003, www.theguardian.com/world/2003/aug/07/italy (accessed June 25, 2014).

Johnson, Madeleine. "The Deeper Woe," *The American*, July 4, 2011, www.theamericanmag.com/article_print.php?article=2877&show_images=1 (accessed August 9, 2014).

Johnston, Bruce, and Julian Coman. "Brussels Horror as Berlusconi Fills In as Foreign Minister," *The Daily Telegraph*, January 13, 2002, http://www.telegraph.co.uk/news/worldnews/europe/italy/1381309/Brussels-horror-as-Berlusconi-fills-in-as-foreign-minister.html (accessed June 26, 2014).

Jones, Gavin, and James Mackenzie. "How Italy Became a Submerging Economy," *Reuters*, July 14, 2014, http://www.reuters.com/article/2014/07/14/us-italy-economy-submerging-specialrepor-idUSKBN0FJ0QT20140714 (accessed July 16, 2014).

Kington, Tom. "Could Barbara Montereale's Revelations Break Silvio Berlusconi's Grip on Power?" *The Observer*, June 21, 2009, http://www.theguardian.com/world/2009/jun/21/berlusconi-italy-barbara-montereale (accessed July 11, 2014).

Kington, Tom. "Italy in Suspense As 'Bunga Bunga' Trial Poised to Lift Lid on Berlusconi's Antics," *The Observer*, April 3, 2011, http://www.theguardian.com/world/2011/apr/03/italy-silvio-berlusconi-trial (accessed July 18, 2014).

Kington, Tom. "Silvio Berlusconi Bribery Case Thrown Out of Court," *The Guardian*, February 25, 2012, http://www.theguardian.com/world/2012/feb/25/silvio-berlusconi-bribery-case-court (accessed September 3, 2014).

Kington, Tom. "Silvio Berlusconi Paid €127,000 to Witnesses in Trial," *The Guardian*, April 12, 2012, http://www.theguardian.com/world/2012/apr/12/silvio-berlusconi-paid-witnesses-ruby-trial (accessed September 3, 2014).

Koff, Stephen. *Italy: From the 1st to the 2nd Republic* (London: Routledge, 2002).

"La 'bomba' di Grillo contro Equitalia," *Tempo*, January 3, 2012, http://www.iltempo.it/politica/2012/01/03/la-bomba-di-grillo-contro-equitalia-1.19450 (accessed July 15, 2014).

"L'Anm: 'Processo breve amnistia permanente che uccide almeno 15 mila processi," *Il Messaggero*, April 14, 2011, http://www.ilmessaggero.it/articolo_app.php?id=37837&sez=HOME_INITALIA&npl=&desc_sez (accessed July 19, 2014).

Latella, Maria. *Tendenza Veronica* (Milan: BurRizzoli, 2009).

Latella, Maria. "Esclusiva con Veronica Lario: 'Vittima di agguati fotografici: Mi attaccano perche non temo di invecchiare,'" *Il Messaggero*, May 18, 2014, www.ilmessaggero.it/societa/persone/veronica_lario_intervista_invecchiare/notizie/695650.shtml (accessed August 12, 2014).

Leney, Fiona. "The Sleaze Factor: Clean Hands Team Fails to Wash Away Tangentopoli Dirt," *The Independent*, October 25, 1994, http://www.independent.co.uk/news/world/the-sleaze-factor-cleanhands-team-fails-to-wash-away-tangentopoli-dirt-fiona-leney-looks-at-italys-cathedral-of-corruption-where-each-day-a-new-sector-of-society-is-investigated-1444839.html (accessed May 20, 2014).

Livini, Ettore. "E nel nome del padre è pace tra le due sorelle," *La Repubblica*, October 20, 2013, http://ricerca.repubblica.it/repubblica/archivio/repubblica/2013/10/29/nel-nome-del-padre-pace-tra.html (accessed September 22, 2014).

Longhini, Doug. "Amanda Knox Prosecutor Giuliano Mignini Back in Court as a Defendant," *CBS News*, November 2, 2011, http://www.cbsnews.com/news/amanda-knox-prosecutor-giuliano-mignini-back-in-court-as-a-defendant/ (accessed July 9, 2014).

Lyman, Eric J. "Newspaper Berlusconi Controls Says Germany's Merkel Is Heading a 'Fourth Reich,'" *The Hollywood Reporter*, August 7, 2012, http://www.hollywoodreporter.com/news/silvio-berlusconi-newspaper-germany-merkel-fourth-reich-359090 (accessed July 16, 2014).

Macrì, Carlo. "Ex-Minister Scajola and Ex-FI Deputy Matacena Arrested," *Corriere della Sera*, May 8, 2014, http://www.corriere.it/english/14_maggio_08/ex-minister-scajola

-and-ex-fi-deputy-matacena-arrested-22c7f4e6-d6a1-11e3-b1c6-d3130b63f531.shtml (accessed July 10, 2014).

"Mafia, politica e affari: Sette domande al cavaliere,"*La Stampa*, January 23, 2011, http://www.lastampa.it/2011/02/23/italia/politica/diritti-mediaset-chiesti-anniper-il-parlamentare-pdl-berruti-nHG6iIHhN6zEJE55cBQ6CK/pagina.html (accessed July 15, 2014).

Maltese, Curzio. *La Bolla: La Pericolosa Fine del Sogno Berlusconiano* (Milan: Feltrinelli, 2009).

Manca, Daniela. "Piersilvio Berlusconi: 'Il nuovo governo? Per Mediaset puo essere boaccata d'ossigeno,'" *Corriere della Sera*, November 19, 2011, http://www.corriere.it/economia/11_novembre_19/manca_buon_senso_6db08818-1283-11e1-b297-12e8887ffed4.shtml (accessed July 10, 2014).

Mancini, Roberto. "Berlusconi's Gift to the Media," *The Guardian*, June 29, 2009, http://www.theguardian.com/commentisfree/libertycentral/2009/jun/29/berlusconi-mafia-wiretapping (accessed July 17, 2014).

"Milan Train Segregation Idea Row," *BBC News*, May 9, 2009, http://news.bbc.co.uk/2/hi/world/europe/8041974.stm (accessed July 21, 2014).

Milosa, Davide. "Fede: 'Ruby? Silvio scopava, scopava. Su Dell'Utri: Solo lui sa sulla mafia,'" *Il Fatto Quotidiano*, July 23, 2014, http://www.ilfattoquotidiano.it/2014/07/23/fede-ruby-silvio-scopava-scopava-su-dellutri-solo-lui-sa-sulla-mafia/1069456/ (accessed August 28, 2014).

Mincuzzi, Angelo. "Diritti tv Mediaset, Berlusconi condannato a quattro anni in appello," *Il Sole 24 Ore*, May 8, 2013, www.ilsole24ore.com/art/notizie/2013-05-08/respinta-giudici-rinvio-udienza-095612.shtml?uuid=Abvuk1tH (accessed September 5, 2014).

Mincuzzi, Angelo. "Processo Ruby, Berlusconi condannato a 7 anni per concussione e prostituzione minorile," *Il Sole 24 Ore*, June 24, 2013, www.ilsole24ore.com/art/notizie/2013-06-24/processo-ruby-berlusconi-giudici-130213.shtml?uuid=AbNsGw7H (accessed September 4, 2014).

Mincuzzi, Angelo. "Ruby bis, Mora e Fede condannati a 7 anni. Nicole Minetti a 5," *Il Sole 24 Ore*, July 19, 2013, www.ilsole24ore.com/art/notizie/2013-07-19/oggi-sentenza-processo-ruby-091708.shtml?uuid=AbnvQYFI (accessed September 6, 2014).

Mola, Giancarlo. "Berlusconi: 'La mia biografia in tutte le famiglie italiane,'" *La Repubblica*, April 11, 2001, www.repubblica.it/online/politica/campagnacinque/libro/libro.html (accessed June 10, 2013).

Moloney, Liam. "Italy's Renzi Presents New Reform Package," *Wall Street Journal*, August 29, 2014, http://online.wsj.com/articles/italys-renzi-presents-new-reform-package-1409340446 (accessed September 25, 2014).

Montanari, Andrea. "Urbani: 'Forza Italia crolla come un castello di carte," *La Reppublica*, April 15, 2014, www.repubblica.it/politica/2014/04/15/news/urbani_forza_italia_crolla_come_un_castello_di_carte-83648804/ (accessed August 14, 2014).

Moore, Malcolm. "Cherie Blair Had Best Night of Her Life with Silvio Berlusconi," *The Daily Telegraph*, June 5, 2008, www.telegraph.co.uk/news/worldnews/europe/italy/2080817/Cherie-Blair-had-best-night-of-her-life-with-Silvio-Berlusconi.html (accessed June 27, 2014).

"Mostro Firenze: Annullate condanne a pm Mignini e Giuttari," *Ansa*, November 22, 2011, http://www.ansa.it/web/notizie/rubriche/cronaca/2011/11/22/visualizza_new.html_15027818.html (accessed September 20, 2014).

Nadeau, Barbie Latza. *Angel Face* (New York: Beast Books, 2010), 94.

Nadeau, Barbie Latza. "Basta! Berlusconi's Wife Bails," *The Daily Beast*, May 4, 2009, http://www.thedailybeast.com/articles/2009/05/04/berlusconis-9-billion-divorce.html (accessed July 10, 2014).

Nadeau, Barbie Latza. "Will Berlusconi Get the Boot?" *The Daily Beast*, November 7, 2011, http://www.thedailybeast.com/articles/2010/11/07/silvio-berlusconis-bunga-bunga-parties.html (accessed July 17, 2014).

Nicoli, Sara. "Cucu, la Merkel e 'inchiavabile,'" *Il Fatto Quotidiano*, September 10, 2011, http://www.ilfattoquotidiano.it/2011/09/10/cucu-la-merkel-e-%E2%80%9Cinchiavabile%E2%80%9D/156545/ (accessed July 18, 2014).

"Notes on a Scandal," *Nature*, vol. 471 (March 9, 2011), 135–136, http://www.nature.com/nature/journal/v471/n7337/full/471135b.html?WT.ec_id=NATURE-20110310 (accessed August 10, 2014).

"On. Niccolò Ghedini," *Openparlamento*, http://parlamento16.openpolis.it/parlamentare/ghedini-niccol%C3%B2/1587 (accessed September 4, 2014).

Onate, Pablo. "Italian Members of Parliament Are Paid Substantially Higher Salaries Than Those in Other Western European Countries," *LSEblogs*, http://blogs.lse.ac.uk/europpblog/2013/09/02/italian-members-of-parliament-are-paid-substantially-higher-salaries-than-those-in-other-west-european-countries/ (accessed September 7, 2014).

Paolini, Alessandra. "Pdl, figuranti pagati per riempire la piazza: 'Ci danno 10 euro, arrotondiamo la pensione,'" *La Repubblica*, March 24, 2013, www.repubblica.it/politica/2013/03/24/news/figuranti_pagati_manifestazione_pdl-55243399/ (accessed September 4, 2014).

"Paolo Borsellino, la sua ultima intervista censurata dale tv," *Controinformazione Indipendente*, August 11, 2013, https://www.youtube.com/watch?v=NDyfC3Z_d5A (accessed May 15, 2014).

Pecorelli, Mino. "Omicidio Pecorelli, Andreotti condannato," *La Repubblica*, November 17, 2002, www.repubblica.it/online/politica/propeco/andreotti/andreotti.html (accessed November 5, 2014).

Pisa, Nick. "Berlusconi 'Paid £300,000 Protection Money to Mafia,'" *The Daily Telegraph*, May 22, 2011, http://www.telegraph.co.uk/news/worldnews/silvio-berlusconi/8529314/Berlusconi-paid-300000-protection-money-to-Mafia.html (accessed May 11, 2014).

Pisa, Nick. "Tessa Jowell's Husband David Mills 'Very Relieved' after Italian Court Quashes Bribery Conviction," *Daily Mail*, February 26, 2010, http://www.dailymail.co.uk/news/article-1253672/Tessa-Jowells-estranged-husband-David-Mills-faces-jail-corruption-charges-Italian-supreme-court-ruling.html (accessed June 2, 2014).

Pisa, Nick. "Tony Blair Begged Wife Cherie to Protect Him from Berlusconi's Bandanna," *The Daily Telegraph*, May 24, 2009, http://www.telegraph.co.uk/news/worldnews/europe/italy/5377843/Tony-Blair-begged-wife-Cherie-to-protect-him-from-Berlusconis-bandanna.html (accessed June 27, 2014).

Politi, Marco. Vatican expert, personal interview with the author, September 10, 2014.

Popham, Peter. "Berlusconi Throws Legal System into Chaos to Save Ally," *The Independent*, October 8, 2005, http://www.independent.co.uk/news/world/europe/berlusconi-throws-legal-system-into-chaos-to-save-ally-318026.html (accessed June 29, 2014).

Popham, Peter. "Hit and Run: Viva Veronica!" *The Independent*, May 6, 2009, http://www.independent.co.uk/news/people/hit-and-run/hit–run-viva-veronica-1679796.html (accessed August 12, 2014).

Portanova, Mario. "Tangenti, truffe, abusi edilizi: L'Incredibile storia del prete-manager Luigi Verzé," *Il Fatto Quotidiano*, January 2, 2012, www.ilfattoquotidiano.it/2012/01/02/tangenti-truffe-abusi-edilizi-lincredibile-storia-prete-manager-luigi-verze/181051/ (accessed May 6, 2014).

Posteraro, Paolo. *Povera Italia. Da Craxi a Renzi: I Peggiori Anni della Nostra Vita* (Rome: Newton Compton Editori, 2014).

"Processo Ruby, i giudici: 'No alla sospensione lle elezioni,'" *Il Fatto Quotidiano*, January 14, 2014, http://www.ilfattoquotidiano.it/2013/01/14/processo-ruby-difesa-berlusconi-chiede-legittimo-impedimento-per-elezioni/468937/ (accessed September 4, 2014).

"Profile: Silvio Berlusconi, Italian Ex-Prime Minister," *BBC News*, May 9, 2014, www.bbc.co.uk/news/world-europe-11981754 (accessed August 12, 2014).

"Restelli: 'Berlusconi aiutera i malati di Alzheimer a mangiare ma non gli fara il bagno, niente ansia di prestazione," *La Repubblica*, May 1, 2014, http://www.repubblica.it

/politica/2014/05/01/news/restelli_berlusconi_aiuter_i_malati_di_alzheimer_a_mangiare_ma_non_gli_far_il_bagno_niente_ansia_da_prestazione-84948521/ (accessed August 14, 2014).

"Results of the 2014 European Elections," *European Parliament*, http://www.results-elections2014.eu/en/country-results-it-2014.html (accessed September 8, 2014).

Rifcolfi, Luca. *Tempo Scaduto. Il 'Contratto con gli Italian' alla Prova dei Fatti* (Bologna: Il Mulino, 2006).

Rizzo, Alessandra. "Berlusconi Attacker Apologizes for 'Superficial, Cowardly and Impetuous' Act," *Huffington Post*, December 14, 2009, http://www.huffingtonpost.com/2009/12/14/berlusconi-attacker-apolo_n_392033.html (accessed July 18, 2014).

Rizzo, Sergio. "Le doppie dimissioni del ministro di sangue dc," *Corriere della Sera*, May 5, 2010, http://archiviostorico.corriere.it/2010/maggio/05/doppie_dimissioni_del_ministro_sangue_co_9_100505011.shtml (accessed August 20, 2014).

"Roberto Maroni (Lega Nord)—Ministro dell'Interno," *MicroMega*, http://temi.repubblica.it/micromega-online/maroni-roberto-lega-nord-ministro-dellinterno (accessed July 20, 2014).

"Ruby, chiesto rinvio a giudizio per Fede, Minetti e Mora," *Il Fatto Quotidiano*, May 6, 2011, http://www.ilfattoquotidiano.it/2011/05/06/ruby-chiesto-rinvio-a-giudizio-per-fede-minetti-e-mora/109438/ (accessed September 3, 2014).

"Ruby si sfoga a Milano. Io utilizzata dai PM per attaccare Berlusconi," *Mnews.it*, April 4, 2013, www.youtube.com/watch?v=ZNo2nqZOW18 (accessed September 4, 2014).

Sallusti, Alessandro. "Un Kennedy ad Arcore," *Il Giornale*, November 22, 2013, www.ilgiornale.it/news/interni/969695.html (accessed August 25, 2014).

Sanderson Rachel. "Berlusconi's Empire Faces a Tricky Future without Him," *Financial Times*, May 28, 2014, http://www.ft.com/cms/s/0/f11b725c-e680-11e3-9a20-00144feabdc0.html#axzz3Bgpw3TLe (accessed August 18, 2014).

Saviano, Roberto. "Il patto scellerato," *La Repubblica*, January 13, 2012, www.repubblica.it/politica/2012/01/13/news/saviano_cosentino-28017990/ (accessed August 8, 2014).

"Scajola arrestato dalla Dia," *La Repubblica*, May 8, 2014, www.repubblica.it/cronaca/2014/05/08/news/arrestato_scajola-85533400/ (accessed August 14, 2014).

Scherer, Steven. "Berlusconi Says Idea That Italy Should Dump Euro Was a 'Joke,'" *Reuters*, June 2, 2012, http://www.reuters.com/article/2012/06/02/us-berlusconi-euro-idUSBRE8510AW20120602 (accessed July 15, 2014).

Severgnini, Beppe. "Il Cavaliere spiegto ai posteri; Dieci motivi per 20 anni di 'regno,'" *Corriere della Sera*, October 27, 2010.

"Silvio Berlusconi vs MRP Schultz; Relive the Moment," *Euractiv*, April 16, 2008, www.youtube.com/watch?v=0bPqaqGJ5Js (accessed June 26, 2014).

Singh, Anita. "Queen Is 'Not Amused' by Berlusconi Gaffe," *Daily Telegraph*, April 3, 2009, www.telegraph.co.uk/finance/g20-summit/5099649/Queen-is-not-amused-by-Berlusconi-gaffe.html (accessed July 14, 2014).

Squires, Nick. "Meet Silvio Berlusconi's New Girlfriend Francesca Pascale—50 Years His Junior," *Daily Telegraph*, Dec. 12, 2012, http://www.telegraph.co.uk/news/worldnews/silvio-berlusconi/9740323/Meet-Silvio-Berlusconis-new-girlfriend-Francesca-Pascale-50-years-his-junior.html (accessed August 19, 2014).

Squires, Nick. "Silvio Berlusconi Paid £100,000 to Showgirls Due to Testify in Trial," *The Daily Telegraph*, April 12, 2012, http://www.telegraph.co.uk/news/worldnews/silvio-berlusconi/9200509/Silvio-Berlusconi-paid-100000-to-showgirls-due-to-testify-in-trial.html (accessed August 5, 2014).

Squires, Nick. "Silvio Berlusconi Picks Starlets for European Elections," *Daily Telegraph*, April 22, 2009, http://www.telegraph.co.uk/news/worldnews/europe/italy/5200992/Silvio-Berlusconi-picks-starlets-for-European-elections.html (accessed July 20, 2014).

Squires, Nick. "Sleaze Threatens to Topple Silvio Berlusconi as Friends Warn Over Scandals," *Daily Telegraph*, June 21, 2009, www.telegraph.co.uk/news/worldnews/europe

/italy/5588183/Sleaze-threatens-to-topple-Silvio-Berlusconi-as-friends-warn-over-scandals.html (accessed July 12, 2014).

Squires, Nick. "Vladimir Plays Ball with Berlusconi Poodle," *Daily Telegraph*, December 4, 2013, http://www.telegraph.co.uk/news/worldnews/silvio-berlusconi/10494736/Vladimir-Putin-plays-ball-with-Berlusconi-poodle.html (accessed September 8, 2014).

Stewart, Phil. "Italy's Berlusconi Wins Immunity from Prosecution," *Reuters*, July 22, 2008, www.reuters.com/article /2008/07/22/us-italy-immunity-idUSL222100720080722 (accessed July 8, 2014).

Stille, Alexander. *The Sack of Rome* (New York: Penguin, 2007).

"Top 10 World Economy Ranking," *Econpost*, February 21, 2011, http://econpost.com/worldeconomy/world-economy-ranking (accessed July 22, 2014).

Travaglio, Marco. *Ad Personam: 1994-2010. Cosi' Destra e Sinistra Hanno Privatizzato la Democrazia* (Milan: Chiarelettere, 2010).

Travaglio, Marco. "Berlusconi, storia dell'evasore-corruttore da Craxi a Mills," *Il Fatto Quotidiano*, August 8, 2013, http://www.ilfattoquotidiano.it/2013/08/08/berlusconi-storia-dellevasore-corruttore-da-craxi-a-mills/679749/ (accessed June 2, 2014).

Travaglio, Marco. *È Stato la Mafia* (Milan: Chiarelettere, 2014).

Travaglio, Marco. Interview with author, June 2, 2014.

Travaglio, Marco. *Montanelli e il Cavaliere: Storia di un Grande e di un Piccolo Uomo* (Milan: Garzanti, 2004).

Travaglio, Marco. *Viva il Re* (Milan: Chiarelettere, 2013).

"Tremonti e Berlusconi, rapporto finito: 'Silvio dimettiti, il problema sei tu,'" *Il Fatto Quotidiano*, November 3, 2011, http://www.ilfattoquotidiano.it/2011/11/03/tremonti-e-berlusconi-volano-gli-stracci-silvio-dimettiti-il-problema-sei-tu/168160/ (accessed July 22, 2014).

Vannucci, Alberto. "The Controversial Legacy of 'Mani Pulite': A Critical Analysis of Italian Corruption and Anti-Corruption Policies," *Bulletin of Italian Politics*, vol.1 (2009): 233-264.

"Vent'anni fa il lancio di monetine contro Craxi all' Hotel Raphael," *Corriere della Sera*, April 30, 2013, http://roma.corriere.it/roma/notizie/politica/13_aprile_30/craxi-raphael-ventanni-dopo-212905795963.shtml (accessed May 18, 2014).

"Via dalla Rai Santoro, Biagi e Luttazzi," *La Repubblica*, April 18, 2002, http://www.repubblica.it/online/politica/rainominedue/berlu/berlu.html (accessed July 30, 2014).

"Visit to Italy: The Gasparri Law—Observations and Recommendations by the OSCE Representative on the Freedom of the Media," June 7, 2005, www.osce.org/fom/15827 (accessed June 27, 2014).

Vivarelli, Nick. "Berlusconi Fuels Rai-Mediaset Rivalry," *Variety*, June 27, 2008, https://variety.com/2008/scene/markets-festivals/berlusconi-fuels-rai-mediaset-rivalry-1117988229/ (accessed July 20, 2014).

Vivarelli, Nick. "Murdoch, Berlusconi Tension Builds," *Variety*, December 3, 2008, http://variety.com/2008/tv/news/murdoch-berlusconi-tension-builds-1117996735/ (accessed July 8, 2014).

Walker, Marcus, Stacy Meichtry and Charles Forelle, "Deepening Crisis over Euro Pits Leader against Leader," *Wall Street Journal*, December 30, 2011, http://online.wsj.com/news/articles/SB10001424052970203391104577124480046463576 (accessed July 25, 2014).

Walston, James. "Berlusconi's Real Woman Problem," *Foreign Policy*, February 14, 2014, http://www.foreignpolicy.com/articles/2011/02/14/berlusconis_real_woman_problem?wp_login_redirect=0 (accessed July 15, 2014).

Westcott, Kathryn. "At Last an Explanation for 'Bunga Bunga,'" *BBC News*, February 5, 2011, http://www.bbc.co.uk/news/world-europe-12325796 (accessed September 16, 2014).

Willan, Philip, in email to author, May 13, 2014.

Willan, Philip. "Meet Ilda Boccassini, the Lady Who Scares the Italian Mob," *Daily Telegraph*, July 18, 2010, http://www.telegraph.co.uk/news/worldnews/europe/italy/7896506/Meet-Ilda-Boccassini-the-lady-who-scares-the-Italian-Mob.html (accessed July 18, 2014).

Willan, Philip. *The Vatican at War: From Blackfriars Bridge to Buenos Aires* (Bloomington: iUniverse, 2013).

"Your Early Business Career," *The Economist*, July 31, 2003, http://www.economist.com/node/1921934 (accessed May 2, 2014).

INDEX